IACOCCA

IACOCCA

An Autobiography

LEE IACOCCA
WITH WILLIAM NOVAK

BANTAM BOOKS
TORONTO · NEW YORK · LONDON · SYDNEY · AUCKLAND

IACOCCA: AN AUTOBIOGRAPHY
A Bantam Book / November 1984

Library of Congress Catalog Card No. 84–45174

ISBN 0-553-05067-2

Published simultaneously in the United States and Canada

Bantam Books are published by Bantam Books, Inc. Its trademark,
consisting of the words "Bantam Books" and the portrayal of a rooster,
is Registered in the United States Patent and Trademark Office and in
other countries. Marca Registrada. Bantam Books, Inc., 666 Fifth Avenue,
New York, New York 10103.

PRINTED IN THE UNITED STATES OF AMERICA

FG   40 39

To my beloved Mary,
for your courage . . .
and your devotion to the three of us.

CONTENTS

STRAIGHT TALK

ACKNOWLEDGMENTS

It's customary for an author to thank all the people who helped him with his book. But since this is an autobiography, I want to begin by thanking some of the people who helped me with my life—my true friends who stuck by me when my world was falling apart: Bishop Ed Broderick, Bill Curran, Vic Damone, Alejandro deTomaso, Bill Fugazy, Frank Klotz, Walter Murphy, Bill Winn, and Gio, my barber. Also my doctor, James Barron, who helped me keep mind and body together.

I want to thank the gang that came out of cozy retirement to give me a hand at Chrysler—Paul Bergmoser, Don DeLaRossa, Gar Laux, Hans Matthias, and John Naughton—and the young Turks like Jerry Greenwald, Steve Miller, Leo Kelmenson, and Ron DeLuca, who left good and secure jobs to pitch in and help save a dying company.

In my thirty-eight years in the auto business, I was blessed with three secretaries who really made me look good. The first was Betty Martin, a woman so talented she made many of the Ford officers look bad by comparison. The second, Dorothy Carr, left Ford the day I was fired and came over to Chrysler out of sheer loyalty, even though she put her pension in jeopardy. And the third, my present secretary, Bonnie Gatewood, a veteran Chrysler employee, ranks right up there with them.

I am grateful to my old friends from Ford, those precious few who stayed my friends during the dark days: Calvin Beauregard, Hank Carlini, Jay Dugan, Matt McLaughlin, John Morrissey, Wes Small, Hal Sperlich, and Frank Zimmerman.

I want to thank Nessa Rapoport, my editor, who made sure this book would have no recalls; the people at Bantam Books who worked so hard, particularly Jack Romanos, Stuart Applebaum, Heather Florence, Alberto Vitale, and Lou Wolfe; and my invaluable collaborator, William Novak.

And, it goes without saying, my daughters, Kathi and Lia, who were really my whole life and still are.

AN OPENING WORD

Wherever I go, people always ask me the same questions. How did you get to be successful? Why did Henry Ford fire you? How did you turn Chrysler around?

I've never had a good quick answer to these questions, so I've slipped into the habit of saying: "When I write my book, you'll find out."

Over the years, I've repeated that phrase so often that I've come to believe my own words. In the end, I had no choice but to write the book I've been talking about for so long.

Why did I write it? Certainly not to become famous. The television ads for Chrysler have already made me more famous than I ever wanted to be.

And I didn't write it to get rich. I already have every material thing a person could need. That's why I'm donating every penny I earn from this book to the Joslin Diabetes Center in Boston.

And I didn't write this book to get back at Henry Ford for firing me. I've already done that the old-fashioned American way—by fighting it out in the marketplace.

The truth is that I wrote this book to set the record straight (and to keep my mind straight), to tell the story of my life at Ford and at Chrysler the way it really happened. While I was working on it and reliving my life, I kept thinking of all those young people I meet whenever I speak at universities and business schools. If this book can give them a realistic picture of the excitement and challenge of big business in America today and some idea of what is worth fighting for, then all of this hard work will have been worth something.

PROLOGUE

You're about to read the story of a man who's had more than his share of successes. But along the way, there were some pretty bad times, too. In fact, when I look back on my thirty-eight years in the auto industry, the day I remember most vividly had nothing at all to do with new cars and promotions and profits.

I began my life as the son of immigrants, and I worked my way up to the presidency of the Ford Motor Company. When I finally got there, I was on top of the world. But then fate said to me: "Wait. We're not finished with you. Now you're going to find out what it feels like to get kicked off Mt. Everest!"

On July 13, 1978, I was fired. I had been president of Ford for eight years and a Ford employee for thirty-two. I had never worked anywhere else. And now, suddenly, I was out of a job. It was gut-wrenching.

Officially, my term of employment was to end in three months. But under the terms of my "resignation," at the end of that period I was to be given the use of an office until I found a new job.

On October 15, my final day at the office, and just incidentally my fifty-fourth birthday, my driver drove me to World Headquarters in Dearborn for the last time. Before I left the house, I kissed my wife, Mary, and my two daughters, Kathi and Lia. My family had suffered tremendously during my final, turbulent months at Ford, and that filled me with rage. Perhaps I was responsible for my own fate. But what about Mary and the girls? Why did they have to go through this? They were the innocent victims of the despot whose name was on the building.

Even today, their pain is what stays with me. It's like the lioness and her cubs. If the hunter knows what's good for him, he'll leave the little ones alone. Henry Ford made my kids suffer, and for that I'll never forgive him.

The very next day I got into my car and headed out to my new office. It was in an obscure warehouse on Telegraph Road, only a few miles from Ford's World Headquarters. But for me, it was like visiting another planet.

I wasn't exactly sure where the office was, and it took me a few minutes to find the right building. When I finally got there, I didn't even know where to park.

As it turned out, there were plenty of people around to show me. Someone had alerted the media that the newly deposed president of Ford would be coming to work here this morning, and a small crowd had gathered to meet me. A TV reporter shoved a microphone in my face and asked: "How do you feel, coming to this warehouse after eight years at the top?"

I couldn't bring myself to answer him. What could I say? When I was safely out of camera range, I muttered the truth. "I feel like shit," I said.

My new office was little more than a cubicle with a small desk and a telephone. My secretary, Dorothy Carr, was already there, with tears in her eyes. Without saying a word, she pointed to the cracked linoleum floor and the two plastic coffee cups on the desk.

Only yesterday, she and I had been working in the lap of luxury. The office of the president was the size of a grand hotel suite. I had my own bathroom. I even had my own living quarters. As a senior Ford executive, I was served by white-coated waiters who were on call all day. I once brought some relatives from Italy to see where I worked, and they thought they had died and gone to heaven.

Today, however, I could have been a million miles away. A few minutes after I arrived, the depot manager stopped by to pay a courtesy call. He offered to get me a cup of coffee from the machine in the hall. It was a kind gesture, but the incongruity of my being there made us both feel awkward.

For me, this was Siberia. It was exile to the farthest corner of the kingdom. I was so stunned that it took me a few minutes before I realized I had no reason to stay. I had a telephone at home, and somebody could bring me the mail. I left that place before ten o'clock and never went back.

This final humiliation was much worse than being fired. It was enough to make me want to kill—I wasn't quite sure who, Henry Ford or myself. Murder or suicide were never real possibilities, but I did start to drink a little more—and shake a lot more. I really felt I was coming apart at the seams.

As you go through life, there are thousands of little forks in the road, and there are a few really big forks—those moments of reckoning, moments of truth. This was mine as I wondered what to do. Should I pack it all in and retire? I was fifty-four years old. I had already accomplished a great deal. I was financially secure. I could afford to play golf for the rest of my life.

But that just didn't feel right. I knew I had to pick up the pieces and carry on.

There are times in everyone's life when something constructive is born out of adversity. There are times when things seem so bad that you've got to grab your fate by the shoulders and shake it. I'm convinced it was that morning at the warehouse that pushed me to take on the presidency of Chrysler only a couple of weeks later.

The private pain I could have endured. But the deliberate public humiliation was too much for me. I was full of anger, and I had a simple choice: I could turn that anger against myself, with disastrous results. Or I could take some of that energy and try to do something productive.

"Don't get mad," Mary reminded me. "Get even." In times of great stress and adversity, it's always best to keep busy, to plow your anger and your energy into something positive.

As it turned out, I went from the frying pan into the fire. A year after I signed up, Chrysler came within a whisker of bankruptcy. There were many days at Chrysler when I wondered how I had got myself into this mess. Being fired at Ford was bad enough. But going down with the ship at Chrysler was more than I deserved.

Fortunately, Chrysler recovered from its brush with death. Today I'm a hero. But strangely enough, it's all because of that moment of truth at the warehouse. With determination, with luck, and with help from lots of good people, I was able to rise up from the ashes.

Now let me tell you my story.

MADE
IN AMERICA

I

THE FAMILY

Nicola Iacocca, my father, arrived in this country in 1902 at the age of twelve—poor, alone, and scared. He used to say the only thing he was sure of when he got here was that the world was round. And that was only because another Italian boy named Christopher Columbus had preceded him by 410 years, almost to the day.

As the boat sailed into New York Harbor, my father looked out and saw the Statue of Liberty, that great symbol of hope for millions of immigrants. On his second crossing, when he saw the statue again, he was a new American citizen—with only his mother, his young wife, and hope by his side. For Nicola and Antoinette, America was the land of freedom—the freedom to become anything you wanted to be, if you wanted it bad enough and were willing to work for it.

This was the single lesson my father gave to his family. I hope I have done as well with my own.

When I was growing up in Allentown, Pennsylvania, our family was so close it sometimes felt as if we were one person with four parts.

My parents always made my sister, Delma, and me feel important and special. Nothing was too much work or too much trouble. My father might have been busy with a dozen other things, but he always had time for us. My mother went out of her way to cook the foods we loved—just to make us happy. To this day, whenever I come to visit, she still makes my two favorites—chicken soup with little veal meatballs, and ravioli stuffed with ricotta cheese. Of all the world's great Neopolitan cooks, she has to be one of the best.

My father and I were very close. I loved pleasing him, and he was always terrifically proud of my accomplishments. If I won a spelling contest at school, he was on top of the world. Later in life whenever I got a promotion, I'd call my father right away and he'd rush out to tell all his friends. At Ford, each time I brought out a new car, he wanted to be the first to drive it. In 1970, when I was named president of the Ford Motor Company, I don't know which of us was more excited.

Like many native Italians, my parents were very open with their feelings and their love—not only at home, but also in public. Most of my friends would never hug their fathers. I guess they were afraid of not appearing strong and independent. But I hugged and kissed my dad at every opportunity—nothing could have felt more natural.

He was a restless and inventive man who was always trying new things. At one point, he bought a couple of fig trees and actually found a way to grow them in the harsh climate of Allentown. He was also the first person in town to buy a motorcycle—an old Harley Davidson, which he rode through the dirt streets of our small city. Unfortunately, my father and his motorcycle didn't get along too well. He fell off it so often that he finally got rid of it. As a result, he never again trusted any vehicle with less than four wheels.

Because of that damn motorcycle, I wasn't allowed to have a bicycle when I was growing up. Whenever I wanted to ride a bike, I had to borrow one from a friend. On the other hand, my father let me drive a car as soon as I turned sixteen. This made me the only kid in Allentown who went straight from a tricycle to a Ford.

My father loved cars. In fact, he owned one of the first Model T's. He was one of the few people in Allentown who knew how to drive, and he was always tinkering with cars and thinking about how to improve them. Like every driver in those days, he used to get a lot of flat tires. For years he was obsessed with finding a way to drive a few extra miles with a flat. To this day, whenever there's a new development in tire technology, I always think of my father.

He was in love with America, and he pursued the American dream with all his might. When World War I broke out, he volunteered for the Army—partly out of patriotism, and partly, he admitted to me later, to have a little more control over his destiny. He had worked hard to get to America and to become naturalized, and he was terrified at the prospect of being sent back to Europe to fight in Italy or France. Luckily for him, he was stationed at Camp

Crane, an army training center just a couple of miles from his home. Because he could drive, he was assigned to train ambulance drivers.

Nicola Iacocca had come to America from San Marco, about twenty-five miles northeast of Naples in the Italian province of Campania. Like so many immigrants, he was full of ambition and hope. In America he lived briefly in Garrett, Pennsylvania, with his stepbrother. There my father went to work in a coal mine, but he hated it so much that he quit after one day. He liked to say it was the only day in his life that he ever worked for anybody else.

He soon moved east to Allentown, where he had another brother. By 1921, he had saved up enough money doing odd jobs, mostly as an apprentice shoemaker, that he could return to San Marco to bring over his widowed mother. As it turned out, he ended up bringing over *my* mother, too. During his stay in Italy this thirty-one-year-old bachelor fell in love with the seventeen-year-old daughter of a shoemaker. Within a few weeks they were married.

Over the years a number of journalists have reported (or repeated) that my parents went to Lido Beach in Venice for their honeymoon and that I was named Lido to commemorate that happy week. It's a wonderful story, except for one problem: it's not true. My father did take a trip to Lido Beach, but it was before the wedding, not after. And since he was with my mother's brother at the time, I doubt that his vacation was very romantic.

My parents' voyage to America wasn't easy. My mother came down with typhoid fever and spent the entire trip in the ship's infirmary. By the time they reached Ellis Island, she had lost all her hair. According to the laws, she should have been sent back to Italy. But my father was an aggressive, fast-talking operator who had already learned how to manage in the New World. Somehow he was able to convince the immigration officials that his new bride was merely seasick.

I was born three years later, on October 15, 1924. By this time, my father had opened a hot-dog restaurant called the Orpheum Wiener House. It was the perfect business for somebody without much cash. All he really needed to get started were a grill, a bun warmer, and a few stools.

My father always drilled two things into me: never get into a capital-intensive business, because the bankers will end up owning you. (I should have paid more attention to this particular piece of advice!) And when times are tough, be in the food business, because no matter how bad things get, people still have to eat. The Orpheum Wiener House stayed afloat all through the Great Depression.

Later, he brought my uncles Theodore and Marco into the business. To this day, Theodore's sons, Julius and Albert Iacocca, are still making hot dogs in Allentown. The company is called Yocco's, which is more or less how the Pennsylvania Dutch used to pronounce our name.

I came pretty close to going into the food business myself. At one point in 1952, I seriously considered leaving Ford to go into food franchising. Ford dealerships operated as independent franchises, and it occurred to me that anyone who could franchise a food operation would get rich in a hurry. My plan was to have ten fast-food outlets with one central buying location. This was long before McDonald's was even a gleam in Ray Kroc's eye, and I sometimes wonder if I missed my true calling in life. Who knows? Maybe today I'd be worth half a billion dollars, with a sign out front proclaiming: Over 10 billion served.

A few years later, I did open my own place, a little sandwich shop in Allentown called The Four Chefs. It served Philadelphia cheese steaks. (That's thinly-sliced steak with melted cheese on an Italian roll.) My father set it up, and I put in the money. It did very well—too well, in fact, because what I really needed was a tax shelter. We made $125,000 the first year, which raised my tax bracket to the point where I had to get rid of it. The Four Chefs was my first exposure to bracket creep and the progressive nature of our tax laws.

Actually I was in the food business long before I got involved with cars. When I was ten, one of the country's first supermarkets opened in Allentown. After school and on weekends, my little pals and I would line up at the door with our red wagons, like a row of taxicabs outside a hotel. As the shoppers came out, we would offer to take home their bags for a small tip. In retrospect, it makes a lot of sense—I was in the transportation end of the food business.

As a teenager, I had a weekend job in a fruit market run by a Greek named Jimmy Kritis. I used to get up before dawn to get to the wholesale market and bring back the produce. He paid me $2.00 a day—plus all the fruit and vegetables I could lug home after a sixteen-hour workday.

By this time, my father had other enterprises besides the Orpheum Wiener House. Early on, he bought into a national company called U-Drive-It, one of the very first car rental agencies. Eventually he built up a fleet of about thirty cars, mostly Fords. My father was also good friends with one Charley Charles, whose son, Edward Charles, worked for a Ford dealership. Later Eddie bought a dealership of his own, where he introduced me to the fascinating world of the retail car business. By the time I was fifteen, Eddie had convinced me to go into the automobile business. From that day forward, all my energies were directed to doing just that.

My father is probably responsible for my instinct for marketing. He owned a couple of movie houses; one of his theaters, the Franklin, is still in use today. Old-timers in Allentown have told me my father was such a great promoter that the kids who came down to the Saturday matinees used to get more excited about his special offers than about the movies. People still talk about the day he announced that the ten kids with the dirtiest faces would be admitted free.

I doubt there are any kids at the Franklin today. It's now called the Jenette, and instead of Tom Mix and Charlie Chaplin, it shows porno flicks.

Economically, our family had its ups and downs. Like many Americans, we did well during the 1920s. My father started making lots of money in real estate, in addition to his other businesses. For a few years we were actually wealthy. But then came the Depression.

No one who's lived through it can ever forget. My father lost all his money, and we almost lost our house. I remember asking my sister, who was a couple of years older, whether we'd have to move out and how we'd find somewhere else to live. I was only six or seven at the time, but the anxiety I felt about the future is still vivid in my mind. Bad times are indelible—they stay with you forever.

During those difficult years, my mother was very resourceful. She was a real immigrant mother, the backbone of the family. A nickel soupbone went a long way in our house, and we always had enough to eat. I remember that she used to buy squabs—three birds for a quarter—and kill the birds herself because she didn't trust the butcher to guarantee their freshness. As the Depression grew worse, she helped out in my father's restaurant. At one point she went to work in a silk mill, sewing shirts. Whatever it took to keep going, she did it gladly. Today she's still a beautiful woman—who looks younger than I do.

Like so many families in those days, our strong belief in God sustained us. We seemed to pray an awful lot. I had to go to Mass every Sunday and take Holy Communion every week or two. It took me a number of years to fully understand why I had to make a good confession to a priest before I went to Holy Communion, but in my teens I began to appreciate the importance of this most misunderstood rite of the Catholic Church. I not only had to think out my transgressions against my friends; I had to speak them aloud. In later years, I found myself completely refreshed after confession. I even began to attend weekend retreats, where the Jesuits, in face-to-face examinations of conscience, made me come to grips with how I was conducting my life.

The necessity of weighing right from wrong on a regular basis turned out to be the best therapy I ever had.

Despite some of the bad times, we had plenty of fun. There was no TV in those days, so people depended more on each other. On Sunday, after church, we'd always have a house full of family and friends, laughing, eating pasta, and drinking red wine. We also read a lot of books back then, and of course every Sunday night we'd gather around the old Philco radio to listen to our favorite shows, like Edgar Bergen and Charlie McCarthy, and *Inner Sanctum.*

For my father, though, the Depression was the shock of his life. He couldn't get over it. After years of struggle he had finally made a pile of money. And then, almost overnight, it was all gone. When I was little, he used to tell me that I had to go to school to learn what the word "depression" meant. He himself had only finished the fourth grade. "If somebody had taught me what a depression was," he used to say, "I wouldn't have mortgaged one business on the next."

This was in 1931. I was only seven, but I knew even then that something serious had gone wrong. Later in college I would learn all about business cycles, and at Ford and Chrysler I would learn how to weather them. But our family's experience was an early inkling of things to come.

My parents were great picture-takers, and our family photo album told me a lot. From birth until I was six, I'm dressed in satin shoes and embroidered coats. My baby pictures show a silver rattle in my hand. Suddenly, around 1930, my clothes start to look a little ragged. My sister and I weren't getting new clothes anymore. I didn't really understand, and it wasn't the sort of thing my father could explain. How can you say to a kid: "I lost my shirt, son, but I don't know why"?

The Depression turned me into a materialist. Years later, when I graduated from college, my attitude was: "Don't bother me with philosophy. I want to make ten thousand a year by the time I'm twenty-five, and then I want to be a millionaire." I wasn't interested in a snob degree; I was after the bucks.

Even now, as a member of the working rich, I put most of my money away in very conservative investments. It's not that I'm afraid of being poor, but somewhere in the back of my mind there's still the awareness that lightning can strike again, and my family won't have enough to eat.

No matter how I'm doing financially, the Depression has never disappeared from my consciousness. To this day, I hate waste. When neckties went from narrow to wide, I kept all my old ones until the style went back to narrow. Throwing out food or scraping half a steak into the disposal still drives me crazy. I've managed to convey some of that awareness to my daughters, and I notice that they don't spend money unless they get a good deal—my goodness, they do go to a lot of sales!

More than once during the Depression, my father's checks were returned to him with that deathless line: Insufficient Funds. This would always throw him for a loop, because he felt a good credit rating was vital to the integrity of an individual or a business. He constantly preached his gospel of fiscal responsibility to Delma and me, urging us never to spend more money than we took in. He believed credit was insidious. Nobody in our family was allowed to have a credit card or to charge *anything*—ever!

In this respect, my father was a little ahead of his time. He foresaw that buying things on time and getting into hock would undermine people's sense of responsibility about money. He predicted that easy credit would eventually permeate and sabotage our entire society and that consumers would get into trouble by treating their little plastic cards as if they were money in the bank.

"If you borrow anything," he used to tell me, "even twenty cents from a kid at school, be sure to write it down so you won't forget to pay it back." I often wonder how he would have reacted if he'd lived long enough to see me go into hock in 1981 to keep the Chrysler Corporation in business. This one was for a lot more than twenty cents: the total came to $1.2 billion. Although I recalled my father's advice, I had a funny feeling that this was one loan I'd remember even without writing it down.

They say that people vote with their pocketbooks, and certainly my father's political views shifted along with his income. When we were poor, we were Democrats. The Democrats, as everybody knew, were the party of the common man. They believed that if you were willing to work hard and not be a deadbeat, you should be able to feed your family and educate your kids.

But when times were good—before the Depression and then again when it was finally over—we were Republicans. After all, we had worked hard for our money and we deserved to hold on to it.

As an adult, I underwent a similar political transformation. As long as I was at Ford and all was right with the world, I was a Republican. But when I took over at Chrysler and several hundred thousand people were suddenly threatened with losing their jobs, the Democrats were the ones who were pragmatic enough to do what was necessary. If the Chrysler crisis had come up during a Republican administration, the company would have gone down the tubes before you could say Herbert Hoover.

Whenever times were tough in our family, it was my father who kept our spirits up. No matter what happened, he was always there for us. He was a philosopher, full of little sayings and homilies about the ways of the world. His favorite theme was that life has its ups and downs and that each person has to come to terms with his own share of misery. "You've got to accept a little sorrow in life," he'd tell me when I was upset about a bad grade in school or some other disappointment. "You'll never really know what happiness is unless you have something to compare it to."

At the same time, he hated to see any of us unhappy and would always try to cheer us up. Whenever I was worried about anything, he'd say: "Tell me, Lido, what were you so upset about last month? Or last year? See—you don't even remember! So maybe whatever you're so worried about today isn't really all that bad. Forget it, and move on to tomorrow."

During hard times, he was always the optimist. "Just wait," he'd tell me whenever things looked bleak, "the sun's gonna come out. It always does." Many years later, when I was trying to save Chrysler from bankruptcy, I missed my father's comforting words. I'd say, "Hey Pop, where's the sun, where's the sun!" He never let any of us surrender to despair, and I confess there was more than one moment in 1981 when I felt ready to throw in the towel. I kept my sanity in those days by recalling his favorite saying: "It looks bad right now, but remember, this too shall pass."

He was really a bird about performing up to your potential—no matter what you did. If we went out to a restaurant and the waitress was rude, he'd call her over at the end of the meal and give her his standard little speech: "I'm going to give you a *real* tip," he'd say. "Why are you so unhappy in this job? Is anyone forcing you to be a waitress? When you act surly, you're telling everybody you don't like what you're doing. We're out for a nice time and you're wrecking it. If you really want to be a waitress, then you should work at being the best damn waitress in the world. Otherwise, find yourself another line of work."

In his own restaurants, he would immediately fire any employee who was rude to a customer. He'd say: "You can't work here, no matter how good you are, because you're scaring the customers away." He got right down to the heart of the matter, and I guess I'm the same way. I still think all the talent in the world doesn't excuse deliberate rudeness.

My father always reminded me that I should *enjoy* life, and he practiced what he preached. No matter how hard he worked, he always made sure to leave enough room to have a good time. He loved bowling and poker as well as good food, drink, and especially good friends. He always made friends with my colleagues at work. During my career at Ford, I think he knew more people there than I did.

In 1971, two years before my father died, I threw a big party for my parents' fiftieth wedding anniversary. I had a cousin who worked in the U.S. Mint, and I commissioned him to sculpt a gold medal depicting my parents on one side and the little church in Italy where they had been married on the other. At the party, each guest was given a bronze version of the medal.

Later that year my wife and I took my parents back to Italy to visit their hometown and to see all their old friends and family. By this time we knew my father had leukemia. He was getting blood transfusions every two weeks and was steadily losing weight. When at one point we lost track of him for several hours, we were afraid he had lost consciousness or collapsed. We finally caught up with him in a tiny shop in Amalfi, where he was excitedly buying up ceramic souvenirs for all his friends back home.

Right up to the end, in 1973, he was still trying to enjoy life. He wasn't dancing as much or eating as much, but he sure was very brave and determined to live. Still, the last couple of years were rough on him, and all of us, too. It was difficult to see him so vulnerable—much less accept it.

        *   *   *

Now when I look back on my father, I only remember a man of great vigor and boundless energy. Once I was in Palm Springs for a Ford dealer meeting and I invited my father to come out for a brief vacation. When the meeting was over, a couple of us went out to play golf. Although my father had never been on a golf course in his life, we asked him to come along.

As soon as he hit the ball, he began to chase after it—seventy years old and running all the way. I had to keep reminding him: "Pop, slow down. Golf is a game of *walking!*"

But that was my father for you. He always preached: "Why walk when you can run?"

II

SCHOOL DAYS

I was eleven before I learned we were Italian. Until then, I knew we came from a real country but I didn't know what it was called—or even where it was. I remember actually looking on a map of Europe for places named Dago and Wop.

In those days, especially if you lived in a small town, being Italian was something you tried to hide. Almost everybody in Allentown was Pennsylvania Dutch, and as a kid I took a lot of abuse for being different. Sometimes I got into fights with kids who called me names. But I always kept in mind my father's warning: "If he's bigger than you are, don't fight back. Use your head instead of your fists."

Unfortunately, the prejudice against Italians wasn't limited to people my own age. There were even a few teachers who called me "little wop" under their breath. My ethnic problems came to a head on June 13, 1933, when I was in the third grade. I'm sure of the date because June 13 is St. Anthony's day, a big event in our family. My mother's name is Antoinette, and Anthony is my middle name, so every year on June 13 we'd throw a big party at our house.

To mark the occasion, my mother would bake pizza. She comes from Naples, the birthplace of pizza. To this day, my mother makes the greatest pizzas in the country, if not the entire world.

That year we had an especially wonderful party with our friends and relatives. As usual, there was a big barrel of beer. Even at age nine I was allowed to swig a little—as long as I did it at home under strict supervision. Maybe that's why I never got pig-drunk in high school and college. In our house alcohol (usually homemade red wine) was accepted as part of life—but always in moderation.

Now, in those days, pizza was virtually unknown in this country. Today, of course, it's pushing hamburgers and fried chicken as one of America's favorite foods. But back then, nobody who wasn't Italian had ever heard of it.

The morning after the party, I started bragging to the other kids at school. "Boy, did we have a party last night!"

"Oh yeah?" somebody asked. "What kind of party?"

"A pizza party," I replied.

"A pizza party? What kind of dumb dago word is that?" And they all started laughing.

"Wait a minute," I said. "You guys like to eat pies." They were all pretty fat, so I knew I was on safe ground. "Well, that's what a pizza is. It's a pie made out of tomatoes."

I should have quit while I was ahead, because now they got hysterical. They didn't have the faintest idea of what I was talking about. But they knew that if it was Italian, it had to be bad. The only good thing about the whole incident was that it took place near the end of the school year. The pizza episode was forgotten over the summer.

But I never forgot it. Those guys grew up on shoofly pie, but I never once laughed at them for eating molasses pie for breakfast. Hell, you don't see shoofly pie huts all over America today. But to think that someday you'll be a trendsetter is no comfort for a nine-year-old kid.

I wasn't the only victim of bigotry in my class. There were also two Jewish kids; I was friendly with both of them. Dorothy Warsaw was always first in the class, and I was usually second. The other Jewish kid, Benamie Sussman, was the son of an Orthodox Jew who wore a black hat and a beard. In Allentown, the Sussmans were treated like outcasts.

The other kids kept their distance from these two as if they had leprosy. At first I didn't understand it. But by the time I was in the third grade, I began to get the message. As an Italian, I was seen as a cut above the Jewish kids—but not by much. I never saw a black person in Allentown until I was in high school.

Being exposed to bigotry as a kid left its mark. I remember it clearly, and it still leaves a bad taste in my mouth.

Unfortunately, I witnessed a lot of prejudice even after I left Allentown. This time it came not from schoolchildren but from men in positions of great power and prestige in the auto industry. In 1981, when I named Gerald Greenwald vice-chairman of Chrysler, I learned that his appointment was unprecedented. Until then, no Jew had ever reached the top ranks of the Big Three automakers. I find it a little hard to believe that none of them was qualified.

Looking back now, I remember certain episodes from my childhood that forced me to reckon with how the adult world operated. When I was in the sixth grade, there was an election for captain of the student patrol. The patrolmen all wore white belts with a silver badge, but the lieutenant and the captain got to wear special uniforms with special badges. In grade school, the captain of the student patrol was the equivalent of the high school quarterback. I loved the idea of wearing that uniform, and I was determined to be the captain.

When the vote came in, I had lost to another kid by a margin of twenty-two to twenty. I was bitterly disappointed. The following day I was at a Saturday afternoon matinee at the local theater, where we used to see Tom Mix movies.

In the row ahead of me sat the biggest kid in our class. He turned around and saw me. "You dumb wop," he said. "You lost the election."

"I know," I said. "But why are you calling me a dummy?"

"Because," he said. "There are only thirty-eight kids in the class. But forty-two kids voted. Can't you dagos even count?"

My opponent had stuffed the ballot box! I went to the teacher and told her that some kids had voted twice.

"Let's leave well enough alone," she said to me. She covered it up. She didn't want any scandals. That incident had a profound effect on me. It was my first dramatic lesson that life wasn't always going to be fair.

In every other respect, however, school was a very happy place for me. I was a diligent student. I was also a favorite of many of my teachers, who were always singling me out to clap the erasers or wash the blackboards or ring the school bells. If you ask me the names of my professors in college or graduate school, I'd have trouble coming up with more than three or four. But I still remember the teachers who molded me in elementary and high school.

The most important thing I learned in school was how to communicate. Miss Raber, our ninth-grade teacher, had us turn in a theme paper of five hundred words every Monday morning. Week in and week out, we had to write that damn paper. By the end of the year, we had learned how to express ourselves in writing.

In class she would quiz us on the Word Power Game from *Reader's Digest*. Without any advance warning she'd rip it out of the magazine and make us take the vocabulary test. It became a powerful habit with me—to this day I still look for the list of words in every issue of the *Digest*.

After a few months of these quizzes, we knew a lot of words. But we still didn't know how to put them together. At that point, Miss Raber started us on extemporaneous speaking. I was good at it, and as a result I joined the debating team, which was sponsored by Mr. Virgil Parks, our Latin teacher. That's where I developed my speaking skills and learned how to think on my feet.

At first I was scared to death. I had butterflies in my stomach—and to this day I still get a little nervous before giving a speech. But the experience of being on the debating team was crucial. You can have brilliant ideas, but if you can't get them across, your brains won't get you anywhere. When you're fourteen years old, nothing polishes your skills like arguing both sides of "Should capital punishment be abolished?" That was the hot issue in 1938—and I must have spoken for each side of the debate at least twenty-five times.

The next year was a turning point. I came down with rheumatic fever. The first time I had a palpitation of the heart, I almost passed out—from fear. I thought my heart was popping out of my chest. My doctor said: "Don't worry. Just put an ice pack on it." I panicked: What the hell was I doing with this chunk of ice on my chest? I must be dying!

Back then people *did* die from rheumatic fever. In those days it was treated with birch bark pills to get the infection out of your joints. They were so strong you had to take antacid pills every fifteen minutes to keep from throwing up. (Today, of course, they use antibiotics.)

With rheumatic fever there's always a threat to the heart. But I was lucky. Although I lost about forty pounds and stayed in bed for six months, I eventually made a full recovery. But I'll never forget those crude splints with cotton wadding wet with oil of wintergreen to quiet down the lousy pain in my knees, ankles, elbows, and wrists. They actually alleviated the pain on the inside by giving you third degree burns on the outside. Sounds primitive today—but Darvon and Demerol weren't invented yet.

Before I got sick, I had been a pretty decent baseball player. I was a great Yankee fan, and Joe DiMaggio, Tony Lazzeri, and

Frankie Crossetti—all Italian—were my real heroes. Like most boys, I dreamed of playing in the major leagues. But my long illness changed all that. I gave up sports and started playing chess, bridge, and especially poker. I still love poker, and I usually win. It's a great game for learning when to exploit an advantage, when to back off, and when to bluff. (It sure came in handy years later during tough union negotiations!)

Most of all, as I lay flat on my back, I turned to books. I read like crazy—everything I could get my hands on. I especially liked the stories of John O'Hara. My aunt had brought me *Appointment in Samarra*, which was a pretty dirty book for those days. When the doctor saw it by my bed, he almost flipped. As far as he was concerned, this wasn't what a teenage boy with a palpitating heart ought to be reading.

Years later, when Gail Sheehy came to interview me for *Esquire*, I happened to mention *Appointment in Samarra*. She pointed out that it was a novel about business executives and asked me whether I thought it had influenced my choice of a career. Hell no! All I could remember about the book was that it got me interested in sex.

I must have read my share of schoolbooks, too, because each year in high school I graduated near the top of my class, with straight A's in math. I was in the Latin club, and I won a prize for being the best kid in Latin for three years running. I haven't used a word of it in forty years! It did help me with my English vocabulary, and I was one of the few kids who could follow the priest at Sunday Mass. Then Pope John switched to English, and that was the end of that.

Being a good student was very important to me—but it wasn't enough. I was always heavily involved in extracurricular activities. In high school I was active in the drama club and the debating society. After my illness, when I could no longer participate in athletics, I became manager of the swim team. That meant I carried the towels and washed out the tank suits.

Back in seventh grade I had developed a passion for jazz and swing. This was the big-band era, and my friends and I spent every weekend going to hear the big bands. Usually I just listened, although I got pretty good at doing the shag and the lindy hop. We would go to the Empire Ballroom in Allentown and to Sunnybrook in Pottstown, Pennsylvania. When I could afford it, I slipped into the Hotel Pennsylvania in New York, or Frank Daley's Meadowbrook on the Pompton Turnpike.

I once saw Tommy Dorsey and Glenn Miller in a Battle of the

Bands—all for eighty-eight cents. In those days music was my life. I subscribed to *Downbeat* and *Metronome,* and I knew the name of every sideman in all of the major bands.

By this time I had started playing the tenor sax. I was even asked to play first trumpet in the school band. But I gave up music in order to go into politics. I wanted to be president of my class in seventh and eighth grade—and I was.

In ninth grade I ran for president of the whole school. Jimmy Leiby, my closest friend, was a genius. He became my campaign manager, and he created a real political machine. I won the election by a landslide and it went to my head. To use the vernacular of the day, I really thought I was hot shit.

But once I was elected, I lost touch with my constituency. I thought I was a cut above the other kids, and I started acting like a snob. I hadn't yet learned what I know now—that the ability to communicate is everything.

As a result, I lost the election in the second semester. It was a terrible blow. I had given up music to be in the student council, and now my political career had come to a halt because I forgot to shake hands and be friendly. It was an important lesson about leadership.

With all my extracurricular activities, I still managed to graduate twelfth in a class of over nine hundred. To show you the kind of expectations I grew up with, my father's reaction was: "Why weren't you first?" To hear him describe it, you'd think I flunked!

By the time I was ready for college, I had a solid background in the fundamentals: reading, writing, and public speaking. With good teachers and the ability to concentrate, you can go pretty far with these skills.

Years later, when my kids asked me what courses to take, my advice was always to get a good liberal arts education. Although I'm a great believer in the importance of learning from history, I really didn't care if they mastered all the dates and places of the Civil War. The key is to get a solid grounding in reading and writing.

Suddenly, in the middle of my senior year, Japan attacked Pearl Harbor. President Roosevelt's speeches had us all riled up, and the entire country was rallying 'round the flag. Overnight all of America was galvanized and united. I learned something from that crisis that has stayed with me ever since: it often takes a shot of adversity to get people to pull together.

Like most young men that December of 1941, I couldn't wait to join up. Ironically, the illness that had almost killed me may have ended up saving my life. To my enormous disappointment, I was classified 4F—a medical deferment—which meant I couldn't join the Air Corps and fight in the war. Although I had pretty well recovered and I felt terrific, the Army had decided not to take anybody with a history of rheumatic fever. But I didn't *feel* sick, and a year or two later, when I had my first physical for life insurance, the doctor turned to me and said: "You're a healthy young fellow. Why aren't you overseas?"

Most of my classmates were called up, and many of them died. We were the class of '42, and the kids who were seventeen or eighteen went to boot camp and then straight across the Atlantic where the Germans were knocking the hell out of us. To this day I sometimes look through my high school yearbook and shake my head in sorrow and disbelief at all the students from Allentown High who died overseas, defending democracy.

Because World War II was nothing like Vietnam, younger readers may not fully understand how it felt to be unable to serve your country when it needed you most. Patriotism was at a fever pitch, and I wanted nothing more than to fly a bomber over Germany to take revenge on Hitler and his troops.

Being burdened with a medical deferment during the war seemed like a disgrace, and I began to think of myself as a second-class citizen. Most of my friends and relatives had gone over to fight the Germans. I felt like the only young man in America who wasn't in combat. So I did the only thing I could: I buried my head in my books.

By this time I had developed an interest in engineering, and I was looking into several colleges that specialized in the field. One of the finest in the country was Purdue. I applied for a scholarship there, and when I didn't get it I was crushed. However, Cal Tech, MIT, Cornell, and Lehigh also had top-rated engineering schools. I finally chose Lehigh because it was only half an hour's drive from my home in Allentown and I wouldn't have to leave my family too far behind.

Lehigh University, in Bethlehem, Pennsylvania, was a kind of satellite school for the Bethlehem Steel Company. Its departments of metallurgy and chemical engineering were among the best in the world. But being a freshman there was the academic equivalent of boot camp. Any student who didn't maintain a sufficiently high average by the end of his sophomore year was politely asked to leave. I had classes six days a week, including a course in statistics that met every Saturday morning at eight. Most of the guys cut it, but I got an

A—not so much for my proficiency in statistics, but for my perseverance in showing up every week while the other guys were sleeping off their Friday-night binges.

I don't mean to imply that I had no fun at all during college. I liked to raise a little hell, and I went to my share of football games and beer parties. There were also trips to New York and Philadelphia, where I had a couple of girlfriends.

But with the war on, I was in no mood to goof off. As a little kid I had learned how to do my homework right after school so that I could play after supper. By the time I got to college, I knew how to concentrate and how to study without a radio or other distraction. I used to tell myself: "I'm going to give this my best shot for the next three hours. And when those three hours are up, I'll set this work aside and go to the movies."

The ability to concentrate and to use your time well is everything if you want to succeed in business—or almost anywhere else, for that matter. Ever since college I've always worked hard during the week while trying to keep my weekends free for family and recreation. Except for periods of real crisis I've never worked on Friday night, Saturday, or Sunday. Every Sunday night I get the adrenaline going again by making an outline of what I want to accomplish during the upcoming week. It's essentially the same schedule I developed at Lehigh.

I'm constantly amazed by the number of people who can't seem to control their own schedules. Over the years, I've had many executives come to me and say with pride: "Boy, last year I worked so hard that I didn't take any vacation." It's actually nothing to be proud of. I always feel like responding: "You dummy. You mean to tell me that you can take responsibility for an $80 million project and you can't plan two weeks out of the year to go off with your family and have some fun?"

If you want to make good use of your time, you've got to know what's most important and then give it all you've got. That's another lesson I learned at Lehigh. I might have had five classes the next day, including an oral quiz where I didn't want to look stupid, so I had to prepare. Anyone who wants to become a problem-solver in business has to learn fairly early how to establish priorities. Of course, the time frame is a little different. In college I had to figure out what I could accomplish in one evening. In business the time frame is more like three months to three years.

From what I've seen, you either get grounded in that kind of positive thinking early on in life or you don't. Establishing priorities and using your time well aren't things you can pick up at the Harvard Business School. Formal learning can teach you a great deal, but many of the essential skills in life are the ones you have to develop on your own.

It wasn't only my ability to concentrate that helped me at college. I was also lucky. As more and more students were drafted, the classes at Lehigh became smaller and smaller. A teacher who was accustomed to a lecture course for fifty was suddenly teaching a seminar of five. As a result, I had a very exclusive college education.

When you have small classes, everybody gets plenty of attention. A professor could afford to say: "Tell me why you can't do that machine design problem, and I'll help you understand it." So by an accident of history, I got terrific training. Right after the war, with the G.I. Bill, the same class at Lehigh might have had seventy guys. In that setting I wouldn't have learned half as much.

I was also motivated by the pressure from my father that was typical among immigrant families, where any kid who was fortunate enough to attend college was expected to compensate for his parents' lack of education. It was up to me to take advantage of all the opportunities they never had, so I had to be at the top of my class.

This, however, was easier said than done. I had an especially rough time during my first semester. When I failed to make the dean's list, my father got on my case—and quick! After all, he reasoned, if I was so smart in high school, where I graduated near the top of my class, how could I be so stupid only a few months later? He assumed that I was playing around. I couldn't get him to understand that college was completely different from high school. At Lehigh, *everyone* was good—or they wouldn't have been there in the first place.

In my freshman year, I almost failed physics. We had a professor named Bergmann, a Viennese immigrant whose accent was so thick that I could hardly understand him. He was a great scholar, but he lacked the patience to teach freshmen. Unfortunately, his course was a requirement for anyone who majored in mechanical engineering.

Somehow, in spite of my difficulties in his class, I got to be good friends with Professor Bergmann. We would walk around the campus, and he would describe the latest developments in physics. He was especially interested in splitting atoms, which at that point seemed still in the realm of science fiction. It all sounded like Greek to me, and I understood only a fraction of what he was saying, although I managed to follow the main argument.

There was something mysterious about Bergmann. Every Friday he'd end the class abruptly and leave campus until the following Monday. It wasn't until several years later that I finally learned his secret. Given the nature of his interests, I probably should have guessed. He used to spend every weekend in New York working on the Manhattan Project. In other words, when Bergmann wasn't teaching at Lehigh, he was working on the atomic bomb.

Despite our friendship and despite the private tutorials, I managed no more than a D in freshman physics—my lowest grade at Lehigh. I had been a good math student in high school, but I simply wasn't prepared for the world of advanced calculus and differential equations.

Eventually I smartened up and switched my major from mechanical to industrial engineering. Before long, my grades started to improve. By my senior year I had moved away from the advanced sciences of hydraulics and thermodynamics and switched over to business courses such as labor problems, statistics, and accounting. I did much better in these subjects, finishing my last year with straight A's. My goal was a 3.5 grade average so I could graduate with high honors. I made it by a hair—ending up at 3.53. They say that this generation is competitive. You should have seen us at work!

In addition to all the engineering and business courses, I also studied four years of psychology and abnormal psychology at Lehigh. I'm not being facetious when I say that these were probably the most valuable courses of my college career. It makes for a bad pun, but it's true: I've applied more of those courses in dealing with the nuts I've met in the corporate world than all the engineering courses in dealing with the nuts (and bolts) of automobiles.

In one course we would spend three afternoons and evenings a week at the psychiatric ward of the Allentown State Hospital, about five miles from the campus. We saw them all—manic-depressives, schizophrenics, and even some violent types. Our teacher was a professor named Rossman, and to see him work with these mental patients was to watch a master in action.

The focus of the course was nothing less than the fundamentals of human behavior. What motivates that guy? How did this woman develop her problems? What makes Sammy run? What led Joe over there to act like an adolescent at the age of fifty? For our final exam we were introduced to a group of new patients. Our assignment was to make a diagnostic analysis of each one within a few minutes.

As a result of this training, I learned to figure people out pretty quickly. To this day, I can usually tell a fair amount about somebody from our first meeting. That's an important skill to have, because the most important thing a manager can do is to hire the right new people.

But there are two really important things about a candidate that you just can't learn from one short job interview. The first is whether he's lazy, and the second is whether he's got any horse sense. There's no qualitative analysis to check out whether he's got some fire in his belly, or whether he will have savvy—or street smarts—when it comes to decision time.

I wish there were some kind of machine that would measure these traits, because they're the ones that separate the men from the boys.

I completed my studies at Lehigh in eight straight semesters, which meant no summer vacations. I wish I had taken some time off to smell the flowers, as my father had always advised me. But the war was raging, and with my friends fighting—and dying—overseas, I had to run at full steam.

In addition to my studies, I got involved in lots of extracurricular activities. By far the most interesting was the time I spent on the school paper, *The Brown and White*. My first assignment as a reporter was to interview a professor who had rigged up a little car that ran on charcoal. (This was years before the energy crisis, of course.) I must have written a pretty good story, because it got picked up by the Associated Press and ran in a hundred papers.

On the strength of that story, I became the layout editor. This, I soon learned, was where the real power of the press resided. Years later, I read Gay Talese's book on *The New York Times*, in which one of the editors said that the most powerful position on any paper is not the editor of the editorial page, but rather the editors in charge of headlines and layout.

That was a lesson I had already learned. As the layout editor, I figured out pretty quickly that most people don't read the stories. Instead, they rely on the headlines and subheads. That means that whoever writes *those* has a helluva lot of influence on people's perception of the news.

In addition, I had to determine the length of each story, based on how much space was available. I did this with impunity, and I often lopped off two inches from a good story because I needed that space for the ads. I also learned how to screw our reporters through the judicious use of headlines and subtitles. Years later, I could see when I'd been had by the layout editors of the country's most prestigious newspapers and magazines. It takes one to know one!

Even before I graduated, I wanted to work for Ford. I drove a beat-up 1938 sixty-horsepower Ford, which is how I got interested in the company. More than once I'd be going up a hill when suddenly the cluster gear in my transmission would go. Some faceless executive at the Ford corporate headquarters in Dearborn, Michigan, had apparently decided they'd get better fuel economy by taking a V-8 engine down to only sixty horsepower. That was a fine idea—if they had restricted the car to places like Iowa. Lehigh was built on a mountain.

"Those guys need me," I used to joke to my friends. "Anybody who builds a car this bad can use some help."

In those days, owning a Ford was an excellent way to learn about cars. During the war, all the auto plants were kept busy making weapons; no new cars were manufactured. Even spare parts became scarce. People used to search for them on the black market or by visiting junkyards. If you were lucky enough to own a car then, you learned how to take good care of it. The wartime shortage of cars was so great that after graduation I sold that Ford for $450. When you consider that my father had bought me the car for only $250, I made out pretty well.

During my college days, gas was selling for only thirteen cents a gallon. But because of the war, there was a real shortage. As an engineering student, I was given a C-card, which meant that my studies were vital to the war effort. (Can you believe that!) It wasn't as patriotic as being overseas, but at least it was a small badge of honor that said I would make a contribution to my country—someday.

In the spring of my senior year, engineers were in great demand. I had about twenty job interviews, and I literally had my pick of where I wanted to work.

But cars were what I cared about. Since I still wanted to go to Ford, I made an appointment to see the company recruiter, whose name, unbelievably, was Leander Hamilton McCormick-Goodheart. He drove through the campus in a Mark I, one of those snazzy Lincoln Continentals that looked as if they were custom-built. That car really turned my head. One glimpse of it and one whiff of the leather interior were enough to make me want to work at Ford for the rest of my life.

Back then, Ford's recruitment policy was to visit fifty universities and select one student from each. This has always struck me as a little dumb. If Isaac Newton and Albert Einstein had been classmates, Ford could have accepted only one of them. McCormick-Goodheart interviewed several Lehigh students, but I was the one he picked for Ford, and I was on cloud nine.

After graduation and before starting the program, I took a brief vacation with my parents in Shipbottom, New Jersey. While we were there, I got a letter from Bernadine Lenky, the placement director at Lehigh. She enclosed a flyer offering a fellowship for graduate work at Princeton, a grant that covered tuition, books, and even spending money.

Bernadine told me that only two of these fellowships were awarded each year and suggested I apply. "I realize that you weren't planning on graduate school," she said, "but this one looks like a winner." I wrote to Princeton to ask for more details, and they wrote back for my records. The next thing I knew, I had won the Wallace Memorial Fellowship.

After one look at the campus I knew I wanted to be there. I figured that a master's degree after my name wouldn't hurt my career, either.

Suddenly I had two terrific opportunities. I called McCormick-Goodheart about my dilemma. "If they want you at Princeton," he told me, "by all means go and get your master's. We'll hold a space for you until you graduate." That was just what I hoped he would say, and I was on top of the world.

Princeton was a delightful place to go to school. Compared to Lehigh's frenetic pace it was almost laid back. I took my electives in politics, and a new field—plastics. Like Lehigh, Princeton had a very favorable teacher-student ratio due to the war. One of my professors, a man named Moody, was the most famous hydraulics expert in the world. He had worked on the Grand Coulee Dam and many other projects, yet there were only four of us in his class.

One day I went to hear Einstein give a lecture. I didn't really understand what he was talking about, but it was exciting just to be in his presence. The graduate school wasn't far from the Institute for Advanced Studies, where Einstein taught, and from time to time I would catch a glimpse of him taking a walk.

I was given three semesters to write my thesis, but I was so eager to begin working at Ford that I finished it in two. My project was to design and build, by hand, a hydraulic dynamometer. A professor named Sorenson offered to work with me. Together we built it and hooked it up to an engine that General Motors had donated to the university. I ran all the tests, completed my thesis, and had it bound—in leather yet, I was so proud of it.

Meanwhile, back in Dearborn, Leander McCormick-Goodheart had been drafted. Foolishly, I had neglected to stay in touch with him during my year at Princeton. Even worse, I had not gotten his promise to me in writing. By the time I was finished at Princeton, nobody at Ford had ever heard of me.

Finally I got McCormick-Goodheart's boss, Bob Dunham, on the phone and explained my predicament. "The training group is closed," he said, "and we already have our fifty guys. But considering the circumstances, it doesn't seem fair. If you can get yourself out here right away, we'll make you number fifty-one." The next day, my father drove me to Philadelphia, where I boarded the *Red Arrow* for Detroit to begin my career.

It was an all-night trip, but I was too excited to sleep. When I arrived at the Fort Street Station, a duffel bag on my shoulder and fifty bucks in my pocket, I went outside and asked the first guy I met: "Which way to Dearborn?"

He said: "Go west, young man—go west about ten miles!"

THE
FORD STORY

III

GETTING MY
FEET WET

In August 1946, I began working at Ford as a student engineer. Our program was known as a loop training course, because the trainees made a complete circuit of the entire operation. We worked in the bowels of the company, spending a few days or a week in each department. When we finished, we were supposed to be familiar with every stage of manufacturing a car.

The company went to great lengths to give us hands-on experience. We were assigned to the famous River Rouge plant, the largest manufacturing complex in the world. The Ford Motor Company actually owned the coal and limestone mines, so we got to see the entire process, start to finish—from hauling the stuff out of the ground to making the steel and then turning the steel into cars.

Our tour of duty included the jobbing foundry, the production foundry, the ore boats, the tool and die shops, the test track, the forging plant, and the assembly lines. But not all of our experience was directly connected to manufacturing. We also spent time in the purchasing department and even in the plant hospital.

It was the best place in the world to learn how cars were really made and how the industrial process worked. The Rouge plant was the pride of the company, and visiting delegations from other countries were always coming over to have a look. It was long before the Japanese showed any interest in Detroit, but eventually they too would make a thousand pilgrimages to the Rouge.

I was finally seeing the practical application of everything I had read about in books. I had studied metallurgy at Lehigh, but now I was actually doing it, working at the blast furnaces and in the open hearths. In the tool and die department I got to run the machinery I had only read about, such as the planers, the milling machines, and the lathes.

I even spent four weeks on the final assembly line. My job was to attach a cap to a wiring harness on the inside of a truck frame. It wasn't hard work, but it was tedious as hell. My mother and father came to visit one day, and when my dad saw me in overalls, he smiled and said: "Seventeen years you went to school. See what happens to the dummies who don't finish first in their class?"

Our supervisors were pretty decent, but the workers treated us with suspicion and resentment. At first we thought the badges we wore, which said "Student Engineer," might be causing the problem. When we complained, our badges were changed to read "Administration." But that only made matters worse.

I soon learned enough history to understand what was going on. By this time, Henry Ford, the founder, had grown old. The company was being run by a group of his henchmen, notably Harry Bennett, who was known as a pretty tough cookie. Relations between workers and management were terrible, and the student engineers, with their "Administration" badges, were caught in the middle. Many of the workers were convinced we were spies who had been sent to keep an eye on them. The fact that we were just out of college and wet behind the ears didn't help.

Despite the tension, we did the best we could to have fun. We were a mix of fifty-one guys from different colleges who roomed together, drank beer together, and tried to enjoy life as much as possible when we weren't working. The training program was pretty disorganized, and if you wanted to take a couple of days off and drive to Chicago, nobody would know the difference.

Halfway through, we had an evaluation meeting with our supervisors. Mine said: "Ah, Iacocca—mechanical engineering, hydraulic dynamometers, automatic transmissions. Let's see, now. We're setting up a new automatic-transmission group. We'll send you over there."

I was nine months into the program with another nine to go. But engineering no longer interested me. The day I'd arrived, they had me designing a clutch spring. It had taken me an entire day to make a detailed drawing of it, and I said to myself: "What on earth am I doing? Is this how I want to be spending the rest of my life?"

I wanted to stay at Ford, but not in engineering. I was eager to be where the real action was—marketing or sales. I liked working with people more than machines. Naturally, my supervisors in the program were not amused. After all, the company had hired me out of engineering school and had invested all this time and money in my training. And now I wanted to be in *sales*?

When I insisted, we settled on a compromise. I told them there was no point in my finishing the training course and that my masters degree from Princeton was equivalent to the second nine months of training. They agreed to let me go and try to find a job in sales. But I had to do it on my own. "We'd like to keep you at Ford," they told me. "But you've got to get out and sell yourself if you choose to go the sales route."

Right away I got in touch with Frank Zimmerman, my best friend in the training program. Zimmie had been the first guy accepted into the program, and he was the first to graduate. Like me, he had decided against engineering and had already talked himself into a sales position in trucks in the New York district. When I went East to visit him, we were like two little kids in the big city, racing to restaurants and nightclubs and taking in the splendor of Manhattan. "God," I thought, "I have just got to come back here." I was from the East, so this was really home.

The New York district manager happened to be out when I arrived in the office, so I had to meet with his two assistant managers. I was nervous. My background was in engineering, not sales. The only way I could possibly land a job here was to make a great impression in the interview.

I had brought a letter of recommendation from Dearborn, which I handed to one of the men. He reached out and took it without taking his eyes off his newspaper. In fact, he spent the entire half hour reading *The Wall Street Journal* and didn't look up once.

The other guy was only slightly better. He glanced at my shoes and checked to see if my tie was straight. Then he asked me a couple of questions. I could tell he didn't like the fact that I had a college education and that I had spent some time in Dearborn. Maybe he thought I was there to check up on him. In any case, it was clear that he wasn't going to hire me. "Don't call us," he said. "We'll call you." I felt like I had just failed my Broadway audition. My only hope was to try another district sales office, so I made an appointment to see the manager of the sales office in Chester, Pennsylvania, not far from Philadelphia. This time I had better luck. The district manager was not only in that day—he was even willing to take a chance on me. I was hired for a low-level desk job in fleet sales.

In Chester, my job was to speak to fleet purchasing agents about the allocation of new cars. It wasn't easy. I was bashful and awkward in those days, and I used to get the jitters every time I picked up the phone. Before each call I'd practice my speech again and again, always afraid of being turned down.

Some people think that good salesmen are born and not made. But I had no natural talent. Most of my colleagues were a lot more relaxed and outgoing than I was. For the first year or two I was theoretical and stilted. Eventually I got some experience under my belt and started to improve. Once I had mastered the facts, I worked on how to present them. Before long, people started listening to me.

Learning the skills of salesmanship takes time and effort. You have to practice them over and over again until they become second nature. Not all young people today understand that. They look at a successful businessman and they don't stop to think about all the mistakes he might have made when he was younger. Mistakes are a part of life; you can't avoid them. All you can hope is that they won't be too expensive and that you don't make the same mistake twice.

Here again, as in college, my timing was lucky. There had been no car production during the war, so between 1945 and 1950, demand was high. Every new car was sold at list price—if not more. And all the dealers were looking for customers with used cars to trade, because even the most decrepit used car could be resold at a handsome profit.

Although I had a lowly position, the backlog for new cars gave my job a lot of clout. If I had wanted to cheat, I could have done very well for myself. There was plenty of shady dealing going on. Almost everywhere you looked, district employees were allocating cars to their friends in return for gifts or financial favors.

The dealers were getting rich. There was no such thing as a sticker price, so people paid what the market would bear. Some of the district guys wanted part of the action and played fast and loose with the rules to get it. As an idealistic, freshly scrubbed kid just a year out of college, I was shocked.

Eventually, I got out from behind the telephone. I went from the desk to the field, visiting dealers as a traveling truck and fleet representative to give them pointers on selling. I loved every minute of it.

Finally I was out of school and into the real world. I spent my days driving around in a brand-new car, sharing my newly found wisdom with a couple of hundred dealers—each one hoping I could turn him into a millionaire.

In 1949, I became a zone manager in Wilkes-Barre, Pennsylvania. My job was to work closely with eighteen dealers. For me, this was a critical learning experience.

It's the dealers who have always been the guts of the car business in this country. While they have a working relationship with the parent company, they're really the quintessential American entrepreneurs. They're the ones who represent the heart of our capitalist system. And, of course, they're the guys who are actually selling and servicing all the cars the factory's turning out.

Because I started out by working directly with the dealers, I knew what they were worth. Later, when I became part of management, I worked hard to keep them happy. If you want to succeed in this business, you all have to operate as a team. And that means the home office and the dealers have to be playing on the same side.

Unfortunately, most auto executives I've known have failed to grasp this concept. The dealers, in turn, have been resentful because they're seldom invited to eat at the head table. To me, it's simple enough to understand: the dealers are really the *only* customers a company has. So it's only common sense to listen very carefully to what they have to say, even if you don't always like what you hear.

During my years in Chester, I learned a great deal about the retail car business, most of it from a sales manager in Wilkes-Barre named Murray Kester. Murray was a real pro at training and motivating salesmen.

One of his little tricks was to call up every customer thirty days after he'd bought a new car. Murray would always ask: "How do your friends like it?" His strategy was simple. He reasoned that if you asked the customer how *he* liked the car, he might feel obliged to think of something that was wrong with it. But if you asked him how his *friends* liked it, he would have to tell you how great the car was.

Even if his friends didn't like his car, he wouldn't be able to admit it. At least not so soon! He still needed to justify in his own mind that he had made a smart buy. If you were really on the ball, you would ask the customer for the names and phone numbers of his friends. After all, they might be interested in buying a similar car.

Remember this: Anybody who ever buys anything—a house, a

car, or stocks and bonds—will rationalize his purchase for a few weeks, even if he made a mistake.

Murray was also a great storyteller. He got most of his material from his brother-in-law, who happened to be Henny Youngman. One time he brought Henny down from New York to address a sales rally at the Broadwood Hotel in Philadelphia. Henny warmed up the crowd, and then I introduced the new cars. It was the first time I ever heard those famous words: "Take my wife—please!"

Following Murray's lead, I used to give the dealers a few tips myself. I would explain that they had to "qualify" a buyer, to ask the right questions that might lead to a sale.

If a guy wanted a red convertible, of course that's what you sold him. But many customers didn't really know what they wanted, and part of the salesman's job was to help them find out. I would say that buying a car isn't all that different from buying a pair of shoes. If you work in a shoe store, first you measure the guy's foot and then you ask whether he's interested in something sporty or dressy. The same thing applies to cars. You've got to learn what he wants to use the car for and who else in his family will be driving it. You've also got to figure out how much he can afford, so that you can put together the best finance plan.

Murray was always talking about the importance of closing the deal. We found that most of our people would do fine in the preliminary stages of selling but then were so afraid of rejection that they would often let potential customers walk right out the door. They just could never bring themselves to say: *Sign here.*

Working in Chester, I came under the influence of another remarkable man, who would have more impact on my life than any person other than my father. Charlie Beacham was Ford's regional manager for the entire East Coast. Like me, he was trained as an engineer but later switched into sales and marketing. He was the closest thing I've ever had to a mentor.

Charlie was a Southerner, a warm and brilliant man, very large and imposing with a wonderful smile. He was a great motivator—the kind of guy you'd charge up the hill for even though you knew very well you could get killed in the process.

He had the rare gift of being tough and generous at the same time. On one occasion, out of the thirteen sales zones in our district, mine had come in last. I was depressed about it, and when Charlie saw me walking through the garage he came over and put his arm around me. "What are you so down about?" he wanted to know.

"Mr. Beacham," I replied, "there are thirteen zones and I ended up number thirteen in sales this month."

"Ah, hell, don't let *that* get you down, somebody's got to be last," he said, and started to walk away. Just as he reached his car, he turned around. "But listen," he told me, "just don't be last two months in a row!"

He had a colorful way of speaking. One time there was talk of sending out some new recruits to visit the dealers in Philadelphia, who were a pretty rough group. Beacham thought that was a terrible idea. He said: "Those kids are so green that in the springtime the cows will eat 'em right up."

He could also be direct: "Make money," he used to say. "Screw everything else. This is a profit-making system, boy. The rest is frills."

Beacham used to talk about street smarts, the things you just *know*, the basic lessons that can't really be taught. "Remember, Lee," he would say, "the only thing you've got going for you as a human being is your ability to reason and your common sense. That's the only real advantage we've got over the apes. Remember, a horse is stronger and a dog is friendlier. So if you don't know a dip of horse-shit from a dip of vanilla ice cream—and a lot of guys don't—that's just too bad, because then you can never really make it."

He accepted mistakes, provided you took responsibility for them. "Always remember," he would say, "that everybody makes mistakes. The trouble is that most people just won't own up to them. When a guy screws up, he will never admit it was his fault, not if he can help it. He will try to blame it on his wife, his mistress, his kids, his dog, the weather—but never himself. So if you screw up, don't give me any excuses—go look at yourself in the mirror. Then come see me."

During sales meetings, Charlie would sometimes take a few minutes to list all the excuses he had heard recently on why cars weren't selling, so nobody would be tempted to use any of them. He respected people who faced up to their own failings. He didn't like the guys who were always making alibis or were still fighting the last war instead of the next one. Charlie was a street fighter and a strategist, always thinking ahead about what he could do next.

He was addicted to cigars, and even after the doctor made him stop smoking, he couldn't bear to part with them. Instead, he'd keep the unlit cigar in his mouth and chew on it. Every so often he would take out his pocket-knife and cut off the well-chewed end. When a meeting was over, you thought a rabbit had been in there with you—on your desk there were ten or fifteen little cigar pieces that looked remarkably like rabbit droppings.

Charlie could be a tough boss when he thought the situation called for it. At a dinner celebrating my election to the presidency of Ford in 1970, I finally got up the nerve to tell Charlie publicly what I thought of him. "There will never be another Charlie Beacham," I said. "He has a special niche in my heart—and sometimes I think he was carving it out by hand. He was not only my mentor, he was more than that. He was my tormentor, but I love him!"

As I became more confident and more successful, Charlie assigned me to teach dealers how to sell trucks. I even produced a little handbook called *Hiring and Training Truck Salesmen*. There was no doubt that I had made the right choice in leaving engineering. This was where the action was, and I loved being right in the middle of it.

As at college, my success in Chester wasn't all my own doing. Here, too, I was lucky enough to be in the right place at the right time. Ford was in the throes of reorganization. As a result, there was plenty of room for advancement. The opportunity was there, and I grabbed it. Before long, Charlie was sending me farther afield.

I would travel up and down the East Coast from city to city like a traveling salesman, lugging around the tools of my trade—slide projectors, posters, and flip charts. I'd get to town on a Sunday night and put on a five-day training course for the Ford truck salesmen in the area. I was talking all day. And like anything else, if you do enough of it, you eventually get the hang of what you're doing.

As part of my job, I had to make a lot of long-distance calls. In those days, there was no direct dialing, so that you always had to go through an operator. They'd ask for my name, and I'd say "Iacocca." Of course, they had no idea how to spell it, so there was always a struggle to get that right. Then they'd ask for my first name and when I said "Lido," they'd break out laughing. Finally I said to myself: "Who needs it?" and I started calling myself Lee.

Once, before my first trip to the South, Charlie called me into his office. "Lee," he said, "you're going down to my part of the country, and I want to give you a couple of tips. First, you talk much too fast for these guys, so slow it down. Second, they won't like your name. So here's what I want you to do. Tell them you have a funny first name—Iacocca—and that your family name is Lee. They ought to like that in the South."

They loved it. I started every meeting with that line, and they'd go wild. I would completely disarm all those Southerners. They'd forget that I was an Italian Yankee. Suddenly I was accepted as a good ole boy.

I worked hard on those trips, riding the trains to places like Norfolk, Charlotte, Atlanta, and Jacksonville. I got to know the dealers and the salesmen all over the South. I ate more grits and red-eyed gravy than I could stand. But I was happy. I had wanted to be in the people part of the car business, and now, at last, I was.

IV

THE
BEAN COUNTERS

After a few good years in Chester, I suffered an unexpected setback. There was a mild recession in the early 1950s, and Ford decided to cut back drastically. One third of the sales force was fired—including some of my best buddies. I guess I was lucky to escape with only a demotion, but I certainly didn't *feel* lucky. For a while I was pretty miserable. That was when I started thinking about the food business.

But if you really believe in what you're doing, you've got to persevere even when you run into obstacles. When I finished sulking, I doubled my efforts and worked even harder. In a few months I had my old job back. Setbacks are a natural part of life, and you've got to be careful how you respond to them. If I had sulked too long, I probably would have got myself fired.

By 1953, I had worked my way up to assistant sales manager of the Philadelphia district. Whether or not the dealers are moving them, the cars keep coming off the assembly lines and you've got to do something about it. You learn to scramble and move quickly. You learn to produce, or you get into trouble—fast!

When it rains, it pours, and for me it rained pretty hard in 1956. That was the year Ford decided to promote auto safety rather than performance and horsepower. The company introduced a safety package that included crash padding for the dashboard. The factory had sent along a film for us to show the dealers, which was supposed to explain just how much safer the new padding was in the event that a passenger hit his head on the dash. To illustrate the point, the narrator in the film claimed the padding was so thick that if you dropped an egg on it from a two-story building, the egg would bounce right off without breaking.

I was hooked. Instead of having the salesmen learn about the safety padding from the film, I would make the point far more dramatically by actually dropping an egg onto the padding. About eleven hundred men sat in the audience at the regional sales meeting as I began to make my pitch about the terrific new safety padding we were offering in our 1956 models. I had spread strips of the padding across the stage, and now I climbed up on a high ladder with a carton of fresh eggs.

The very first egg I dropped missed the padding altogether and splattered on the wooden floor. The audience roared with delight. I took more careful aim with the second egg, but my assistant, who was holding the ladder, chose this moment to move in the wrong direction. As a result, the egg bounced off his shoulder. This, too, was greeted with wild applause.

The third and fourth eggs landed exactly where they were supposed to. Unfortunately, they broke on impact. Finally, with the fifth egg, I achieved the desired result—and got a standing ovation. I learned two lessons that day. First, never use eggs at a sales rally. And second, never go before your customers without rehearsing what you want to say—as well as what you're going to *do*—to help sell your product.

I had plenty of egg on my face that day, and it turned out to be a prophetic symbol for our 1956 cars. The safety campaign was a bust. Our campaign was well conceived and highly promoted, but the consumers failed to respond.

While sales of 1956 Fords were poor everywhere, our district was the weakest in the entire country. Shortly after the egg incident, I came up with another—and, I hoped, better—plan. I decided that any customer who bought a new 1956 Ford should be able to do so for a modest down payment of 20 percent, followed by three years of monthly payments of $56. This was a payment schedule that almost anyone could afford, and I hoped that it would stimulate sales in our district. I called my idea "56 for '56."

At that time, financing for new cars was just coming into its own. "56 for '56" took off like a rocket. Within a period of only three months, the Philadelphia district moved from last place in the country all the way to first. In Dearborn, Robert S. McNamara, vice-president in charge of the Ford Division—he would become secretary of defense in the Kennedy administration—admired the plan so much that he made it part of the company's national marketing strategy. He later estimated it was responsible for selling 75,000 extra cars.

And so, after ten years of preparation, I became an overnight success. Suddenly I was known and even talked about in national headquarters. I had toiled in the pits for a good decade, but now I had a big break. My future suddenly looked a lot brighter. As a reward, I was promoted to district manager of Washington, D.C.

In the midst of all this excitement, I also got married. Mary McCleary had been a receptionist in the Ford assembly plant in Chester. We had first met eight years earlier, at a reception following the introduction of our 1949 models at the Bellevue Stratford Hotel in Philadelphia. We dated on and off for several years, but I was constantly traveling, which made for a difficult and extended courtship. Finally, on September 29, 1956, we were married in Chester at St. Robert's Catholic Church.·

Mary and I had spent several months looking for a house in Washington, but no sooner had we bought one than Charlie Beacham called me in and said: "You're getting moved." I said: "You gotta be kidding. I'm getting married next week and I just bought a house." He said: "I'm sorry, but if you want to get paid, your paycheck will be in Dearborn." Not only did I have to tell Mary that all of a sudden we were moving to Detroit, but I also had to tell her on our honeymoon that when we got back to our beautiful home in Maryland I would spend one night with her and then I was off!

Charlie Beacham, who himself had been promoted to head of car and truck sales for the Ford Division, brought me to Dearborn as his national truck marketing manager. Within a year I was head of car marketing, and in March of 1960 I took over both functions.

The first time that I met Robert McNamara, my new boss, we talked about carpeting. Although I was thrilled about the promotion to national headquarters, I was worried about the amount of money tied up in our new house in Washington. McNamara tried to put me at ease by explaining that the company would buy the house from me. Unfortunately, Mary and I had just spent two thousand dollars to install carpeting, a considerable sum of money in those days. I was hoping that Ford would reimburse me for that, too, but McNamara shook his head. "Just the house," he told me. "But don't worry," he added. "We'll take care of the rugs in your bonus."

That sounded fine to me, but when I got back to my office I had second thoughts. "Wait a minute," I said to myself. "I don't even know what the bonus would have been *without* the carpeting, so how can I be sure I'm getting a good deal?" In retrospect, the whole incident seems ridiculous, and McNamara and I had a few laughs about it in later years. At the time, however, it wasn't prestige or power I wanted. It was money.

Robert McNamara had arrived at Ford eleven years earlier as one of the famous Whiz Kids. In 1945, when Henry Ford II came out of the Navy to take over his grandfather's huge but ailing company, what he needed most was managerial talent. As fate would have it, the solution to his problems fell into his lap. And he was smart enough to seize the opportunity.

Shortly after the war ended, Henry received an unusual and intriguing telegram from a group of ten young Air Force officers. They were interested in talking with him about "a matter of management importance," as they put it in the cable. As their reference, they named the secretary of defense. These ten officers, who had run the Air Force Office of Statistical Control, wanted to continue working as a team—this time in the private sector.

Henry Ford invited them out to Detroit, where their leader, Colonel Charles (Tex) Thornton, explained that his men could improve cost efficiency at Ford just as they had in the Air Force. Thornton also made clear that he was offering Henry a package deal. If he was interested, Henry would have to hire the whole gang. Wisely, Henry agreed. Although none of the men had a background in automobiles, two of them, McNamara and Arjay Miller, would eventually become presidents of Ford.

The Air Force officers came to Ford at the same time I joined up as a student engineer. They completed a loop course of their own, but instead of learning all about manufacturing, as we did, they studied the company's administration and management. They spent their first four months moving from one department to the next, and they asked so many questions that people started calling them the Quiz Kids. Later, when their success at Ford became obvious, they became known as the Whiz Kids.

Robert McNamara was noticeably different from the other Whiz Kids and also from his fellow executives at Ford. Many people thought he lacked warmth, and I guess he did project a degree of coolness. Certainly he didn't laugh very easily, except when he was with Beacham.

Charlie relaxed him, and although the two men couldn't have been more different—or perhaps because of it—they got along famously. Despite McNamara's reputation as a human robot, he was really a very kind man as well as a loyal friend. But his intelligence was so formidable and so disciplined that it often overshadowed his personality.

He wasn't always easy to get along with, and his high standards of personal integrity could sometimes drive you crazy. Once, for a skiing vacation he planned, he needed a car with a ski rack. "No problem," I told him. "I'll put a rack on one of our company cars out in Denver, and you just pick it up." But he wouldn't hear of it. He insisted that we rent him a car from Hertz, pay extra for the ski rack, and send him the bill. He resolutely refused to use a company car on his vacation, even though we loaned out hundreds of courtesy cars every weekend to other VIPs.

McNamara used to say that the boss had to be more Catholic than the Pope—and as clean as a hound's tooth. He preached a certain aloofness, and he practiced what he preached. He was never one of the boys.

Whereas most auto executives lived in the residential suburbs of Grosse Pointe and Bloomfield Hills, McNamara and his wife lived in Ann Arbor, near the University of Michigan. Bob was an intellectual and preferred to socialize with academics, not car men. He was equally independent in his politics. In a world that automatically supported big-business Republicans, McNamara was both a liberal and a Democrat.

He was also one of the smartest men I've ever met, with a phenomenal IQ and a steel-trap mind. He was a mental giant. With his amazing capacity to absorb facts, he also retained everything he learned. But McNamara knew more than the actual facts—he also knew the hypothetical ones. When you talked with him, you realized that he had already played out in his head the relevant details for every conceivable option and scenario. He taught me never to make a major decision without having a choice of at least vanilla or chocolate. And if more than a hundred million dollars were at stake, it was a good idea to have strawberry, too.

When it came to spending large amounts of money, McNamara calculated the consequence of every possible decision. Unlike anyone else I've met, he could carry a dozen different plans in his head and could spin out all the facts and figures without ever consulting his notes.

Nevertheless, he taught me to put all my ideas into writing.

"You're so effective one on one," he used to tell me. "You could sell anybody anything. But we're about to spend one hundred million dollars here. Go home tonight and put your great idea on paper. If you can't do that, then you haven't really thought it out."

It was a valuable lesson, and I've followed his lead ever since. Whenever one of my people has an idea, I ask him to lay it out in writing. I don't want anybody to sell me on a plan just by the melodiousness of his voice or force of personality. You really can't afford that.

McNamara and the other Whiz Kids were part of a new breed of managers who brought to Ford something the company urgently needed: financial controls. For many years, this area had been Ford's major weakness, dating from the time that old Henry Ford himself used to manage the accounts by scribbling numbers on the back of an envelope.

The Whiz Kids brought the Ford Motor Company into the twentieth century. They set up a system of controls so that for the first time each operation in the company could be measured in terms of profit and loss—and each manager could now be held responsible for the financial success or failure of his own area.

In addition to the Whiz Kids, Henry Ford II hired dozens of Harvard Business School graduates. Those of us in sales, product planning, and marketing thought of the financial planners as the longhairs—men with M.B.A.'s who formed an elitist group within the company. They had been brought in to clean up a bad mess, and they did their job well. By the time they were finished, however, they also held most of the power at Ford.

In the business world, financial men are often referred to as bean counters. McNamara was the quintessential bean counter, and he epitomized both the strengths and weaknesses of the breed. At their best—and Bob was as good as they came—the bean counters had great financial minds and impressive analytical skills. In the days before computers, these guys *were* the computers.

By their very nature, financial analysts tend to be defensive, conservative, and pessimistic. On the other side of the fence are the guys in sales and marketing—aggressive, speculative, and optimistic. They're always saying, "Let's do it," while the bean counters are always cautioning you on why you shouldn't do it. In any company you need both sides of the equation, because the natural tension between the two groups creates its own system of checks and balances.

If the bean counters are too weak, the company will spend itself into bankruptcy. But if they're too strong, the company won't meet the market or stay competitive. That's what happened at Ford during the 1970s. The financial managers came to see themselves as the only prudent people in the company. Their attitude was: "If we don't stop them, these clowns are going to break us." They saw their mandate as saving the company from the wild-eyed dreamers and radicals who would spend Ford into oblivion. What they forgot was how quickly things can change in the car business. While their company was dying in the marketplace, they didn't want to make a move until next year's budget meeting.

Robert McNamara was different. He was a good businessman, but he had the mentality of a consumerist. He believed strongly in the idea of a utilitarian car, a car whose purpose was simply to meet people's basic needs. He looked upon most luxury models and options as frivolous and accepted them only because of the higher margins they commanded. But McNamara was so skillful a manager and so valuable to the company that he continued to rise in the system despite his ideological independence.

Although he had his eye on the presidency of Ford, he never expected to reach it. "I won't get there," he once told me, "because Henry and I don't see eye to eye on *anything*." He was right in his assessment and wrong in his prediction.

But I don't think he would have been wrong in the long run. Bob was a strong man who fought hard for what he believed in. Henry Ford, as I would learn firsthand, had a nasty habit of getting rid of strong leaders. McNamara became president on November 10, 1960, and I was promoted the same day to fill his old position of vice-president and general manager of the Ford Division. Our appointments coincided with the election of J.F.K. A few days later, when Kennedy was putting together his cabinet, representatives of the President-elect flew to Detroit to meet with Bob. McNamara, who among his other accomplishments had been a professor at the Harvard Business School, was offered secretary of the treasury. He turned it down, but Kennedy was clearly impressed with him. When Kennedy later offered him the defense post, Bob said yes.

In 1959 McNamara had brought out his own car. The Falcon was the first American compact, and to quote a good line from the Subaru people, it was inexpensive—and built to stay that way. It was also extremely successful, selling a fabulous 417,000 units during the first year alone. This achievement was unprecedented in automobile history and more than enough to earn McNamara the presidency of Ford.

McNamara believed in basic transportation without gimmicks, and with the Falcon, he put his ideas into practice. Although I didn't care for the car's styling—I don't really think it had any—I had to admire its success. Here was a car priced to compete with the small imports, which were starting to come on strong and had already reached nearly 10 percent of the American market. But unlike the imports, the Falcon carried six passengers, which made it large enough for most American families.

We at Ford weren't the only ones to challenge the imports. Around the same time, General Motors came out with the Corvair, and Chrysler offered the Valiant. But the Falcon was the easy winner, in part because it carried the lowest price tag.

In addition to a good price, the Falcon also represented good value. Although fuel economy was certainly not a high-priority item in 1960, the Falcon had excellent mileage. More important, it boasted a fine reputation as a trouble-free, rattle-free, and carefree car. Its simple design made repairs relatively inexpensive when they did occur—so much so that insurance companies were willing to offer discounts to drivers who owned one.

But despite its enormous popularity, the Falcon did not bring in as much money as we had hoped. As an economical small car, its profit margin was limited. Nor did it offer many options, which would have greatly increased our revenues. After my promotion to head of the Ford Division, I began to develop my own ideas about doing a car that would be popular *and* make us a ton of money. Within a couple of years, I would have the opportunity to put these ideas into practice.

V

THE KEY
TO MANAGEMENT

At the age of thirty-six, I was the general manager of the biggest division in the world's second largest company. At the same time, I was virtually unknown. Half the people at Ford didn't know who I was. The other half couldn't pronounce my name.

When Henry Ford called me over to his office in December of 1960, it was like being summoned to see God. We had shaken hands a few times, but this was the first time we ever had a real conversation. McNamara and Beacham had already told me they had sold Henry on the idea of making me head of the Ford Division, but they asked me to play dumb. They knew that Henry would want to give me the impression it was his idea.

I was thrilled by the promotion, but I could see that it put me in a delicate position. On the one hand, I was suddenly running the company's elite division. Henry Ford had personally entrusted me with the crown jewels. On the other hand, I had bypassed a hundred older and more experienced people on my way up the ladder. Some of them, I knew, were resentful of my quick success. In addition, I still had no real credentials as a product man. At this point in my career there was no car that people could point to and say: "Iacocca did that one."

That left me with the area I did know: the people side of the business. I had to find out whether all my training in sales and marketing could be applied to working with people. I had to use everything I had learned from my father, from Charlie Beacham, and from my own experience and common sense. It was testing time.

One of my first ideas came from Wall Street. The Ford Motor Company had finally gone public only four years earlier, in 1956. Now we were owned by a large group of stockholders, who were keenly interested in our health and productivity. Like other publicly-held corporations, we sent those stockholders a detailed financial report every three months. Four times a year they kept tabs on us through these quarterly reports, and four times a year we paid them a dividend out of our earnings.

If our stockholders had a quarterly review system, why shouldn't our executives? I asked myself. I began to develop the management system I still use today. Over the years, I've regularly asked my key people—and I've had them ask *their* key people, and so on down the line—a few basic questions: "What are your objectives for the next ninety days? What are your plans, your priorities, your hopes? And how do you intend to go about achieving them?"

On the surface, this procedure may seem like little more than a tough-minded way to make employees accountable to their boss. It is that, of course, but it's also much more, because the quarterly review system makes employees accountable to *themselves*. Not only does it force each manager to consider his own goals, but it's also an effective way to remind people not to lose sight of their dreams.

Every three months, each manager sits down with his immediate superior to review the manager's past accomplishments and to chart his goals for the next term. Once there is agreement on these goals, the manager puts them in writing and the supervisor signs off on it. As I'd learned from McNamara, the discipline of writing something down is the first step toward making it happen. In conversation, you can get away with all kinds of vagueness and nonsense, often without even realizing it. But there's something about putting your thoughts on paper that forces you to get down to specifics. That way, it's harder to deceive yourself—or anybody else.

The quarterly review system sounds almost too simple—except that it works. And it works for several reasons. First, it allows a man to be his own boss and to set his own goals. Second, it makes him more productive and gets him motivated on his own. Third, it helps new ideas bubble to the top. The quarterly review forces managers to pause and consider what they've accomplished, what they expect to accomplish next, and how they intend to go about it. I've never found a better way to stimulate fresh approaches to problem-solving.

Another advantage of the quarterly review system—especially in a big company—is that it keeps people from getting buried. It's very hard to get lost in the system if you're reviewed every quarter by your superior and, indirectly, by his boss and his boss's boss. This way, good guys don't get passed over. And equally important, bad guys don't get to hide.

Finally, and this is perhaps most important of all, the quarterly review system forces a dialogue between a manager and his boss. In an ideal world, you wouldn't need to institute a special structure just to make sure that kind of interaction takes place. But if a manager and his boss don't get along very well, at least four times a year they still have to sit down to decide what they're going to accomplish together in the months ahead. There's no way they can avoid this meeting, and over time, as they gradually come to know each other better, their working relationship usually improves.

During these quarterly meetings, it's the boss's responsibility to respond to each manager's plan. The boss might say: "Listen, I think you're shooting a little high, but if you think you can do all that in the next ninety days, why not give it a shot?" Or: "This plan makes good sense, but there are some priorities here that I don't agree with. Let's talk it over." Whatever the nature of the discussion, the boss's role begins to shift. Gradually he becomes less of an authority figure and more of an adviser and senior colleague.

If I'm Dave's supervisor, I might begin by asking Dave what he hopes to get done in the next three months. He might tell me he wants to raise our market penetration by half a point. At that point I'll say: "Fine. Now, how do you intend to do that?"

Before I ask that question, Dave and I have to agree on the specific goal he's working for. But that's rarely a problem. If there's any conflict between us, it's much more likely to center on *how* rather than on *what*. Most managers are reluctant to let their people run with the ball. But you'd be surprised how fast an informed and motivated guy can run.

The more Dave feels he has set his own goals, the more likely it is that he'll go right through a brick wall in order to reach them. After all, he's decided on them himself, *and* he has the boss's stamp of approval. And because Dave wants to do things his own way, he'll do his utmost to prove his way makes good sense.

The quarterly review system works equally well when Dave doesn't measure up. At that point the boss usually doesn't have to say anything.

More often than not, Dave will bring it up himself, because his failure is so painfully obvious.

In my experience, after the ninety days are up, the guy who hasn't succeeded will usually come in and explain apologetically that he didn't make his goal before the boss says anything. If that happens for several quarters in a row, the guy begins to doubt himself. He comes to realize that this is *his* problem—and not the boss's fault.

Even then, there's usually still time to take some constructive action. Often the guy himself will say: "Look, I can't handle my job. I'm in over my head. Can you move me somewhere else?"

It's far better for everybody when an employee comes to this decision on his own. Every company has lost good people who have simply been in the wrong job and who might have found more satisfaction as well as greater success if they could have been moved to another area instead of being fired. Obviously, the earlier you can detect this kind of problem, the better your chances of solving it.

Without a regular system of review, a manager who isn't working out in a particular area may build up resentment against his boss. Or the manager may imagine that the reason he failed to reach his target is that the boss holds a grudge against him. I've seen too many cases where somebody was in the wrong job for years. More often than not, there was no way for management to find that out until it was too late.

Normally, I'm not in favor of switching people around. I'm skeptical of the current fad of rotating people through various departments of a company as though all skills were interchangeable. They're not. It's like taking a cardiologist and saying: "He's a great heart surgeon. Next week, let's have him deliver a baby." He'll be the first to tell you that obstetrics is a completely different line of work and that having some expertise in one area doesn't translate into skill or experience in another. The same thing is true in the business world.

At Ford and later at Chrysler, I've always tried to get the people who worked for me to use my quarterly review system. "This is the way I control things," I explain. "And I'll show you how it works. I'm not saying you have to do it my way. But if you don't, you better find something else that produces the same results."

After using this system for many years, I've learned to watch for two potential problems. First, people sometimes bite off more than they can chew. In some cases that's a blessing in disguise, because it indicates that the guy is stretching, and for him, even a partial success may be worth a great deal. Any supervisor worth his salt would rather deal with people who attempt too much than with those who try too little.

The other problem is the boss's tendency to interfere too early. And as I came up through the ranks, I was one of the worst. I couldn't resist the temptation to get into a guy's hair, but through patience I learned. For the most part, the quarterly review system is self-regulating; it works best when I don't interfere. When it runs itself, it keeps people glued together in a constructive way, headed toward appropriate and agreed-upon objectives. You can't ask for more than that.

If I had to sum up in one word the qualities that make a good manager, I'd say that it all comes down to decisiveness. You can use the fanciest computers in the world and you can gather all the charts and numbers, but in the end you have to bring all your information together, set up a timetable, and *act*.

And I don't mean act rashly. In the press, I'm sometimes described as a flamboyant leader and a hip-shooter, a kind of fly-by-the-seat-of-the-pants operator. I may occasionally give that impression, but if that image were really true, I could never have been successful in this business.

Actually, my management style has always been pretty conservative. Whenever I've taken risks, it's been after satisfying myself that the research and the market studies supported my instincts. I may act on my intuition—but only if my hunches are supported by the facts.

Too many managers let themselves get weighed down in their decision-making, especially those with too much education. I once said to Philip Caldwell, who became the top man at Ford after I left: "The trouble with you, Phil, is that you went to Harvard, where they taught you not to take any action until you've got *all* the facts. You've got ninety-five percent of them, but it's going to take you another six months to get that last five percent. And by the time you do, your facts will be out of date because the market has moved on you. That's what life is all about—timing."

A good business leader can't operate that way. It's perfectly natural to want all the facts and to hold out for the research that guarantees a particular program will work. After all, if you're about to spend $300 million on a new product, you want to be absolutely sure you're on the right track.

That's fine in theory, but real life just doesn't work that way. Obviously, you're responsible for gathering as many relevant facts and projections as you possibly can. But at some point you've got to take that leap of faith. First, because even the right decision is wrong if it's made too late. Second, because in most cases there's no such thing as certainty. There are times when even the best manager is like the little boy with the big dog waiting to see where the dog wants to go so he can take him there.

What constitutes enough information for the decision-maker? It's impossible to put a number on it, but clearly when you move ahead with only 50 percent of the facts, the odds are stacked against you. If that's the case, you had better be very lucky—or else come up with some terrific hunches. There are times when that kind of gamble is called for, but it's certainly no way to run a railroad.

At the same time, you'll never know 100 percent of what you need. Like many industries these days, the car business is constantly changing. For us in Detroit, the great challenge is always to figure out what's going to appeal to customers three years down the road. I'm writing these words in 1984, and we're already planning our models for 1987 and 1988. Somehow I have to try to predict what's going to sell three and four years from now, even though I can't say with any certainty what the public will want next *month*.

When you don't have all the facts, you sometimes have to draw on your experience. Whenever I read in a newspaper that Lee Iacocca likes to shoot from the hip, I say to myself: "Well, maybe he's been shooting for so long that by this time he has a pretty good idea of how to hit the target."

To a certain extent, I've always operated by gut feeling. I like to be in the trenches. I was never one of those guys who could just sit around and strategize endlessly.

But there's a new breed of businessmen, mostly people with M.B.A.'s, who are wary of intuitive decisions. In part, they're right. Normally, intuition is not a good enough basis for making a move. But many of these guys go to the opposite extreme. They seem to think that every business problem can be structured and reduced to a case study. That may be true in school, but in business there has to be somebody around who will say: "Okay, folks, it's time. Be ready to go in one hour." When I read historical accounts of World War II and D-Day, I'm always struck by the same thought: Eisenhower almost blew it because he kept vacillating. But finally he said: "No matter what the weather looks like, we have to go ahead now. Waiting any longer could be even more dangerous. So let's move it!"

The same lesson applies to corporate life. There will always be those who will want to take an extra month or two to do further research on the shape of the roof on a new car. While that research may be helpful, it can wreak havoc on your production plans. After a certain point, when most of the relevant facts are in, you find yourself at the mercy of the law of diminishing returns.

That's why a certain amount of risk-taking is essential. I realize it's not for everybody. There are some people who won't leave home in the morning without an umbrella even if the sun is shining. Unfortunately, the world doesn't always wait for you while you try to anticipate your losses. Sometimes you just have to take a chance—and correct your mistakes as you go along.

Back in the 1960s and through most of the 1970s, these things didn't matter as much as they do now. In those days the car industry was like a golden goose. We were making money almost without trying. But today, few businesses can afford the luxury of slow decision-making, whether it involves a guy who's in the wrong job or the planning of a whole new line of cars five years down the road.

Despite what the textbooks say, most important decisions in corporate life are made by individuals, not by committees. My policy has always been to be democratic all the way to the point of decision. Then I become the ruthless commander. "Okay, I've heard everybody," I say. "Now here's what we're going to do."

You always need committees, because that's where people share their knowledge and intentions. But when committees replace individuals—and Ford these days has more committees than General Motors—then productivity begins to decline.

To sum up: nothing stands still in this world. I like to go duck hunting, where constant movement and change are facts of life. You can aim at a duck and get it in your sights, but the duck is always moving. *In order to hit the duck, you have to move your gun.* But a committee faced with a major decision can't always move as quickly as the events it's trying to respond to. By the time the committee is ready to shoot, the duck has flown away.

In addition to being decision-makers, managers also have to be motivators.

When I was general manager of the Ford Division, I was invited to speak to the Sloan Fellows at MIT's Alfred P. Sloan School of Management. The Sloan Fellows were a very talented group with a first-rate program that gave them a week in Europe studying the

Common Market, a week on Wall Street, a week in the Pentagon, and so on.

Every Thursday night, a guest speaker from business or industry would meet with the students. When they asked me to address one of those gatherings back in 1962, I was honored but also a little nervous. "Just relax," I was told. "The students meet after dinner in the lounge. You'll say a few words about the car business, and then they'll ask you some questions."

So I spoke briefly about manufacturing and selling automobiles, and then I asked for questions and comments. With such a bright group, I was expecting some very abstract and theoretical queries, so I was surprised when somebody said to me: "How many people work in the Ford Division?"

"We have about eleven thousand people," I responded.

"Well," he said, "you're spending today and tomorrow here in Cambridge. While you're away from the office, who motivates those eleven thousand people?"

It was a very important question, and I still remember the face of the young man who asked it. He hit the nail on the head, because management is nothing more than motivating other people.

Obviously, I couldn't know the names of all eleven thousand people who worked for me. So there had to be something else in addition to the quarterly review system that was motivating them all.

The only way you can motivate people is to communicate with them. Although I was a member of the debating team in high school, I used to be afraid of public speaking. For the first few years of my working life, I was an introvert, a shrinking violet.

But that was before I took a course in public speaking at the Dale Carnegie Institute. At the time, I had just been appointed national truck training manager at Ford. The company sent a group of us to Dale Carnegie to learn the ins and outs of public speaking.

The course started off by trying to get us out of our shells. Some people—and I was one of them—can talk all day in front of one or two people, but speaking before a whole group makes them pretty nervous.

One exercise I remember was that we had to talk off the cuff for two minutes about something we knew nothing about—such as Zen Buddhism, for example. You could start off by saying you didn't know what it was, but then you'd have to keep going—and pretty soon you'd find *something* to say. The point was to train you to think on your feet.

We learned some basic techniques of public speaking that I still practice. For example, you may know your subject, but you have to keep in mind that your audience is coming in cold. So start by telling them what you're going to tell them. Then tell them. Finally, tell them what you've already told them. I've never deviated from that axiom.

Another technique we learned was that you should always get your audience to *do* something before you finish. It doesn't matter what it is—write your congressman, call your neighbor, consider a certain proposition. In other words, don't leave without asking for the order.

As the weeks went by, I started to feel more relaxed. Pretty soon I was willing to get up and speak without being asked. I liked the challenge. The whole point was to make us less inhibited, and in my case it certainly worked. Once I started speaking, I couldn't get enough of it. (I'm sure there are those who wish I hadn't learned to like it so much!)

To this day, I'm a great believer in the Dale Carnegie Institute. I've known a lot of engineers with terrific ideas who had trouble explaining them to other people. It's always a shame when a guy with great talent can't tell the board or a committee what's in his head. More often than not, a Dale Carnegie course would make all the difference.

Not every manager has to be an orator or a writer. But more and more kids are coming out of school without the basic ability to express themselves clearly. I've sent dozens of introverted guys to Dale Carnegie at the company's expense. For most of them it's made a real difference.

I only wish I could find an institute that teaches people how to *listen.* After all, a good manager needs to listen at least as much as he needs to talk. Too many people fail to realize that real communication goes in both directions.

In corporate life, you have to encourage all your people to make a contribution to the common good and to come up with better ways of doing things. You don't have to accept every single suggestion, but if you don't get back to the guy and say, "Hey, that idea was terrific," and pat him on the back, he'll never give you another one. That kind of communication lets people know they really count.

You have to be able to listen well if you're going to motivate the people who work for you. Right there, that's the difference between a mediocre company and a great company. The most fulfilling thing for me as a manager is to watch someone the system has labeled as just average or mediocre really come into his own, all because someone has listened to his problems and helped him solve them.

Of course, the more common way to communicate with your people is to talk to them as a group. Public speaking, which is the best way to motivate a large group, is entirely different from private conversation. For one thing, it requires a lot of preparation. There's just no way around it—you have to do your homework. A speaker may be very well informed, but if he hasn't thought out exactly what he wants to say *today, to this audience*, he has no business taking up other people's valuable time.

It's important to talk to people in their own language. If you do it well, they'll say, "God, he said exactly what I was thinking." And when they begin to respect you, they'll follow you to the death. The *reason* they're following you is not because you're providing some mysterious leadership. It's because you're following them.

That's what Bob Hope is doing when he sends an advance man to scout his audience so that he can make jokes that are special to them and their situation. If you're watching on television, you might not understand what he's saying. Nevertheless, the live audience always appreciates it when a speaker has taken the trouble to learn something about who they are. Not everyone can afford an advance man, but the message is clear: public speaking does not mean impersonal speaking.

Although I could probably speak off the cuff for two hours, I always work from a script. Speaking extemporaneously is simply too exhausting. I compromise by using a prepared text and deviating from it whenever I feel the need.

When I speak to a group at Chrysler, I'm less likely to be entertaining than when I'm on the dinner circuit. With my own people, my goal is to be as direct and as straightforward as possible. I've found that the best way to motivate them is to let them know the game plan so they can all be part of it. I have to explain my own goals, just as the other executives have to set their own objectives with their supervisors. And if they meet these objectives, they should be rewarded with more than kind words. Money and a promotion are the tangible ways a company can say: most valuable player.

When you give a guy a raise, that's the time to increase his responsibilities. While he's in a good frame of mind, you reward him for what he's done and, at the same time, you motivate him to do even more. Always hit him with more while he's up, and never be too tough on him when he's down. When he's upset over his own failure, you run the risk of hurting him badly and taking away his incentive to improve. Or, as Charlie Beacham used to say, "If you want to give a man credit, put it in writing. If you want to give him hell, do it on the phone."

Charlie Beacham would preach against trying to be a one-man band. "You want to do everything yourself," he used to say. "You don't know how to delegate. Now, don't get me wrong. You're the best guy I've got. Maybe you're even as good as two guys put together. But even so—that's still only two guys. You've got a hundred people working for you right now. What happens when you get ten thousand?"

He had foresight, because at the Ford Division I had eleven thousand. He taught me to stop trying to do everybody's job. And he taught me how to give other people a goal—and how to motivate them to achieve it.

I've always felt that a manager has achieved a great deal when he's able to motivate one other person. When it comes to making the place run, motivation is everything. You might be able to do the work of two people, but you can't *be* two people. Instead, you have to inspire the next guy down the line and get him to inspire *his* people.

Once, at a private dinner with Vince Lombardi, the legendary football coach and a friend of mine, I asked him about his formula for success. I wanted to know exactly what made a winning team. What he told me that evening applies as much to the business world as it does to sports.

"You have to start by teaching the fundamentals," Lombardi said. "A player's got to know the basics of the game and how to play his position. Next, you've got to keep him in line. That's discipline. The men have to play as a team, not as a bunch of individuals. There's no room for prima donnas."

He continued: "But there have been a lot of coaches with good ball clubs who know the fundamentals and have plenty of discipline but still don't win the game. Then you come to the third ingredient: if you're going to play together as a team, you've got to care for one another. You've got to *love* each other. Each player has to be thinking about the next guy and saying to himself: 'If I don't block that man, Paul is going to get his legs broken. I have to do my job well in order that he can do his.'

"The difference between mediocrity and greatness," Lombardi said that night, "is the feeling these guys have for each other. Most people call it team spirit. When the players are imbued with that special feeling, you know you've got yourself a winning team."

Then he blurted out almost self-consciously: "But Lee, what am I telling *you* for? You run a company. It's the same thing, whether you're running a ball club or a corporation. After all, does one man build a car all by himself?"

Lombardi told me he'd like to visit Ford and see how cars are made, and I promised to invite him out to Detroit. But shortly after our dinner together, he was hospitalized with a fatal illness. I had met him only a couple of times, but his words have stayed with me: "Every time a football player goes out to ply his trade, he's got to play from the ground up—from the soles of his feet right up to his head. Every inch of him has to play. Some guys play with their heads, and sure, you need to be smart to be number one in anything you try. But most important, you've got to play with your heart. If you're lucky enough to find a guy with a lot of head and a lot of heart, he's never going to come off the field second."

He was right, of course. I've seen too many guys come along who are smart and talented but who just can't play on a team. These are the managers about whom other people say: "I wonder why he didn't go further?" We all know such people, the ones who seem to have it all and yet never make much progress. I'm not talking here about the guys who don't really want to move ahead, or those who are just plain lazy. I'm thinking of the go-getters who followed a plan, went to school, got a good job, worked hard—and then nothing came of it.

When you speak to these guys, they'll often tell you that they've had some bad breaks or perhaps a boss who didn't like them. Invariably, they present themselves as victims. But you have to wonder why they had only bad breaks and why they never seemed to look for good ones. Certainly luck plays a part. But a major reason capable people fail to advance is that they don't work well with their colleagues.

I know a man who's been working in the car business all his life. He's highly educated and well organized. He's a brilliant strategist, probably one of the most valuable people in his company. Yet he's never risen to the top ranks, because he just doesn't have the ability to handle people.

Or look at my own career. I've seen a lot of guys who are smarter than I am and a lot who know more about cars. And yet I've lost them in the smoke. Why? Because I'm tough? No. You don't succeed for very long by kicking people around. You've got to know how to talk to them, plain and simple.

Now, there's one phrase that I hate to see on any executive's evaluation, no matter how talented he may be, and that's the line: "He has trouble getting along with other people."

To me, that's the kiss of death. "You've just destroyed the guy," I always think. "He can't get along with people? Then he's got a real problem, because that's all we've got around here. No dogs, no apes—only people. And if he can't get along with his peers, what good is he to the company? As an executive, his whole function is to motivate other people. If he can't do that, he's in the wrong place."

Then there's the prima donna. Nobody likes this type, although if he's sufficiently talented he may be tolerated. At Ford, there was one executive who wanted to have his office refurbished in antiques. He put through a request to have it redecorated to the tune of $1.25 million. (That's one room and half a bath!) I happened to see Henry Ford's response, and I could tell he was angry by the message he scrawled on the memo, which said simply: "Make do with three-quarters of a million." This executive knows a lot about the car industry, but in my opinion his style makes him ineffective as a manager.

I recall another case many years ago in which Ford hired a top executive to help straighten out the marketing department. Eventually he got himself fired by doing the unthinkable—he hired his own personal PR man. He tried to make it look as though the guy were coming in as a consultant, but the truth emerged soon enough. This executive's biggest concern was that his own accomplishments would be chronicled in the newspaper. Not surprisingly, he didn't last very long.

At the same time, a certain degree of self-promotion is natural and even necessary. I've seen managers who are too shy or too scared to deal with the press, or who don't want anyone to know how much they've done. Although General Motors has encouraged this kind of faceless personality with some success, it's not for me. If your top executives don't have some ego drive, how will your company stay stirred up and competitive?

There's a world of difference between a strong ego, which is essential, and a large ego—which can be destructive. The guy with a strong ego knows his own strengths. He's confident. He has a realistic idea of what he can accomplish, and he moves purposefully toward his goal.

But the guy with a large ego is always looking for recognition. He constantly needs to be patted on the back. He thinks he's a cut above everybody else. And he talks down to the people who work for him.

The Wall Street Journal once said that I had "an ego as big as all outdoors." But if that were really true, I don't think I'd be effective in a business that depends so highly on the ability to work well with other people.

I've already said that I believe in writing things down. But this, too, can be carried to extremes. Some people seem to enjoy turning a company into a paper mill. In part, it's human nature. There are always situations in an office where some people feel a strong need to cover their ass by producing a memo for the file. True, putting your ideas on paper is usually the best way of thinking them through. But that doesn't mean everything you write should be circulated to your colleagues.

The best way to develop ideas is through interacting with your fellow managers. This brings us back to the importance of teamwork and interpersonal skills. The chemistry among two or three people sitting down together can be incredible—and it's been a big part of my own success.

So I'm a great believer in having executives spend time together talking—not always in formal meetings but simply shooting the breeze, helping each other out, and solving problems.

People who visit my office at Chrysler are often surprised that I don't have a computer terminal on my desk. Maybe they forget that everything that comes out of a computer, somebody has to put in. The biggest problem facing American business today is that most managers have too much information. It dazzles them, and they don't know what to do with it all.

The key to success is not information. It's people. And the kind of people I look for to fill top management spots are the eager beavers. These are the guys who try to do more than they're expected to. They're always reaching. And reaching out to the people they work with, trying to help them do their jobs better. That's the way they're built.

Then there are the other guys, the nine-to-five gang. They just want to get along and be told what to do. They say: "I don't want to be in the rat race. It might affect my heartbeat."

Just because you get involved and excited and really tear into things doesn't mean you'll die of hypertension next week!

So I try to look for people with that drive. You don't need many.

With twenty-five of these guys, I could run the government of the United States.

At Chrysler I have about a dozen. What makes these managers strong is that they know how to delegate and how to motivate. They know how to look for the pressure points and how to set priorities. They're the kind of guys who can say: "Forget that, it'll take ten years. Here's what we gotta do *now*."

VI

THE MUSTANG

My years as general manager of the Ford Division were the happiest period of my life. For my colleagues and me, this was fire-in-the-belly time. We were high from smoking our own brand—a combination of hard work and big dreams.

In those days, I couldn't wait to get to work in the morning. At night I didn't want to leave. We were continually playing with new ideas and trying out models on the test track. We were young and cocky. We saw ourselves as artists, about to produce the finest masterpieces the world had ever seen.

In 1960, the whole country was optimistic. With Kennedy in the White House, a fresh breeze was blowing across the land. It carried an unspoken message that anything was possible. The striking contrast between the new decade and the 1950s, between John Kennedy and Dwight Eisenhower, could be summed up in a single word—youth.

But before I could act on my own youthful dreams, there were other matters to take care of. After the spectacular success of the Falcon, Robert McNamara had authorized the development of another new car, a German-built compact known as the Cardinal. It was scheduled to be introduced in the fall of 1962, and when I took over the Ford Division, one of my responsibilities was to oversee its production.

Because McNamara was concerned with fuel efficiency and basic transportation, the Cardinal was conceived to be the American response to the Volkswagen. Like the Falcon, it was small, plain, and inexpensive. Both models expressed McNamara's deep conviction that a car was a means of transportation and not a toy.

A few months into my new job, I flew over to Germany to check on the progress of McNamara's car. It was my first time in Europe, and that alone was quite a thrill. But when I finally saw the Cardinal, I was underwhelmed.

It was a fine car for the European market, with its V-4 engine and front-wheel drive. But in the United States there was no way it could have sold the three hundred thousand units we were counting on. Among other problems, the Cardinal was too small and had no trunk. And while its fuel economy was great, that wasn't yet a selling point for the American consumer. In addition, the styling was lousy. The Cardinal looked like it was designed by committee.

As usual, McNamara was ahead of his time—ten years, to be exact. A decade later, after the OPEC crisis, the Cardinal would have been a world-beater.

In some industries, being ahead of your time is a great advantage. But not in Detroit. Just as the car industry can't afford to lag too far behind the consumer, it also can't afford to be too far ahead of him. Coming out with a new product too early is just as bad as being too late.

There's a widespread myth that those of us who run the car industry somehow manipulate the public, that we tell people what kind of cars they should buy—and that they listen. Whenever I hear this, I always smile and think: "If only it were true!"

The truth is that we can only sell what people are willing to buy. In fact, we follow the public far more than we lead it. Naturally, we do our best to persuade people to buy our products. But sometimes our best efforts aren't good enough.

I didn't need any reminder of that in 1960. The company was still reeling from the Edsel fiasco a couple of years back. This isn't the place to go into the various reasons for that sad story, but suffice it to say that the Edsel—which neither McNamara nor I had anything to do with—failed on so grand a scale that "Edsel" has come to be synonymous with failure.

When I returned from Germany I went straight to Henry Ford. "The Cardinal is a loser," I told him. "To bring out another lemon so soon after the Edsel would bring this company to its knees. We simply can't afford a new model that won't appeal to younger buyers."

I stressed the youth angle for two reasons. First, I was becoming increasingly aware of the economic power of the younger generation, a power that had not yet been recognized in our industry. Second, I knew that the boss liked to think of himself as a with-it guy, a swinger who understood what young people wanted.

Then I met with top management and our board of directors to discuss the fate of the Cardinal. In these talks, I got the impression that the entire company was confused about the car and that the senior people were only too pleased to have a young upstart like me make the decision for them. That way, none of them would have to take direct responsibility if stopping the Cardinal turned out to be a gigantic mistake. Although the company had already invested $35 million in the car, I argued that it wouldn't sell and that we should cut our losses and run.

I must have been convincing, because my decision was accepted with only two dissenters: John Bugas, head of our international operations, and Arjay Miller, our controller. Bugas, although he was my close friend, naturally wanted the Cardinal to come out because it was made overseas. Miller was concerned about the $35 million we had already invested. Like a true bean counter, he saw mainly the $35 million loss in that quarter.

With the Cardinal out of the way, I was free to work on my own projects. Right away, I brought together a group of bright and creative young guys from the Ford Division. We started getting together once a week for dinner and conversation at the Fairlane Inn in Dearborn, about a mile from where we worked.

We met at the hotel because a lot of people back at the office were just waiting for us to fall on our faces. I was a young Turk, a new vice-president who hadn't yet proved himself. My guys were talented, but they weren't always the most popular people in the company.

Don Frey, our product manager and now head of Bell and Howell, was a key member of that group. So was Hal Sperlich, who is still with me today in a top position at Chrysler. The others included Frank Zimmerman from marketing; Walter Murphy, our public-relations manager and my loyal friend throughout my years at Ford; and Sid Olson from J. Walter Thompson, a brilliant writer who was once a speech writer for F.D.R. and, among other things, coined the phrase "The Arsenal of Democracy."

The Fairlane Committee, as we called ourselves, had a lot on the ball. We were dimly aware that the car market would be stood on its ear in the next few years, although there was no way of knowing exactly how that would happen. We also knew that General Motors had taken the Corvair, an economy car, and transformed it into the hot-selling Corvair Monza simply by adding a few sporty accessories such as bucket seats, stick shift, and fancy interior trim. We at Ford had nothing to offer to the people who were considering a Monza, but it was clear to us that they represented a growing market.

Meanwhile, our public-relations department was receiving a steady stream of letters from people who wanted us to bring out another two-passenger Thunderbird. This was a surprise to us, because that car had not been very successful, selling only fifty-three thousand units over three years. But the mail was telling us consumer tastes were changing. Maybe the two-passenger Thunderbird was simply ahead of its time, we said to ourselves. We were starting to get the strong impression that if that car were still on the market, we'd be selling a lot more than eighteen thousand a year.

At the same time, our market researchers confirmed that the youthful image of the new decade had a firm basis in demographic reality. For one thing, the average age of the population was falling at an unusually rapid rate. Millions of teenagers born in the baby boom that followed World War II were about to surge into the national marketplace. The twenty- to twenty-four-year-old group would increase by over 50 percent during the 1960s. Moreover, young adults between eighteen and thirty-four would account for at least half the huge increase in car sales that was predicted for the entire industry during the next ten years.

The researchers added an obscure but interesting footnote. Not only would there be *more* young people than ever before, but they would also be better educated than previous generations. We already knew that college-educated people bought cars at a much higher rate than their less-educated counterparts, and our projections showed that the number of college students was going to double by 1970.

There were equally interesting changes going on among older car buyers. We were now starting to see a perceptible shift away from the preoccupation with economy cars that had characterized the late 1950s and had helped the Falcon set new records. Consumers were beginning to look beyond the austere and the purely functional to consider more sporty and luxury models—just as they are again in 1984.

When we analyzed all this information, the conclusion was inescapable. Whereas the Edsel had been a car in search of a market it never found, *here was a market in search of a car.* The normal procedure in Detroit was to build a car and then try to identify its buyers. But we were in a position to move in the opposite direction—and tailor a new product for a hungry new market.

Any car that would appeal to these young customers had to have three main features: great styling, strong performance, and a low price. Developing a new model with all three would not be easy. But if it could be done, we had a shot at a major success.

We went back to the research and learned a little more about the changing market for new cars. First, there was an enormous growth in two-car families, with the second car typically smaller and more sporty than the first. Second, a growing number of cars were being bought by women, who preferred small cars with easy handling. Single people, too, were increasingly represented among new-car buyers, and they were choosing smaller and sportier models than their married friends. Finally, it was becoming clear that in the next few years, Americans would have more money than ever before to spend on transportation and entertainment.

As we processed this information, we began to look at the sales figures from the Falcon to see what we could find out about our own customers. The results were surprising. Although the Falcon was marketed as a low-priced economy car, far more customers than we expected were starting to order such options as automatic transmission, white-wall tires, and more powerful engines. This was my first inkling of an important fact about small cars that remains as true today as it was twenty years ago: the American car buyer wants economy so badly he'll pay almost anything to get it!

The Fairlane Committee began to get more specific about the car we wanted to build. It had to be small—but not *too* small. The market for a two-seat car may have been growing, but it was still limited to around a hundred thousand, which meant that a two-seater would never have mass appeal. Our car, then, had to hold four passengers. For performance it also had to be light—twenty-five hundred pounds was our limit. And finally, it had to be inexpensive. Our goal was to have it sell for no more than $2,500 with equipment.

In terms of styling, I had an idea of what I wanted. I used to go home and pore through the pages of a book called *Auto Universum*, which features pictures of all the cars ever built. The one that always jumped out at me was the first Continental Mark. That was everyone's dream car—or at least it had been mine ever since Leander Hamilton McCormick-Goodheart drove up to Lehigh in 1945. What distinguished the Mark was its long hood and short deck. The length of the hood gave the appearance of verve and performance, and that, I decided, was what people were looking for.

The more our group talked, the more concrete our ideas became. Our car had to be obviously sporty and distinctively styled, with just a dash of nostalgia. It had to be easy to identify and unlike anything else on the market. It had to be simple to maneuver but still capable of seating four people, with enough room left for a fair-sized trunk. It had to be a sports car but more than a sports car. We wanted to develop a car that you could drive to the country club on Friday night, to the drag strip on Saturday, and to church on Sunday.

In other words, our intention was to appeal to several markets at once. We had to broaden our base of potential customers because the only way we could afford to produce this car at a terrific price was to sell a ton of them. Rather than offer several different versions of the same product, we agreed that the only sensible course was to develop one basic car with a wide range of options. That way, the customer could buy as much economy, luxury, or performance as he wanted—or could afford.

But the question was: could *we* afford the car? An all-new car from the ground up would cost $300 to $400 million. The answer lay in using components that were already in the system. That way we could save a fortune in production costs. The engines, transmissions, and axles for the Falcon already existed, so if we could adapt them, we wouldn't have to start from scratch. We could piggyback the new car onto the Falcon and save a fortune. In the end, we would be able to develop the new car for a mere $75 million.

All this sounded great, but not everyone thought it could be done. Dick Place, a product planner, said that making a sporty car out of a Falcon was like putting falsies on Grandma. Still, I assigned Don Frey and Hal Sperlich to play with the idea. They experimented with several different models but in the end concluded that the new car's design and exterior had to be completely original. We could keep the platform and the engine from the Falcon, but as we say in Detroit, the car needed a whole new skin and greenhouse—the windshield, side glass, and backlite.

By late 1961, we had a target date. The New York World's Fair was scheduled to open in April 1964, which sounded to us like the ideal place to launch our car. Although new models are traditionally introduced in the fall, we had in mind a product so exciting and so different that we would dare to bring it out in the middle of the season. Only the World's Fair had enough scale and drama for the car of our dreams.

There was one big piece missing from the puzzle: we still didn't have a design. During the first seven months of 1962, our styling people produced no less than eighteen different clay models, in the hope that one of them might be the car we were after. Several of these models were exciting, but none of them seemed exactly right.

By now I was growing impatient. If our new car was going to be ready in April 1964, we needed a design right away. There were twenty-one months left in which to get the idea approved, agree on a final styling model, decide on a plant, buy equipment, locate supply sources, and arrange for dealers to sell the finished product. We were well into the summer of 1962, and the only way we could still have a shot at the World's Fair was to come up with a fully approved clay model by September 1.

With time running out, I decided to stage a competition among our designers. On July 27, Gene Bordinat, our styling director, summoned three of his top stylists to his office. He explained that each of their studios would take part in an unprecedented open competition by designing at least one model of the small sports car we were determined to build.

The designers were told to have their clay models ready for review by top management on August 16. We were asking a great deal of these guys, because normally you can't design a car that quickly. But after two weeks of 'round-the-clock work, there were seven models to choose from on the day of the review.

The clear winner was designed by Dave Ash, the assistant to Ford studio head Joe Oros. When it was about half done, Joe had invited me down to have a look. As soon as I saw it, one thing hit me instantly: although it was just sitting there on the studio floor, this brown clay model looked like it was moving.

Because they saw their car as feline in nature, Joe and Dave had started calling it the Cougar. The model they had prepared for the August 16 showing was painted white with red wheels. The Cougar's back bumper turned up to form a bustling little rear end. The grille on the front had a stylized cougar inside, giving the model an aura that was both handsome and powerful.

Immediately after the presentation, the Cougar was rolled to the Ford studios for feasibility studies. At long last we had an active proposal under consideration. But we still didn't have a car. For that, we needed approval from the styling committee—which was made up of the top executives in the company.

I knew I was facing an uphill battle when I went in to try to sell the Cougar. To begin with, the senior executives were not yet convinced, as we were, that the youth market was real. And because the Edsel was still fresh in their minds, they were cautious and wary about introducing another new model. To make matters worse, they had already committed themselves to the huge expense of retooling the regular line of Ford products for 1965. There was some question as to whether the company could really afford another car—even one that could be produced for relatively little money.

Arjay Miller, who would soon become the new president, ordered a study of our proposal. He was somewhat optimistic about sales, but he worried about cannibalism—that the new car's success might come at the expense of other Ford products, especially the Falcon. The study he commissioned projected that the Cougar would sell eighty-six thousand units. That was a respectable figure, but it wasn't quite high enough to justify the huge expense of starting up a new model.

Fortunately, Henry Ford was now more receptive to the plan. This openness was in sharp contrast to his reaction the first time I had described the idea to a committee of high-level executives. In the middle of my pitch, Henry had suddenly said, "I'm leaving," and walked out of the room. I had never seen him so cold to a new idea. I went home and told Mary: "I got shot down today on my favorite project. Henry walked out on me."

I was really crushed. But the very next day, we learned that Henry's abrupt departure had nothing to do with my presentation. He had been feeling weak so he went home early—and spent the next six weeks in bed with mononucleosis. When he came back, he was feeling much better about everything, including the plans for our new car.

Later, as we were building the prototype, Henry came by one day to have a look. He climbed into the car and announced: "It's a little tight in the back seat. Add another inch for leg room."

Unfortunately, adding even an inch to the interior of a car can be a very expensive proposition. An extra inch also had implications for styling, and all of us were against the change. But we also knew that Henry's decisions were not open to debate. As he liked to remind us, his name was on the building. Besides, at that point we would have added another *ten* inches if it would make the difference between doing the car and losing it.

* * *

Although he probably didn't know it at the time—and in fact, he may *still* not know it—Henry also played a role in the new car's name. Before we decided to call it the Mustang, it was known by several other designations. During the early planning stages, we called it the Special Falcon. Then, after the Oros-Ash model was accepted, the Cougar. Henry wanted to call it T-Bird II, but nobody else liked that one.

At a product strategy meeting in May, we narrowed our choices down to Monte Carlo, Monaco, Torino, and Cougar. When we learned that the first two had already been registered with the Automobile Manufacturers Association by other companies, it came down to Torino and Cougar. Finally we settled on Torino, which happens to be the Italian spelling of the industrial city of Turin. Torino was also in keeping with the vaguely foreign flavor we had worked so hard to capture. As a kind of compromise, we decided to keep the stylized cougar as the Torino's emblem.

While we were preparing the ad campaign for the Torino, I got a call from the top guy in public relations, Charlie Moore. "You'll have to pick another name for your car," he said. He explained that Henry was in the midst of a divorce and was keeping company with Cristina Vettore Austin, an Italian jet-set divorcée he had met at a party in Paris. Some of Henry's underlings felt that giving the new car an Italian name would lead to unfavorable publicity and gossip, which would embarrass the boss.

We had to come up with another name in a hurry. When it comes to naming a car, there's always a battle. And for good reason: the name is often the toughest part of the car to get right. It's easier to design doors and roofs than to come up with a name, because the choice is inevitably subjective. Sometimes the process can get pretty emotional.

John Conley, who worked for J. Walter Thompson, our ad agency, was a name specialist. In the past, he had researched bird names for the Thunderbird and the Falcon. This time we sent him to the Detroit Public Library to look up the names of animals—from aardvark to zebra. John came up with thousands of suggestions, which we narrowed down to six: Bronco, Puma, Cheetah, Colt, Mustang, and Cougar.

Mustang had been the name of one of the car's prototypes. Curiously, it was not named for the horse but for the legendary World War II fighter plane. No matter. We all liked Mustang, and as the ad agency said: it "had the excitement of wide-open spaces and was American as all hell."

In my library at home, I still have a die casting of the emblem of the Cougar, which the designers sent me in a little walnut box with a scroll saying: "Please don't fool around. Don't name it anything but Cougar." It was a request I couldn't honor, but we did use the name Cougar a few years later for a fine new car in the Lincoln-Mercury division.

Ever since the Mustang was introduced, people have enjoyed pointing out that the emblem of the horse on the front of the car was facing the wrong way, because it gallops in a clockwise direction instead of counterclockwise, the way horses run on American racetracks. My answer to that has always been that the Mustang is a wild horse, not a domesticated racer. And no matter which way it was running, I felt increasingly sure that it was headed in the right direction.

Once we settled on the styling, we had to make some basic decisions about the interior. We were eager to provide for those customers who wanted luxury, but we didn't want to cut out the people who were more interested in performance or economy. At the same time, we didn't want to produce a totally stripped car. The Mustang was already being seen as a poor man's Thunderbird; there would be little point in bringing out a poor man's Mustang. We decided that even the economy model had to be comparable to the luxury and performance versions, and so we included such items as bucket seats, vinyl trim, wheel covers, and carpeting as standard features in each car.

Beyond that, we had in mind a kind of do-it-yourself car that would appeal to all segments of the market. If a customer could afford luxury, he could buy extra accessories and more power. If he loved luxury but couldn't afford these extras, he would still be happy because several options he'd normally have to pay for were available here at no extra charge.

Long before the car came out, we started doing market research. One of our final tests was especially encouraging. We invited a select group of fifty-two Detroit area couples to our styling showroom. Each of these couples already owned a standard-sized car and earned average incomes, which meant they were not prime candidates for a second car. We brought them in small groups into our styling studio to view the prototype of the Mustang, and we recorded their impressions on tape.

What we found was that white-collar couples were impressed by the car's styling, while blue-collar workers saw the Mustang as a symbol of status and prestige. When we asked them to estimate the price of the car, almost everybody guessed a figure that was at least $1,000 too high. When we asked if they would buy a Mustang, most said they wouldn't. They explained that it was too expensive, or too small, or too difficult to handle.

But when we told them the actual price of the car, a funny thing happened. Most people said: "The hell with my objections, I want it!" Suddenly their excuses vanished. They came up with all sorts of innovative reasons why this particular car made good sense after all. One fellow said: "If I parked that car in my driveway, all my neighbors would wonder what gravy train I fell into." Another one told us: "It doesn't look like an ordinary car—and at that price what you get is an ordinary car."

The lesson was clear. When it came time to market the Mustang, we had to make sure to emphasize its low price.

The final sticker price on the Mustang reflected our early decision to hold the price under $2,500. We ended up with a car that was an inch and a half longer than we had originally planned and 108 pounds heavier. But we held the line on price, and the Mustang sold for $2,368.

The good omens continued. By January 1964, only a few weeks from the launch, economic conditions had become unusually favorable. We would later learn that the first quarter of 1964 marked the highest level of auto sales in history. In addition, Congress was about to enact an income-tax cut, and disposable income was on the rise. All things considered, the national mood reflected high confidence and optimism.

On March 9, 1964, 571 days after the Oros-Ash Cougar had been selected over its six rivals, the first Mustang rolled off the assembly line. We had arranged to produce a minimum of 8,160 cars before introduction day—April 17—so that every Ford dealer in the country would have at least one Mustang in his showroom when the car was officially launched.

We promoted the Mustang to the hilt. We invited the editors of college newspapers to Dearborn, and we gave them a Mustang to drive for a few weeks. Four days before the car was officially launched, a hundred members of the press participated in a giant seventy-car Mustang rally from New York to Dearborn, and the cars demonstrated their reliability by breezing through the seven-hundred-mile trip without any problems. The press recorded its enthusiasm in a massive and lyrical outpouring of words and photographs that appeared prominently in hundreds of magazines and newspapers.

On April 17, Ford dealerships everywhere were mobbed with customers. In Chicago, one dealer had to lock his showroom doors because the crowd outside was so large. A dealer in Pittsburgh reported that the crush of customers was so thick he couldn't get his Mustang off the wash rack. In Detroit, another dealer said that so many people who had come to see the Mustang had arrived in sports cars that his parking lot looked like a foreign-car rally.

In Garland, Texas, a Ford dealer had fifteen potential customers bidding on a single Mustang in his display window. He sold it to the highest bidder—a man who insisted on spending the night in the car so that nobody else could buy it while his check was clearing. At a dealership in Seattle, the driver of a passing cement truck became so fascinated by the Mustang on display that he lost control of his vehicle and crashed through the showroom window.

The Mustang was destined to be an incredible hit. During the first weekend it was on sale, an unprecedented four million people visited Ford dealerships. The car's public reception was exceeding our wildest hopes.

The press played an important role in creating this excitement. Due to the tireless efforts of Walter Murphy in public relations, the Mustang was featured simultaneously on the covers of both *Time* and *Newsweek*. This was an astounding publicity coup for a new commercial project. Both magazines sensed we had a winner, and their added publicity during the very week of the Mustang's introduction helped make their prediction a self-fulfilling prophecy. I'm convinced that *Time* and *Newsweek* alone led to the sale of an extra 100,000 cars.

The twin cover stories had the effect of two gigantic commercials. After telling its readers that my name "rhymes with try-a-Coke-ah," *Time* noted that "Iacocca has produced more than just another new car. With its long hood and short rear deck, its Ferrari flair and openmouthed air scoop, the Mustang resembles the European racing cars that American sports-car buffs find so appealing. Yet Iacocca has made the Mustang's design so flexible, its price so reasonable, and its options so numerous that its potential appeal reaches toward two-thirds of all U.S. car buyers. Priced as low as $2,368 and able to accommodate a small family in its four seats, the Mustang seems destined to be a sort of Model A of sports cars—for the masses as well as the buffs." I couldn't have said it better myself.

The automotive press was no less enthusiastic. "A market which had been looking for a car has it now," began the story in *Car Life*. Even *Consumer Reports*, generally no great fan of Detroit, noted the Mustang's "almost complete absence of poor fit and sloppy workmanship in a car being built at a hell-for-leather pace."

But we hadn't been counting on the press to do our advertising for us. On introduction day we ran full-page ads in twenty-six hundred newspapers. We used what I call the Mona Lisa approach: a simple profile of the car in white, listing the price along with a simple line, "The Unexpected." When the product is right, you don't have to be a great marketer.

We also blanketed the television networks with Mustang commercials. J. Walter Thompson produced a whole series of ads using a Walter Mitty theme, based on the James Thurber character who dreams of being a race driver or a jet pilot. In one of these ads, Henry Foster, a conservative, mild-mannered antiques dealer, leaves his shop carrying a lunch bag. "Have you heard about Henry Foster?" asks the lady in the next store. Henry walks around the corner and gets into his red Mustang. He throws away his derby and replaces it with a sporty tweed hat from his bag. Then he takes off his coat to reveal a bright red vest. Finally he exchanges his old-fashioned glasses for racing goggles.

"Something's happened to Henry," the lady's voice continues.

"A Mustang's happened to Henry," announces another woman. She's young, attractive, and waiting for Henry in a green meadow with a picnic lunch and a bottle of wine.

We also ran hard-hitting national promotion programs. We displayed Mustangs in fifteen of the country's busiest airports and in the lobbies of two hundred Holiday Inns from coast to coast. At the University of Michigan football games, we contracted for several acres of space in the parking lot and put up huge signs that said: "Mustang Corral." We also did a lot of direct mail, sending out millions of pieces to small-car owners across the country.

After only a few weeks it became clear to me that we had to open up a second plant. The initial assumption had been that the Mustang would sell seventy-five thousand units during the first year. But the projections kept growing, and before the car was introduced we were planning on sales of two hundred thousand. To build even that many cars, we had to convince top management to convert a second plant, in San Jose, California, into producing more Mustangs.

Because the cars were in such short supply, it was hard to know how many we could really sell. So a few weeks after the Mustang was introduced, Frank Zimmerman arranged for an experiment in Dayton, Ohio, known as a GM town because GM had several plants in the area.

He met with the Ford dealers in Dayton and told them: "Look, you guys are in a tough, competitive market here, and the Mustang's a hot car. We want to see how hot it really is, so we're going to give each of you ten cars to put in stock and we'll honor your retail orders as quickly as you get them."

The results were amazing. We got something like 10 percent of the entire car market in Dayton. That was all the ammunition we needed, and by September we were starting to convert the San Jose plant.

Our annual capacity was now 360,000 cars, and soon we were converting a third plant, in Metuchen, New Jersey. These two conversions represented an expensive risk, but we had been burned on the Falcon when we'd set our sights too low and then didn't have the capacity to produce all the cars we needed. We weren't going to make that mistake twice.

People were buying Mustangs in record numbers. The options and accessories were moving just as quickly. Our customers reacted to the long list of options like hungry lumberjacks at a Swedish smorgasbord. Over 80 percent ordered white sidewall tires, 80 percent wanted radios, 71 percent took eight-cylinder engines, and 50 percent bought the automatic transmission. Every tenth Mustang was sold equipped with a tachometer and a clock that comprised a special "Rallye Pack." For a car that cost $2,368, our customers were spending an average of $1,000 each just on options!

I had a target in mind for the first year. During *its* first year, the Falcon had sold a record 417,174 cars, and that was the figure I wanted to beat. We had a slogan: "417 by 4/17"—the Mustang's birthday. Late in the evening of April 16, 1965, a young Californian bought a sporty red Mustang convertible. He had just purchased the 418,812th Mustang, and we finished our first year with a new record.

The bean counters went back into the bunkers muttering that there was evidently more than one way to build a car. It was the styling that did it, which was something they hadn't counted on. But they weren't shy when it came time to count the money. In the first two years alone, the Mustang generated net profits of $1.1 billion. And that's in 1964 dollars!

*   *   *

Within weeks of the Mustang's introduction, we were flooded with letters from satisfied customers. I always read customer mail, so I'm well aware that most people write to the manufacturer only when there's a problem. With the Mustang, however, people wrote to express their gratitude and their enthusiasm. Just about the only complaint I got had to do with the scarcity of Mustangs and the long waiting list.

One of my favorite letters came from a Brooklyn man only four days after the car was launched. "I'm not much on cars," he wrote, "and I haven't been since most cars got pregnant. Furthermore, New York is no place to have a car. Pet owners urge their dogs to urinate on the wheels. Slum kids steal the hubcaps. Cops give parking tickets. Pigeons roost on the car, and worse. Streets are always torn up. Buses crush you, taxis bump you, and inside parking requires a second mortgage on the house. Gas costs 30 percent more than anyplace else. The insurance rates are incredible. The garment district is impassable, the Wall Street area impenetrable, going to New Jersey impossible."

And here's his final line: "So as soon as I can raise the nut, I'm buying a Mustang."

When we surveyed the ranks of Mustang owners, we found that their average age was thirty-one, but that one in every six owners was in the forty-five-to-fifty-four group, which meant that the car wasn't limited to young people. Almost two thirds of the buyers were married, and more than half of them had been to college.

Before the first year was over, there were Mustang clubs—hundreds of them—as well as Mustang sunglasses, key chains, and hats, along with toy Mustangs for kids. I knew we had it made when somebody spotted a sign in a bakery window that read: "Our hotcakes are selling like Mustangs."

I could easily devote the rest of this book to Mustang stories, but I'll add just one more.

During one of my fifty-two round trips to Europe, I was asleep on the company plane one Sunday morning over the iceberg route—where the *Titanic* sank. Beneath us was a weather ship with one poor, godforsaken soul giving weather reports to airplanes. When our guys went over the ship, they radioed down: "How're things?"

"I can't stand up," the weatherman answered. "It's such a rough day, the swells are twelve feet high."

They kibitzed about it, and then the guy found out who we were. "I got a Mustang," he said immediately. "You got Iacocca on board?"

While they were crackling this out, a KLM plane crossed our path and their pilot said: "Hold it. Is that the Ford plane with Iacocca? I'd like to talk to him."

Just then a Pan Am plane flew by and *their* guy jumped in.

This all happened while I was asleep. Our pilot comes in and says to me: "You're wanted on the phone. We've got a ship and two airplanes all wanting to talk to you at the same time."

I said: "Is nothing sacred? It's Sunday morning, I'm in the middle of nowhere, and I can't get away from this Mustang mania!"

I'm generally seen as the father of the Mustang, although, as with any success, there were plenty of people willing to take the credit. A stranger asking around Dearborn for people who were connected with the Edsel would be like old Diogenes with his lantern searching for an honest man. On the other hand, so many people have claimed to be the father of the Mustang that I wouldn't want to be seen in public with the mother!

They say all good things must come to an end, and the Mustang was no exception. In 1968, at Ford's annual meeting, one of our stockholders took the floor to voice a complaint: "When the Thunderbird came out," she said, "it was. a beautiful sports car. Then you blew it up to the point where it lost its identity. The same thing is happening to the Mustang. Why can't you leave a small car small? You keep blowing them up and then starting another little one, blowing that one up and starting another one."

Unfortunately, she was right. Within a few years of its introduction, the Mustang was no longer a sleek horse. It was more like a fat pig. In 1968, Bunkie Knudsen came in as the new president of Ford. Right away he added a monster of an engine with double the horsepower to the Mustang. To support the engine, he had to widen the entire car. By 1971, the Mustang had grown eight inches longer, six inches wider, and almost six hundred pounds heavier than the original 1965 model.

It was no longer the same car, and our declining sales figures were making the point very clearly. In 1966, we sold 550,000 Mustangs. By 1970, sales had plummeted to 150,000—a disastrous decline. Our customers had abandoned us because we had abandoned their car. Instead of the original $2,368, the Mustang was now closer to $3,368, and not all of that rise could be blamed on inflation.

Late in 1969 we began planning the Mustang II, a return to the small car that had been so successful. A lot of people in Detroit could hardly believe we were doing this, because it violated an unwritten rule that an established car could only be made bigger—never smaller. To put out a smaller Mustang was tantamount to admitting we had made a mistake.

Of course we had. To plan Mustang II, I turned once more to Hal Sperlich, who had played a major role in creating the original Mustang. Hal and I flew over to Italy to visit the Ghia studios in Turin, where we met with Alejandro deTomaso, the studio head. Within two months, deTomaso's prototype arrived in Dearborn, and we had ourselves a terrific design.

Mustang II was very successful, although it wasn't quite the hit that the original had been. But then, as we knew only too well, that was a tough act to follow.

VII

ENCORE!

The success of the Mustang was apparent so quickly that even before its first birthday I was given a major promotion. In January 1965, I became vice-president of the corporate car and truck group. I was now in charge of the planning, production, and marketing of all cars and trucks in both the Ford and Lincoln-Mercury Divisions.

My new office was in the Glass House, which is how everybody at Ford referred to World Headquarters. I was finally one of the big boys, part of that select group of officers who ate lunch every day with Henry Ford. Until now, as far as I was concerned, Henry had simply been the top boss. Suddenly I was seeing him almost every day. Not only was I part of the rarefied atmosphere of top management, but I was also the new kid on the block, the young comer who was responsible for the Mustang.

Moreover, I was His Majesty's special protégé. After McNamara left in 1960 to join the Kennedy administration, Henry had more or less adopted me, and he kept a close eye on what I was up to from the start.

As a group vice-president, I had a number of new assignments and responsibilities, especially in the area of advertising and promotion. But my chief mandate, as Henry made clear, was to "rub some of that Mustang ointment onto the Lincoln-Mercury Division."

For years, Lincoln-Mercury had been the weak sister of the Ford family and a burden to the rest of the company. The division had been started in the 1940s, but twenty years later it still hadn't come into its own. There had even been talk of dropping the Lincoln and selling off that part of the company.

This was the division that featured high-priced, upscale cars. The company's hope and expectation had been that the customer who had purchased a Ford Division product would eventually "graduate" to a Mercury or a Lincoln, much as a General Motors customer might trade up from a Chevrolet or Pontiac to a Buick or Oldsmobile.

So much for theory. In practice, most Ford owners ended up jumping ship. Those who could afford to trade up were more likely to graduate to a Buick, Oldsmobile, or Cadillac rather than a Mercury or Lincoln. All we were doing was growing future customers for GM's luxury cars.

When I took a good look around the Lincoln-Mercury Division, I understood why. The cars simply weren't exciting. It's not that they weren't *good*; they just weren't distinctive. The Comet, for example, was really only a fancy Falcon, while the Mercury resembled an oversized Ford. What Lincoln-Mercury cars were lacking was their own unique style and identity.

Over the years, sales had languished. The Lincoln was supposed to be competing with Cadillac, but it was consistently outsold by Cadillac by something like five to one. The Mercury suffered a similar fate and was unable to mount much of an assault on GM's duo of Buick and Oldsmobile. Now, in 1965, the Lincoln-Mercury Division was virtually dead and in urgent need of a resurrection.

It would have been easy enough to blame the dealers, but that would have been grossly unfair. In fact, those dealers who were able to survive until 1965 *had* to be good, because they didn't have the benefit of a first-rate product. Still, they suffered from low morale. They needed motivation. They needed a new team of district sales managers. And they needed somebody in the Glass House who could really look after their interests.

But most of all, they needed new products. We got right to work, and by 1967 we were ready with two new entries. The Mercury Cougar was a luxury sports car designed to appeal to the Mustang driver who was ready for something a little plusher. The Mercury Marquis was a full-sized luxury car to compete with Buick and Oldsmobile.

It was symptomatic of our problems that Gar Laux, the head of the Lincoln-Mercury Division, didn't even want the Marquis to carry the Mercury name. As far as he was concerned, the Mercury name was the kiss of death, so bad that it would drag down even a great car. I had to convince him that by starting with the new Marquis, we were going to upgrade Lincoln-Mercury's image.

*   *   *

To create a sense of excitement about these two new cars, it was important to unveil them to the dealers in the most dramatic way. Until around ten years ago, the annual introduction of new-car models from Detroit was a major event for both the dealers and the general public. As introduction day approached, the dealers would keep their new cars under wraps. All across the land, kids would peek into the windows in the hope of getting an early glimpse of the new Fords or Chevys. Today that ritual is just a fond memory.

Also long gone are the big dealer shows, which we used to arrange each year in Las Vegas. Every summer we would wine them and dine them and spend millions on a spectacular show where we would introduce the new models. There would be cars coming out of fountains, girls jumping out of cars, lots of smoke bombs and strobe lights, and all sorts of dazzling displays. These shows were sometimes better than Broadway, but here the cars were the stars.

We also used to run dealer incentive programs. Back then, the Big Three were rolling in big bucks. Everything we did was first class. When it came to impressing the dealers, the sky was the limit. Many of them were making $1 million a year, and even the guys who weren't so good were doing well.

During the 1960s, we used to run a lot of trips as incentives and bonuses for the dealers. No matter how wealthy they were, there was something about a well-planned trip to an exotic spot that was very difficult to pass up. These trips were always a big hit, and many of the dealers became very friendly with each other, which raised their morale even higher and gave them a heightened sense of purpose and belonging.

Sometimes I used to go along as an official host. For me, the trips were a perfect opportunity to touch base with a lot of dealers over a short time. They were also an ideal way of combining work with a good time, and Mary and I always had fun.

In September 1966, Lincoln-Mercury scheduled a spectacular cruise for those dealers who had reached a certain sales quota. We leased the S. S. *Independence* at a cost of $44,000 a day and set sail from New York for the Caribbean, where we planned to show our new models. At sunset on the second day, we assembled all the dealers at the stern of the ship. At a predetermined moment we released hundreds of helium balloons, which floated skyward to reveal the 1967 Mercury Marquis. Together with Matt McLaughlin, who had become head of the division, I introduced the car and described its features.

Two nights later, on the island of St. Thomas, we unveiled the new Cougar. At a beach lit by clusters of brilliant torches, a World War II landing craft pulled up to the shore and lowered its ramp. The audience was breathless as a shining white Cougar drove onto the sand. The door opened, and out stepped singer Vic Damone, who began to entertain. I've seen some pretty fancy dealer introductions in my time, but this one really took the cake.

The dealers hadn't had anything to get excited about in years. They went nuts over the Cougar. Like the Mustang, it had a sporty look, with a long hood and a short deck. As the dealers expected, it was an immediate success and soon became the most visible part of the Lincoln-Mercury Division. Today a 1967 Cougar in good condition is a collector's item.

A lot of the credit for these spectacular introductions has to go to Frank Zimmerman, our resident promotion genius. Zimmie, who is now retired in South Carolina, is an unforgettable character—thin as a reed, endlessly energetic, and very funny.

Working with Zimmie was a joy, but it presented its own special challenge because he used to have a new idea every five minutes. About 10 percent of his ideas were splendid, but some of the rest bordered on the absurd.

To promote the Cougar, for example, Zimmie wanted to have a trained bear drive the car from New York to California. According to one scenario, a trainer would sit in front beside him. Another plan called for a midget to crouch under the dash and do the driving using special equipment. The way Zimmie described it, the car would make dozens of stops each day as the public crowded around and the press took pictures. "Think of the headlines," said Zimmie. "Bear Drives Cougar Coast to Coast!"

I love bold ideas, but this one was a little wild even for me. Some years later, Henry Ford received a letter from a guy who claimed to have trained his horse to drive a Lincoln Continental. The horse even blew the horn by pressing on it with its nose! Henry passed the letter on to me, and I gave it to Zimmie. That was the last I heard of it, which is probably just as well.

We did use a live animal to promote the Cougar. At the suggestion of Kenyon & Eckhardt, the advertising agency for Lincoln-Mercury, we tried the obvious—a real cougar. The agency's New York office was charged with the awesome responsibility of finding a trained cougar and filming it on top of a Lincoln-Mercury sign. This was no easy task, but within about a month we had a few precious seconds of film depicting a growling cougar on top of the logo. The Ford Division had been successful with a wild horse. Now Lincoln-Mercury would see what a wild cat could do.

The cougar turned out to be such an effective symbol that the ad agency recommended we use "the sign of the cat" to represent the entire division. We did, and it became a vital step in creating a new identity for Lincoln-Mercury. Before long, the picture of the cougar perched on top of the sign became almost as widely known as Ford's oval and Chrysler's pentastar.

Whenever you're trying to promote a brand name, your first task is to make clear where the brand is available. That's why the McDonald's arch is so effective. Even a little kid knows that's where you go to get a hamburger. Before the cougar went up on the signs, most people had never heard of Lincoln-Mercury. Today almost everybody knows what it is.

Meanwhile, Zimmie was continuing to come up with promotion ideas. At one point he scouted the country for people with the same names as famous explorers, like Christopher Columbus or Admiral Byrd. When he tracked them down, he hired them to appear in our ads, which would claim, for example, that "Christopher Columbus has just discovered the new Mercury."

Kenyon & Eckhardt did a great job in advertising the Cougar. With the Marquis, we all decided the strong selling point was the smoothness of its ride. The Marquis had achieved a new level in ride engineering, and the result was the softest, plushest ride in the world.

But how could we get this across to the public? Our engineers had told the advertising people that the ride of the Marquis was better than the competition's more expensive cars. The agency's response was: "Prove it!" So the engineers invited a group from the agency to our test track, blindfolded them, and then drove them around in Oldsmobiles, Buicks, Cadillacs, and Marquis. All but one guy voted for the Marquis as the best ride of them all.

Eventually the blindfold test found its way into the advertising campaign. Kenyon & Eckhardt made several commercials where blindfolded consumers, and in one case chauffeurs, were asked to rate the cars on smoothness and quiet.

Before long, the agency came up with other commercials that made the point equally well. In one ad, a container of dangerous acid was suspended over an expensive fur coat. In another, a record was playing on a phonograph that was sitting on the front seat. In a third, Bart Starr, the football player, was being shaved by a barber. Then there was the one that showed a container of nitroglycerin on the back seat. To show that it was real, at the end of the commercial we blew up the car!

In the most famous commercial of all, the agency filmed a Dutch diamond cutter busy at his craft while the car twisted its way down some pretty bumpy roads. Those too young to remember that ad might have seen a classic parody of it that appeared a few years later on *Saturday Night Live*. In this version, the diamond cutter was replaced by a rabbi about to perform a ritual circumcision on an infant while being driven in the rain over bad country roads. Believe me, the suspense in the diamond-cutter ad was nothing compared to the tension in this one.

With the Marquis and the Cougar in place, the Mercury line was now in pretty good shape. But we still had nothing special at the high end. We needed a new Lincoln that would really give Cadillac a run for the money.

One night when I was in Canada for a meeting, I was lying in bed in my hotel room unable to sleep. Suddenly I had an idea. I put through a call to Gene Bordinat, our chief stylist. "I want to put a Rolls-Royce grille on the front of a Thunderbird," I told him.

At the time, we had a four-door Thunderbird that was dying in the marketplace. My plan was to create a new car using the same platform, engine, and even the roof, but to make enough changes so that the car really *looked* new and not like a spinoff of the T-Bird.

While I was trying to imagine this new luxury car, I remembered a good precedent. Some years earlier, in the late 1930s, Edsel Ford had produced the Mark, a quiet and understated luxury car that appealed to a small, discriminating audience. In the middle 1950s, his son William Clay had built the Mark II, a derivative of the original Mark. Both of these cars were classics, the Rolls-Royce of American automobiles. They were the kind of car that most people dreamed about but only a select few could afford.

I decided it was time for us to revive the Mark line with a Mark III, based on our Thunderbird but with enough changes to make it fresh and different. The Mark III had a very long hood, a short rear deck, a powerful V-8 engine, and the same continental spare tire in the back that had been part of the original Marks. It was big, dramatic, and very distinctive. I had mixed feelings when one reporter compared it to a German staff car from World War II.

We brought out the Mark III in April 1968, and in its very first year it outsold the Cadillac Eldorado, which had been our long-range goal. For the next five years we had a field day, in part because the car had been developed on the cheap. We did the whole thing for $30 million, a bargain-basement price, because we were able to use existing parts and designs.

Our initial plan was to introduce the Mark III at Cartier's, the prestigious Fifth Avenue jeweler in Manhattan. The management of Cartier's was very interested, so Walter Murphy flew to New York to meet with them. We wanted to stress the elegance and good taste of the car by inviting the press to a midnight supper right in the store. So far, so good. But when Walter explained that we'd have to tear down a couple of walls and expand a window or two to get the car in, Cartier's had second thoughts. (They did agree to let us use their name on the Mark III's clock.)

Instead, we brought out the Mark III in several different cities. In Hollywood, we put it on a stage on the set of *Camelot*, so people had to walk up the steps as though they were paying homage to a king. In Detroit, we unveiled the car at a dinner of American newspaper publishers. Rather than placing the car on a turntable, which was the normal way of introducing a new model, we put the *publishers* on a turntable. As their viewpoint shifted, they saw a series of historic Lincolns and Marks. Finally the curtains opened and there was the new Mark III. The publishers were so impressed that many of them ordered one on the spot.

Before the Mark III, the Lincoln-Mercury Division was actually losing money on every luxury car. We were selling only about eighteen thousand Lincolns a year, which wasn't enough to amortize the fixed costs. In our business, these costs are enormous. Whether you produce one car or a million, you've got to have a plant and you have to develop the dies to stamp out the metal. If your volume projections are wrong and you don't hit your objective, you have to pay off these fixed expenses over a smaller number of cars. Simply stated: you lose your shirt.

The old cliché is certainly true: bigger cars do mean bigger profits. We made as much from selling one Mark as we did from ten Falcons. Our profit worked out to an astonishing $2,000 per car. Moreover, the money started coming in so quickly we could barely keep track of it. In our best year, we made almost $1 billion from the

Lincoln Division alone, which is as big a success as I've ever had in my career.

We followed with the Mark IV in 1971. Ford is still making the series—they're currently up to the Mark VII. The Mark is Ford's biggest moneymaker, just as Cadillac is for General Motors. It's the Alfred Sloan theory: you have to have something for everybody. To hedge your bets, you always need a poor man's car—that's all the first Henry Ford ever envisioned—but then you need upscale cars, too, because you never know when the blue-collar guy is going to be laid off. It seems that in the United States the one thing you can count on is that even during a depression, the rich get richer. So you always have to have some goodies for them.

VIII

THE ROAD TO
THE TOP

By 1968, I was the odds-on favorite to become the next president of the Ford Motor Company. The Mustang had shown I was someone to watch. The Mark III made it clear I was no flash in the pan. I was forty-four, Henry Ford had taken me under his wing, and my future never looked better.

But just as it seemed that nothing could stop me, fate intervened. General Motors presented Henry with an opportunity he couldn't resist.

In those days, GM had a highly regarded executive vice-president named Semon Knudsen, known to the world as "Bunkie." Knudsen was an MIT graduate in engineering who had been made head of the Pontiac Division at the age of forty-four. This made him the youngest division head in GM's history—the kind of distinction that definitely gets noticed in Detroit.

One reason for Knudsen's notability was that his father had once been president of GM. Many people expected Bunkie to follow in the elder Knudsen's footsteps. But when, despite Bunkie's strong reputation as a product man, GM chose Ed Cole as its next president, Bunkie soon understood that he had reached the end of his career at GM.

As Avis watches Hertz, as Macy's watches Gimbel's, we at Ford always kept a close eye on General Motors. Henry in particular was a great GM watcher and admirer. For him, the sudden availability of

Bunkie Knudsen was a gift from heaven. Perhaps Henry believed that Knudsen had all of that famous GM wisdom locked in his genes. In any event, he wasted no time in making his approach. When Henry heard that Bunkie was thinking of resigning, he called him immediately.

Henry couldn't very well ask Bunkie to come to the office, because there are no secrets in the Glass House. Within half an hour, the press would have known all about the visit. And he ruled out inviting Bunkie home when he realized his Grosse Pointe neighbors might notice. But Henry loved intrigue, so he rented an Oldsmobile from Hertz, put on a raincoat, and in his best 007 style, he drove over to Bunkie's house in Bloomfield Hills.

A week later, they had a deal. Knudsen would take over immediately as president at an annual salary of $600,000—the same as Henry's.

To make room for Knudsen, Henry had to get rid of Arjay Miller, who had been our president for the past five years. Miller was abruptly kicked upstairs to become the vice-chairman, a new position created especially for the occasion. A year later, he resigned and went on to become dean of the Business School at Stanford University.

Bunkie was hired during the early winter of 1968, while I was away on a skiing vacation with my family. In the middle of the trip, I got a call from Henry's office asking me to come in the next day. The company even sent a DC-3 to bring me back.

On the day after my return, I went in to see the boss. Henry knew I would be upset that he was bringing in Bunkie as president, and he wanted to explain his reasons. He was sure that the addition of a high-level GM man to our team at Ford would make a big difference in the next few years. And he took pains to assure me that Bunkie's arrival did not mean my career was over. On the contrary. "Look," he told me, "you're still my boy. But you're young. There are things you have to learn."

As Henry saw it, Bunkie would be bringing in a wealth of information about the GM system. I was twelve years younger than Knudsen, he reminded me, asking me to be patient. He made it clear he didn't want to lose me. And he strongly implied that my patience now would be amply rewarded in the future.

A few days later, I got a call from Sidney Weinberg, one of our senior board members and a legendary Wall Street wizard. He had been Henry's mentor for years, but he was also a big fan of mine. He always called me "Lehigh."

Over lunch in his New York apartment, Weinberg told me that
he assumed I was angry about Knudsen's arrival. But he advised me to
sit tight. Sidney had heard the same rumors I had: that GM was
secretly delighted to be rid of Knudsen. Weinberg had gotten the
word straight from a top executive at GM, who said: "You solved one
helluva problem for us. We didn't know what to do with Knudsen
until good old Henry picked him up. We couldn't be more grateful."

"If Bunkie's as bad as they say," Sidney told me, "your turn will
come soon enough."

I wasn't so sure. In those days I was in a mad rush to the top.
Despite Henry's reassurances, Bunkie's arrival was a big blow to me. I
wanted the presidency badly, and I didn't agree I had much left to
learn. As I saw it, I had been exposed to every test the company had
to offer. And I had passed each one with flying colors.

For a few weeks I seriously considered resigning. There had been
an attractive offer from Herb Siegel, a Lehigh graduate who was head
of ChrisCraft. Herb wanted to expand ChrisCraft into a small con-
glomerate in the leisure business. He liked me and respected what I
had accomplished at Ford.

"Look," said Herb, "if you stay here, you're always going to be at
the mercy of Henry Ford, and if he was dumb enough to pass you
over for president, he'll probably zap you again."

I was tempted. I even went so far as to look for houses in New
York and Connecticut. Mary, too, liked the idea of going back East.
"If nothing else, we can get fresh seafood again," she said with a
twinkle in her eye.

In the end, I decided to stay at Ford. I loved the car business and
I loved the Ford Motor Company. I really couldn't imagine being
anywhere else. With Henry on my side, the future still looked bright.
I was also counting on the prospect that Bunkie would not work out as
president and that my turn would come sooner rather than later.

In Detroit, Knudsen's move from GM to Ford was the talk of the
town. In our industry, jumping ship and going to work for a competitor has always been pretty rare. It was almost unheard of at GM,
which even by Detroit standards had a reputation for being inbred.

What made the story even more appealing was that Bunkie wasn't
the first Knudsen to work for the Ford Motor Company. More than
half a century earlier, William Knudsen, Bunkie's father, had worked
for Henry's grandfather. The elder Knudsen had supervised the establishment of fourteen Model T plants in two years, including the

famous River Rouge plant. After World War I, he was sent over to Europe, where he was instrumental in developing Ford's operations overseas.

After rising to the top ranks of the company, the senior Knudsen ran into problems with the senior Ford, who fired him in 1921. When Knudsen left Ford, he was making $50,000 a year, a huge salary in those days. A year later, he signed on with General Motors.

And now the Knudsen-Ford relationship had come full circle. Detroit loved the drama of the Knudsen hiring, and the press had a field day with Bunkie's appointment. It made for a great story: Henry Ford, the grandson of the man who had fired William Knudsen, was now bringing back Knudsen's son as *his* president.

When Bunkie's appointment was first announced, many of us in top positions at Ford were resentful that a GM man was going to be our boss. I was especially concerned, as there were rumors that Knudsen was going to bring in John Z. DeLorean to put me in my place. (In those days, DeLorean was a creative young maverick at GM who had worked with Bunkie in the Pontiac Division.)

My colleagues and I were pretty sure that the GM system of management wouldn't work very well at Ford. But as Henry saw it, the mere presence of Bunkie Knudsen in the Glass House would cause some of GM's great success to rub off on us.

It never happened. Ford had its own way of doing things. We liked to move quickly, and Bunkie seemed to have trouble keeping up. Besides, administration was not his strong point. It soon became clear to me that GM probably had a good reason for passing him over as president.

Knudsen was always suspicious of me. He assumed that I had been after the presidency before he came and that I was still gunning for it after he arrived. He was right on both counts. Fortunately, we were both too busy to spend much time on office politics. But we did have our share of disagreements, especially about the styling of new models.

As soon as Knudsen arrived at Ford, he began adding weight to the Mustang and making it bigger. He was a racing nut, but he failed to understand that the heyday of racing had already passed. Knudsen also took it upon himself to redesign our Thunderbird so that it would look like a Pontiac, which was a complete disaster.

As a leader, Bunkie Knudsen had little impact on the company. Among other things, he failed to bring over any of his top people from GM to help him put his plans into operation. Nobody at Ford felt much loyalty to Knudsen, so he was without a power base. As a result, he found himself alone in an alien atmosphere, never really accepted. A decade later, when I went to Chrysler, I made sure not to repeat that mistake.

The press has often reported that I led a revolt against Knudsen. But his failing had little to do with me. Bunkie Knudsen tried to run Ford without using the system. He ignored the existing lines of authority and alienated me and a lot of other top people by making policy in areas that were ours to decide.

From the very start, Ford and GM have been completely different companies. GM has always been clubby and genteel, with dozens of committees and multiple levels of management. Ford, by contrast, has a more competitive environment. We always made decisions more quickly, with less staff review and more of an entrepreneurial spirit. In the slow, well-ordered world of GM, Bunkie Knudsen had flourished. At Ford, he was a fish out of water.

Knudsen lasted only nineteen months. Henry Ford had achieved a great publicity coup by hiring a top GM man, but he soon learned that success in one car company does not always guarantee success in another.

I wish I could say that Bunkie got fired because he ruined the Mustang or because his ideas were all wrong. But the actual reason for the firing was nothing like that. Bunkie Knudsen was fired because he used to walk into Henry's office without knocking. That's right—without knocking!

Ed O'Leary, one of Henry's aides, used to say: "That drives Henry nuts! The door opens, and there's Bunkie just standing there."

Of course, this minor transgression was merely the last straw in a relationship that had never been very good to begin with. Henry was a king who could tolerate no equals, a point Bunkie never seemed to grasp. He tried to get palsy-walsy with Henry, and that was a big mistake. The one thing you could never do at Ford was to get too close to the throne. "Give Henry a wide berth," Beacham had advised me years earlier. "Remember, he has blue blood. Yours is only red."

The way that Henry Ford fired Bunkie Knudsen makes for a good story. It also reveals a great deal about Henry. On Monday evening of the Labor Day weekend, he sent Ted Mecke, his vice-president of public relations, to Bunkie's house. Mecke's assignment: to let Knudsen know he was about to be fired.

But Mecke couldn't bring himself to spill the beans. All he could say was: "Henry sent me here to tell you that tomorrow will be a rough day at work."

"Wait a minute," said Florence Knudsen, a very strong-willed lady. "What is it you're really here for? Who sent you and what's your message? Did you come to fire my husband?" She guessed the truth instantly, and Mecke had no choice but to confirm it.

The next morning Henry came running down the hall. He was looking for an ally, and he knew that I'd be pleased to see Knudsen go. But Henry still hadn't told Bunkie he was fired.

Finally Mecke said to Bunkie: "I guess you're supposed to see Mr. Ford."

When Bunkie went in to Henry's office, Henry asked him: "Did Mecke talk to you?"

"Now, what the hell's going on here?" demanded Bunkie. "Are you firing me?"

Henry nodded. "Things just didn't work out," he said. That kind of vague statement was vintage Henry.

A few minutes later, Henry came into my office again. "Bunkie's calling a press conference," he said.

"What happened?" I asked. By this time I had a pretty good idea, but I wanted to hear it from the horse's mouth.

Henry tried to tell me that he had just fired Bunkie. But as I stood there looking at him, he couldn't seem to get the words out. Finally he said: "Bunkie doesn't understand. We've got problems here."

It was Keystone Kops time. The next thing I knew, Bunkie was in my office, saying: "I think I've been fired, but I'm not sure."

As soon as Knudsen left, Henry came back in, asking: "What did he tell you?"

A few minutes later, Henry returned again. "What are we going to do?" he said. "Bunkie's going to hold his press conference right here!"

"Well," I replied, "if he's been canned, he's got to say something."

"Sure he's been canned," said Henry. "But I think he should have his press conference at a hotel, not right here in the building."

I had mixed feelings about the whole episode. On the one hand, I was delighted that Bunkie was out. At the same time, I felt real compassion for him. I didn't want anybody's term as president of the company to end like *this*.

But Henry Ford could never bring himself to fire anybody directly. He always had a hatchetman do the dirty work for him.

I couldn't help but wonder: is this what lay in store for me? I spent that evening talking with Mary. "Why don't you pack it in?" she said. Once again I was tempted. And once again I decided to stay on.

The day Bunkie was fired there was great rejoicing and much drinking of champagne. Over in public relations, one of our people coined a phrase that soon became famous throughout the company: "Henry Ford [the first] once said that history is bunk. But today, Bunkie is history."

Even with Bunkie gone, Henry was still not ready to offer me the job. Instead, he set up a three-man office of the president. I was in charge of Ford's North American operations, which made me first among equals. Robert Stevenson was head of Ford International, and Robert Hampson led nonautomotive operations.

Fortunately, the troika didn't last very long. The following year, on December 10, 1970, I finally got what I was waiting for: the presidency of Ford.

A few days before he made the announcement, Henry came into my office to tell me what he had in mind. I remember thinking: "This is the greatest Christmas present I've ever had!" We just sat there for a moment or two, he with a cigarette and me with a cigar, and blew smoke at each other.

The moment Henry walked out the door I called my wife. Then I called my father in Allentown to tell him the good news. During his long and active life my father had a lot of happy moments, but I'm sure my phone call that day ranks near the top.

When I became president, the Ford Motor Company had approximately 432,000 employees. Our total payroll came to more than $3.5 billion. In North America alone, we were building close to 2.5 million cars a year and 750,000 trucks. Overseas, the combined total came to another 1.5 million vehicles. Our total sales for 1970 added up to $14.9 billion, on which we made a profit of $515 million.

Now, while $515 million was certainly nothing to sneeze at, it represented only 3.5 percent of total sales. In the early 1960s, our return on sales had never dipped below 5 percent. I was determined to get it back up.

As everyone knows, there are only two ways to make more money:

you can sell more goods or spend less on overhead. I was satisfied with our sales—at least for the moment. But the closer I looked at our operations, the more I was convinced we could do a lot more to reduce our expenses.

One of the first moves I made as president was to convene a meeting of top managers to establish a cost-cutting program. I called it "four fifties," as its purpose was to cut operating expenses by $50 million in each of four areas—timing foul-ups, product complexity, design costs, and outmoded ways of doing business. If we could reach our goal within three years, we could improve our profits by $200 million—a gain of almost 40 percent—even before selling a single additional car.

There was plenty of room for improvement. For example, it took us two weeks out of each year to prepare our factories for the production of the next year's models. During that time the factories were simply not operating, which meant that both the machinery and the workers were idle.

Through more vigorous computer programing and more sophisticated scheduling, it was possible to reduce the changeover period from two weeks to two days. Of course that kind of change doesn't take place overnight. But by 1974, we had reached the point where our plants were converted during the course of a single weekend—when production lines were down anyway.

Another area where we cut costs was shipping. Freight came to only a small percentage of our total expenses, but at over $500 million a year, it was still a figure worth a second look. This wasn't something I had ever thought about before. But when I checked into it, I found that the railroads were really taking us for a ride. They were charging us by volume rather than weight, and we weren't planning accordingly.

We began packing the freight cars much more tightly. At one point, I recall, we trimmed a fender design by two inches to allow a few more cars to fit onto each train. With huge sums of money at stake, the last thing I wanted was to be shipping air. When you're dealing with figures like $500 million for freight, even a minuscule saving of half of one percent came to $2.5 million.

I also instituted a program called Shuck the Losers. In a company as large as ours, there were dozens of operations that either lost money or made only minimal profits. I've always believed that every operation in a car company could be measured in terms of its profitability. Each plant manager knew—or should have known—whether his operation was making money for the company, or whether the parts he was building cost more than they could be purchased for on the outside.

And so I announced that managers had three years to either make their departments profitable or sell them off. It was simple common sense, like a large department store whose manager says: "We're losing a ton of money in that boutique over there, so let's close it."

Many of our biggest losers were part of Philco-Ford, the appliance and electronics firm we had bought in 1961. Philco was a terrible mistake, and it lost millions of dollars a year for ten years before finally starting to turn a profit. Many in top management had argued against buying it, but Henry had insisted. And at Ford, what Henry wanted, Henry got.

We ended up dropping close to twenty major losers in the early 1970s. One of them was an operation that made laundry equipment. To this day, I don't know what on earth we were doing in laundry equipment. But somehow it had taken us ten years to bite the bullet on that one, which had never earned us a dime.

These programs to reduce expenses and cut losses represented a new area for me. Until now I had concentrated on selling, marketing, and design. But as president my first concern was the relatively unglamorous task of searching out hundreds of different ways to cut costs and increase profits. As a result, I was finally earning the respect of the one group that had always been suspicious of me—the bean counters.

I now had so many diverse responsibilities that I had to learn a different style of operating. I didn't like to admit it, but I no longer had the stamina of the Mustang years, when I thought nothing of grabbing a hamburger for dinner and staying at the office until midnight.

The Ford Motor Company had close to half a million employees around the world, and I had to keep in mind that I was only one of them. Sometimes this meant that I wouldn't be able to return a phone call for a couple of weeks. But I decided it was more important to preserve my mental health than to give everybody curb service.

Instead of driving home a different car every night to become more familiar with our various products, I now had a driver. I used the commuting time to read and answer my mail. But I continued to follow my old weekly routine. Unless I was out of town, my weekends were devoted to the family. I wouldn't open my briefcase until Sunday night. At that point I would sit in my library at home, do the serious company reading, and plan out the week ahead. By Monday morning I was ready to hit the ground running. I expected no less of the people who worked for me: I've always found that the speed of the boss is the speed of the team.

During my years as president of Ford, I was constantly meeting people who would tell me: "I wouldn't want your job for all the money in the world." I never knew how to respond to that kind of remark. I loved my job, even though many people viewed it as the kind of position that grinds you up and kills you off. But I never saw it that way. To me, it was sheer excitement.

Actually, after reaching the presidency I experienced a certain letdown. I had spent years climbing the mountain. When I finally made it to the top, I started to wonder why I had been in such a hurry to get there. I was only in my mid-forties, and I had no idea what I would do for an encore.

I certainly enjoyed the prestige and the power of my position. But being a public figure was definitely a mixed blessing. This was brought home to me very dramatically one Friday morning as I was riding to work. The radio was on and I was half listening when suddenly the announcer interrupted the regular program with a special bulletin. Apparently a group of the nation's top business leaders, myself included, had been marked for assassination by the Manson "family."

This cheerful news had come from Sandra Good, roommate of "Squeaky" Fromme, the young lady who had been arrested for trying to kill President Ford in Sacramento. If you ever want a quick waker-upper in the morning, all you've got to hear is that you've made somebody's hit list!

But I don't want to complain too much about one of the best jobs in the world. If Henry was king, I was the crown prince. And there was no question that the king liked me. Once he and his wife, Cristina, came to our house for dinner. My parents were there, too, and Henry spent half the night telling them how great I was and that without me there wouldn't be a Ford Motor Company. On another occasion, he took me to meet his good friend L.B.J. Henry really thought of me as his protégé, and he treated me that way.

Those were the days of wine and roses. All of us who constituted top management in the Glass House lived the good life in the royal court. We were part of something beyond first class—royal class, perhaps, where we had the best of everything. White-coated waiters were on call throughout the day, and we all ate lunch together in the executive dining room.

Now, this was no ordinary cafeteria. It was closer to being one of the country's finest restaurants. Dover sole was flown over from England on a daily basis. We enjoyed the finest fruits, no matter what the season. Fancy chocolates, exotic flowers—you name it, we had it. And everything was served up by those professional waiters in their white coats.

At first we paid all of $2.00 each for those lunches. The price had started at $1.50, but inflation hiked it to $2.00. When Arjay Miller was still vice-president in charge of finance, he complained about the cost. "We really shouldn't have to pay for these lunches," he said one day. "Feeding employees is deductible for the company. A lot of companies feed their people without charging them at all. But if we pay for it ourselves, it's after-tax money." We were all in the 90 percent bracket, so every time we spent $2.00 we had to earn $20.

At that point a few of us got into a discussion of how much those lunches really did cost the company. In typical Ford style, we ran a study to determine the real expense of serving lunch in the executive dining room. It came out to $104 dollars a head—and this was twenty years ago!

You could order anything you wanted in that room, from oysters Rockefeller to roast pheasant. But Henry's standard meal was a hamburger. He rarely ate anything else. One day at lunch he turned to me and complained that his personal chef at home, who was earning something like $30,000 or $40,000 a year, couldn't even make a decent hamburger. Furthermore, no restaurant he had ever been to could make a hamburger the way he liked it—the way it was prepared for him in the executive dining room.

I like to cook, so I was fascinated by Henry's complaint. I went into the kitchen to speak to Joe Bernardi, our Swiss-Italian chef. "Joe," I said, "Henry really likes the way you make hamburgers. Could you show me how?"

"Sure," said Joe. "But you have to be a great chef to do it right, so watch me very carefully."

He went over to the fridge, took out an inch-thick New York strip steak, and dropped it into the grinder. Out came the ground meat, which Joe fashioned into a hamburger patty. Then he slapped it onto the grill.

"Any questions?" he asked.

Then he looked at me with a half smile and said: "Amazing what you can cook up when you start with a five-dollar hunk of meat!"

IX

TROUBLE IN PARADISE

Until I became president, Henry Ford had always been a pretty remote figure. But now my office was right next to his in the Glass House, and we saw quite a lot of each other, although only in meetings. The better I got to know Henry Ford, the more I worried about the company's future—and my own.

The Glass House was a palace, and Henry reigned supreme. Whenever he entered the building, the word would go out: *The king has arrived*. Executives would linger in the halls, hoping to run into him. If they were lucky, Mr. Ford might notice them and say hello. At times he might even deign to speak to them.

Each time Henry walked into a meeting, the atmosphere changed abruptly. He held the power of life and death over all of us. He could suddenly say "off with his head"—and he often did. Without a fair hearing, one more promising career at Ford would bite the dust.

It was the superficial things that counted for Henry. He was a sucker for appearances. If a guy wore the right clothes and used the right buzz words, Henry was impressed. But without the right veneer, forget it.

One day Henry ordered me to fire a certain executive who was, in his judgment, "a fag."

"Don't be silly," I said. "The guy's a good pal of mine. He's married and has a kid. We have dinner together."

"Get rid of him," Henry repeated. "He's a fag."

"What are you talking about?" I said.

"Look at him. His pants are too tight."

"Henry," I said calmly, "what the hell do the guy's pants have to do with anything?"

"He's queer," said Henry. "He's got an effeminate bearing. Get rid of him."

In the end, I had to demote a good friend. I moved him out of the Glass House and into the boondocks, hating every minute of it. But the only alternative was to fire him.

This arbitrary use of power wasn't merely a character flaw. It was something Henry actually *believed* in.

Early in my presidency, Henry told me his management philosophy. "If a guy works for you," he said, "don't let him get too comfortable. Don't let him get cozy or set in his ways. Always do the opposite of what he expects. Keep your people anxious and off-balance."

Now, one might wonder why on earth the chairman of the Ford Motor Company, one of the most powerful men in the world, would behave like a spoiled brat? What made him so insecure?

Perhaps the answer is that Henry Ford never had to work for anything in his life. Maybe that's the bane of rich kids who inherit their money. They go through life tripping through the tulips, wondering what they would have become without Daddy. Poor people complain that nobody gave them a break, but the rich guy never knows if he's accomplished anything on his own. Nobody ever tells him the truth. They only tell him what he wants to hear.

It seemed to me that Henry Ford II, grandson of the founder of the Ford Motor Company, had spent his whole life worrying that he would screw things up.

Maybe that's why he seemed to feel so threatened. And why he was always on the lookout for palace revolts. He'd see two guys talking together in the hall, and right away—they must be planning a conspiracy!

I don't want to play psychiatrist here, but I had a theory about where his fears came from. When Henry was young, his grandfather was fanatically frightened of kidnappers. Those kids grew up with locked gates and bodyguards, wary of everyone who wasn't part of their immediate family.

So Henry got a little paranoid about some things. For example, he hated to put anything in writing. Although the two of us ran the company together for nearly eight years, almost nothing in my archives from those days carries his signature. Henry actually used to boast that he never kept any files. Every now and then he would burn all his papers.

"That stuff can only hurt you," he'd tell me. "Any guy who holds on to his own files is asking for trouble. Eventually the wrong person will read them and you or the company will pay the price."

He was even worse after Watergate, which had a deep effect on him. "See?" he said. "I was right—look what can happen to you!"

Once on one of his rare visits to my office, he glanced around at my various scrapbooks and files. "You're nuts," he said. "Some day you could be crucified for keeping all this stuff."

He lived by his grandfather's motto: "History is bunk." It became an obsession with him. His attitude was: destroy everything you can.

At one point during my presidency, Henry sat for a portrait by Karsh of Ottawa, the great Canadian photographer. As always, Karsh's work was superb. The photograph was so flattering that Henry sent out autographed copies to his friends and relatives.

One day Ted Mecke, Henry's aide, saw me admiring the portrait. "What do you think of the boss's new picture?" he asked.

"It's outstanding," I replied. "By the way," I added, "I don't have any pictures of Henry. Do you think I could have one of these?"

"Sure," said Ted. "I'll get him to sign it."

A few days later Mecke told me: "Mr. Ford didn't want to sign that picture right away, so I left it with him."

The next time I went in to see Henry, I noticed one of the prints on his desk. "That's a great picture," I said.

"Thank you," he replied. "Actually, this one is for you. I just haven't gotten around to signing it yet."

He never mentioned it again, and I never received the picture. It just evaporated. For Henry, autographing that picture was too intimate a gesture—even for his own president.

Henry didn't seem to want any lasting, concrete reminders of our friendship—even though in those days we were still friends. It was as if he knew that someday he would have to turn against me, and he didn't want any evidence that we were once on good terms.

Even during those first years we had our share of disagreements. But I always took great care to exercise restraint. If I had any major problems with him, I just blocked them out. If we had any serious arguments, I made sure to air them only in private, when I thought he would give me a fair hearing.

As president I couldn't afford to waste energy on petty disputes. I had to think of the big picture. Where was the company going to be five years from now? What were the major trends we had to pay attention to?

After the Arab-Israeli war of 1973 and the subsequent oil crisis, the answers to those questions became very clear. The world had turned upside down, and we had to respond immediately. Small, fuel-efficient, front-wheel-drive cars were the wave of the future.

You didn't have to be a genius to figure this out. All you had to do was read the sales figures for 1974, a terrible year for Detroit. Sales at GM dropped by a million and a half vehicles. Sales at Ford were off by half a million. The Japanese had most of the small cars, and they were selling like crazy.

Gearing up to produce small cars in the United States was a very expensive proposition. But there are times when you have no choice but to make a big investment. General Motors was spending billions of dollars to "downsize" the entire company. Even Chrysler was investing a small fortune in fuel-efficient models.

But for Henry, small cars were a dead end. His favorite expression was "minicars, miniprofits."

Now, it's true that you can't make money on small cars—at least not in this country. And it's becoming more true every day. The margins on small cars just aren't high enough.

But that didn't mean we shouldn't be building them. Even without the prospect of a second oil shortage, we had to keep our dealers happy. If we didn't provide them with the small cars people wanted, those dealers would drop us and sign up with Honda and Toyota, where the action was.

It's a simple fact of life that you've got to take care of the low end of the market. And if there's an energy crisis to boot, that clinches the argument. For us not to be offering small, fuel-efficient cars was like owning a shoe store where you tell the customer: "Sorry, we only handle size nine and up."

Small cars became the bone in Henry's throat. But I insisted that we had to do a small, front-wheel-drive car—at least in Europe. There, gas prices were much higher and the roads were narrower. Even Henry could tell that a small car in Europe made good sense.

I sent Hal Sperlich, our top product planner, across the Atlantic. In only a thousand days, Hal and I put together a brand-new car. The Fiesta was very small, with front-wheel drive and a transverse engine. And it was fabulous. I knew we had a winner.

For twenty years, the bean counters at Ford had given us reasons why we should never build this car. Now even the top people in our

European Division opposed the Fiesta. My vice-president of international operations told me that Phil Caldwell, then president of Ford of Europe, was violently against it, saying that I must be smoking pot, because the Fiesta would never sell, and even if it did, it would never make a dime.

But I knew we had to go for it. I went to Henry's office and confronted him. "Look," I told him, "our guys in Europe don't want to do this car. So you've got to back me up. I don't want any second-guessing like you did on the Edsel. If you're not with me heart and soul, let's just forget it."

Henry saw the light. He finally agreed to spend $1 billion to do the Fiesta. And it's a good thing he did. The Fiesta was a tremendous hit. Whether Henry knew it or not, it saved him in Europe and was as important to our turnaround there as the Mustang had been to the Ford Division in the 1960s.

Right away, Sperlich and I started talking about bringing the Fiesta over to America for the 1979 model year. We saw the Japanese imports on the rise. We knew GM front-wheel-drive X-cars were well on the way. Chrysler was coming out with its Omni and Horizon, and Ford had nothing to offer.

As it stood, the Fiesta was a little too small for the American market. So Hal and I decided to modify it by expanding the sides a little to add more room in the interior. We called our car the "blown Fiesta." Its code name was the Wolf.

By this time, however, a combination of Japanese trade advantages and impossibly high labor rates had made it almost impossible for an American company to build small cars on a competitive basis. It would have cost us $500 million just to build new plants for the four-cylinder engines and transmissions. And Henry wasn't willing to take the gamble.

But Sperlich and I were too hot on this project to give it up without a fight. There just had to be some way to build the Wolf and still make a profit.

On my next trip to Japan, I set up a meeting with the top management of Honda. Back then, Honda didn't really want to make cars. They preferred to stay with motorcycles. But they were already equipped to make small engines and they were eager to do business with us.

I got along wonderfully with Mr. Honda. He invited me to his house and he threw a great party, with a massive display of fireworks. Before I left Tokyo, we had worked out a deal. Honda would supply us with three hundred thousand power trains a year at a price of $711 each. It was a fantastic opportunity—$711 for a transmission and engine in a box, ready to drop into any car we wanted to make.

I was on fire when I came back from Japan. The Wolf just couldn't miss. This was going to be the next Mustang! Hal and I put together a black-and-yellow prototype that was a smash. This car would have knocked the country on its ear.

But when I told Henry about the deal with Honda, he promptly vetoed it. "No car with my name on the hood is going to have a Jap engine inside!" he said. And that was the end of a great opportunity.

Henry may not have liked the Japanese, but he was crazy about Europe. Back home, especially after Vietnam, there was less and less respect for authority. More to the point, there was less and less respect for the Ford name. But Europe was altogether different. Over there, family money still meant something. Europe still had its old class system. It was the home of the landed aristocracy, of palaces and royal families. In Europe people still cared who your grandparents were.

One night to remember, I was with Henry in Germany at a castle on the Rhine. Money was no object when it came to entertaining Henry Ford. When we pulled up, my eyes popped. There was a brass band—all these guys in lederhosen—lined up to welcome him. As Henry walked slowly across the moat and up the steps of the castle, the band followed close behind, serenading. I kept waiting for them to strike up "Hail to the Chief."

Wherever Henry went in Europe, he met with royalty. He hob-nobbed with them, drank with them, and loved to hang around them. He was so crazy about Europe that he often talked of retiring there. Once at a party of jet-setters in Sardinia, he came with an American flag sewed to the seat of his pants. Even the Europeans were offended. But Henry thought it was just jolly good fun.

That's why my success with the Fiesta may have been a nail in my coffin. In America, my achievements weren't threatening. But Europe was his domain. When they started applauding me in the great halls of the Old Country, he got worried.

Henry never said so explicitly, but certain constituencies were definitely off limits. Europe was one of them. Wall Street was another.

In 1973 and early 1974, we started making a ton of money, even after the OPEC crisis. Our top management went to New York to speak to a group of a hundred key bankers and stock analysts. Henry was always opposed to these meetings. "I don't want to go touting the stock," he used to say. But *every* public company used to hold meetings with members of the financial community. It was a routine part of business.

When Henry got up to speak at that meeting, he was well into his cups. He actually started to babble about how the company was unraveling. Ed Lundy, our top finance guy, leaned over to me and said: "Well, Lee, you better do your darnedest now. Try to save the day for us, or we'll all look like idiots."

I got up and spoke, which may have been the beginning of the end for me.

The next morning Henry called me in. "You're talking to too many people outside," he said. What he meant was it was all right for me to talk to the dealers or suppliers, but steer clear of Wall Street. Otherwise, they might think I was running the company, and that didn't sit too well with him.

That same day, similar meetings scheduled for Chicago and San Francisco were canceled. "That's it," Henry said. "We're never doing that again. No more going out to tell the world what we're up to."

Henry didn't mind if I got publicity—as long as it was tied to product. When I was featured on the cover of *The New York Times Magazine*, he sent a cable of congratulations to my hotel in Rome. But when I got praised in his spheres of influence, he couldn't handle it.

Now, just about everybody in this world is accountable to somebody. Some people are accountable to their parents—or their children. Others are accountable to their spouses, or their bosses, or even their dogs. Still others see themselves as accountable to God.

But Henry Ford has never been accountable to anyone. In a publicly held company, the chairman is morally accountable to his employees and his stockholders. He's legally accountable to his board of directors. But Henry always seemed to get his way with them.

The Ford Motor Company had gone public in 1956, but Henry never really accepted the change. As he saw it, he was like his grandfather, the rightful owner—Henry Ford, Prop.—and the company was his to do as he pleased. When it came to the board, he, more than most CEO's, believed in the mushroom treatment—throw manure on them and keep them in the dark. That attitude, of course, was fostered by the fact that Henry and his family, with only 12 percent of the stock, held on to 40 percent of the voting rights.

His attitude toward the government was not very different from his attitude toward the company.

One day he said to me: "Do you pay any income tax?"

"Are you kidding?" I replied. "Of course!" No matter how I sliced it, I was paying 50 percent of everything I earned.

"Well," he said, "I'm getting worried. This year I'm paying eleven thousand dollars. And that's the first time in six years that I'm paying *anything*!"

I was incredulous. "Henry," I said, "how on earth do you do it?"

"My lawyers take care of it," he replied.

"Look," I said, "I'm not against using whatever loopholes the government allows us. But the guys who work in our factories are paying almost as much as you are! Don't you think you should be paying your way? What about the national defense? What about the Army and the Air Force?"

But he didn't see the point. While I have no reason to believe he was breaking the law, as far as he was concerned, the name of the game was: take the government for all you can.

In all the years we worked together, I never saw him spend a penny of his own money. Eventually a group of Ford stockholders hired Roy Cohn, the prominent New York attorney, to represent them in a suit charging that Henry had used corporate funds for all sorts of personal expenses. On trips to London, for example, when he stayed at his own house there, he still billed the company. In fact, he went out of his way to ask me what the company was paying for my suite at Claridge's—just so his charges wouldn't be out of line.

The Roy Cohn suit also charged that Henry had used company planes to fly his own furniture from Europe to Detroit, to transport his sister's dogs and cats whenever she felt her pets needed a trim or a shampoo, and to take Dom Perignon champagne and Château Lafite wine from one home to another.

I don't know if all these charges were true, but I once did carry a fireplace on the company plane from London to Grosse Pointe for him.

Henry had a real thing about airplanes. At one point the company bought from Nippon Airways a 727 jet that Henry converted into a luxury cruiser. The lawyers told Henry it was improper for him to use the plane for his vacations and his jaunts to Europe—unless he paid for the trips himself. But he'd sooner *swim* to Europe than agree to reimburse the company out of his own pocket.

I, meanwhile, was using the 727 regularly for my business trips overseas. That plane became a thorn in Henry's side. He just hated to see me flying in it when he couldn't.

One day Henry suddenly gave an order to sell the plane to the Shah of Iran for $5 million.

The guy in charge of our fleet was shocked. "Shouldn't we at least get bids on it?" he asked.

"No," said Henry. "I want that plane out of here *today!*" The company lost a bundle on the deal.

After an internal audit, Henry had to pay back $34,000 to the company. He had been caught with his hand in the cookie jar, and not even his own auditing people would let him off the hook. Henry's only defense was to hold his wife responsible, but the fact that he admitted to *any* wrongdoing was remarkable in itself.

Ultimately the Roy Cohn suit was settled out of court. Although the stockholders didn't get anything, Cohn collected his legal fees for the effort—some $260,000. Henry got off easy once again.

But all of this was small stuff compared to Renaissance Center.

RenCen, as it's commonly known, is a dazzling complex of office buildings, stores, and the world's tallest hotel. It was designed as an elaborate plan to save downtown Detroit, which had become increasingly bleak and dangerous as more and more businesses had moved out to the suburbs.

Henry decided he would construct this monument to himself and raise the money for it. The official Ford commitment was $6 million—from corporate funds, of course. This was soon doubled to $12 million. Eventually the company funding swelled to about $100 million. At least that was the official story. But all told, I would estimate that we probably invested another couple of hundred million dollars in RenCen—when you count the costs involved in moving hundreds of our employees downtown to try to fill those huge office towers. Naturally, only a fraction of our huge investment was ever made public.

I was plain disgusted. We should have been spending that money on keeping up with General Motors. Instead of fancy real estate, GM was putting *its* profits into small cars. Several times, in private, I let Henry know how I felt. But he ignored me.

Henry's involvement in RenCen would have been very different if he had operated along the lines of the Carnegies, the Mellons, or the Rockefellers. These families used a lot of their own money for the public good.

But unlike the great philanthropists, Henry's generosity too often seemed to come from *other people's money*—money that belonged not to him but to the company and its stockholders. Not surprisingly, the stockholders were never consulted.

From the very start, RenCen was a failure. By 1974, when it was only half complete, it was already short by $100 million.

To make up the difference, Henry assigned Paul Bergmoser, vice-president in charge of purchasing, to fly around the country putting pressure on other companies to "invest" in RenCen. Fifty-one companies put up the money. Of these, thirty-eight depended on the auto industry and Ford in particular for a lot of their business.

Bergmoser would go to see the heads of companies such as U.S. Steel and Goodyear. With a straight face, he'd have to say to them: "Now, I'm not here in my capacity as head of purchasing"—even though we were doing millions of dollars of business with these companies each year. "I'm coming to you as the personal representative of Henry Ford," he'd tell them, "and my visit here has nothing to do with the Ford Motor Company."

The executives of companies such as Budd, Rockwell, and U.S. Steel would burst out laughing at Bergie's disclaimer. Ed Speer, the chief executive of U.S. Steel, told Bergie that the only proper symbol for Renaissance Center was a twisted arm.

Because of the Ford name, some of the finest stores in the United States and Europe agreed to come into RenCen. But they all insisted on financial guarantees by the company. This led to the totally ridiculous situation of the Ford Motor Company's having to be in the boutique or jewelry or fancy chocolate business and cover their losses for the first couple of years. And losses they were.

As I write these words, RenCen is on the verge of economic collapse. Today it offers little more than confusing architecture and a very ordinary shopping mall—with high-priced parking to boot. Oh, yes—there is also a $2.7 million office, complete with a winding staircase and a fireplace, that was built for Henry Ford as a downtown office.

I often wonder: Where was the press? There was a lot of talk about investigative reporting in those days, but nobody in Detroit was digging for the real story behind Renaissance Center.

One reason is that Henry made for good copy, and everybody indulged his excesses. Besides, we were a major advertiser. Nobody in Detroit—or anywhere else, for that matter—wanted to run the risk of offending such a big spender.

The way I saw it, Henry was always a playboy. He never worked hard. He *played* hard. What he cared about was wine, women, and song.

Actually, I always thought he hated women—except for his mother. When Henry's father died, Eleanor Clay Ford had taken over the family and put her son Henry in charge. She also kept him somewhat in line.

But when she died in 1976, his whole world came tumbling down. The only woman in his life he had any respect for was gone. Henry was the ultimate chauvinist, who believed that women were put on earth only for the pleasure of men.

He once complained to me that women would take over the Ford Motor Company one day—and wreck it. That's what happened at Gulf Oil, he would say. He added that the thirteen grandchildren at Ford now held more voting power than he and his brother and sister. But the really sad part, he felt, was that of the thirteen grandchildren, seven were girls and only six were boys. And that was the problem, he'd tell me: women can't run a damn thing.

As usual, Mary was wise to him from the very beginning. She used to say to me: "Liquor destroys all inhibitions and out comes the real man. So beware: this guy is *mean!*"

Actually, Mary was one of the few women he didn't scorn. Once, at a fiftieth birthday party for a close friend of ours, Katie Curran, Henry and Mary got into a long discussion while everyone else was getting bombed. At the time, Henry was on the wagon, and Mary didn't drink because she had diabetes.

They were talking about meetings of top management, which generally took place in fancy resorts. When Mary told Henry that the wives should be invited, too, Henry disagreed. "You girls just try to outdo each other," he said. "All you care about are your clothes and your jewels."

"You're totally wrong," she told him. "When the wives are there, your guys get to bed on time. They aren't out fooling around. The liquor bill is cut in half, and in the morning, guys get to the meetings when they're supposed to. You'll accomplish a lot more if you invite the wives along."

He really listened to her. Afterward, he said to me: "Your wife has horse sense." You had to get to Henry in those moments of sobriety. You had to grab him by the nose and twist it. Mary was always able to do that without getting into trouble.

Henry tried to be sophisticated and European. He knew how to be charming. He even knew something about wine and art.

But it was all a façade. After the third bottle of wine, all bets were off. He would change before your eyes from Dr. Jekyll to Mr. Hyde.

Because of his drinking, I kept my distance from him on social occasions. Beacham and McNamara, my two mentors, had both warned me. "Stay away from him," they said. "He'll get drunk, and you'll find yourself in trouble over nothing."

Ed O'Leary gave me similar advice. "You'll never get fired for losing a billion dollars," he told me. "You'll get fired some night when Henry's drunk. He'll call you a wop and you'll get into a fight. Mark my words—it will be over nothing. So always stay out of his line of fire."

I tried to. But Henry began to reveal himself as more than merely crude.

For me, a turning point in seeing the man for what he was came in 1974, at a management meeting on the equal opportunity program. Each division was asked to report its progress in hiring and promoting blacks. After listening to the reports, which were not impressive, Henry got angry. "You guys are only giving this thing lip service," he told us.

He then proceeded to make an impassioned plea for us to do more on behalf of blacks. He even said that executive bonuses might soon be tied to our progress in this area. "That way," he concluded, "you'll be sure to get off your asses and do what needs to be done for the black community."

His remarks at that meeting were so moving that they literally brought tears to my eyes. "Maybe he's right," I said to myself. "Maybe we really aren't doing enough. Maybe I'm dragging my feet. If the boss feels that strongly, I guess we ought to make a bigger push."

When the meeting was over, we all went up to the penthouse for lunch in the executive dining room. As usual, I was sitting at Henry's table. As soon as we sat down, he started spouting off about the blacks. "Those goddamn coons," he said. "They drive up and down Lake Shore Drive in front of my house. I hate them, I'm scared of them, and I think I'll move to Switzerland, where there just aren't any."

It was one of those moments I'll never forget. My antennae shot up. The guy had practically made me cry, and one hour later he was raving against the blacks. It had all been for show. Deep down, he must have hated their guts.

That's when I realized I was working for a real bastard.

Bigotry is bad enough, as I had learned in Allentown. At least the kids in my school didn't pretend to be anything else. But Henry was more than a bigot. He was also a hypocrite.

Publicly, he tried to be the world's most progressive businessman, but behind closed doors he showed disdain for just about everybody. Until 1975, the only group that Henry hadn't slandered in my presence were the Italians. But before long, he would be making up for lost time.

X

1975: THE FATEFUL YEAR

In 1975, Henry Ford started his month-by-month premeditated plan to destroy me.

Until then, he had pretty well left me alone. But in that year he started having chest pains, and he really didn't look well. It was then that King Henry began to realize his mortality.

He turned animal. I imagine his first impulse was: "I don't want that Italian interloper taking over. What's going to happen to the family business if I get a heart attack and die? Before I know it, he'll sneak in here one night, take my name off the building, and turn this place into the Iacocca Motor Company. Where does that leave my son, Edsel?"

When Henry thought I'd steal the family jewels, he had to get rid of me. But he didn't have the guts to just go ahead and do his own dirty work. Besides, he knew he'd never get away with it. Instead, he played Machiavelli, determined to humiliate me into quitting.

Henry dropped his first bomb while I was away. Early in 1975, I was out of the country for a couple of weeks on a whirlwind tour of the Middle East, part of a delegation of business leaders brought over by *Time* magazine to get a better understanding of Israel and the Arab world.

When I returned to the United States on February 3, I was surprised to find Chalmers Goyert, my executive assistant, waiting for me at J.F.K. Airport in New York.

"What's up?" I asked.

"We've got big problems," he told me.

We sure did. I listened as Goyert outlined the incredible events that had taken place during my absence. Just a few days earlier, while a group of us had been meeting with King Faisal in Saudi Arabia, King Henry had suddenly called a special meeting of top management.

The effects of that meeting are still being felt today. Henry was worried about the OPEC situation. The man who had taken the credit for turning the Ford Motor Company around after World War II was beside himself with fear. The Arabs had come charging up the hill, and he just couldn't take it.

Convinced that a major depression was imminent, he ordered $2 billion scratched from future product programs. With this decision, he summarily eliminated many of the products that would have made us competitive—such necessities as small cars and front-wheel-drive technology.

During the meeting, Henry had announced: "I am the Sewell Avery of the Ford Motor Company." It was an ominous reference.

Sewell Avery had been the head of Montgomery Ward, an ultra-conservative manager who had decided not to allocate any money for future development after World War II. He was sure the world was coming to an end and America was doomed. His decision proved to be a disaster for Montgomery Ward, because Sears started knocking the hell out of them.

Henry's announcement had similar implications for us.

As for me, it wasn't hard to read the writing on the wall. Henry had waited until I was thousands of miles away in order to call a meeting where he usurped my power and responsibility—and where he also went against everything I believed in.

Henry did enormous damage to the company that day. Ford's Topaz and Tempo, the small, front-wheel-drive cars that finally went on sale in May of 1983, should have been ready four or five years earlier when the public was clamoring for small cars. But Ford's response to the 1973 oil crisis wasn't even *planned* until 1979.

I was furious. OPEC had already made clear that without small cars we were dead. GM and Chrysler were working fast and furious to bring out their own subcompacts. And while this was going on, the head of the Ford Motor Company had stuck his head in the sand.

Every month like clockwork, after the board meeting, I used to get a visit from Franklin Murphy, the dean of our board, former chancellor of UCLA, chairman of the board of the *Los Angeles Times-Mirror* Company—and senior confidant of Henry Ford.

Murphy was always giving me sincere advice, not on how to run the company, but on how to handle Henry. "He's under a lot of pressure," he told me one day. "You have to be charitable. He's having a helluva time with his wife."

We all knew that Henry's marriage to Cristina was coming apart. He had just been arrested for drunk driving in Santa Barbara—together with his girlfriend, Kathy DuRoss—while Cristina was off in Katmandu with her good friend Imelda Marcos, the first lady of the Philippines.

Just a few days later, I was home sick with the flu and fatefully missed a meeting about an amazing event.

On February 14, while I was absent, Henry called a summit meeting to discuss "the Indonesian situation." Henry had apparently authorized Paul Lorenz, an executive vice-president and one of the top officers of the company, to pay a "commission" of $1 million to an Indonesian general. In return, Ford was to get a $29 million contract to build fifteen satellite ground stations.

But when word of the "commission" leaked out, Henry sent two of our guys from Dearborn to Djakarta to tell the general this wasn't the way we did business.

Lorenz worked for me. When I learned of the incident I called him into my office. "Paul," I said, "why the hell did you offer that general a million bucks?"

Paul was a very proper and competent guy. He was also loyal, and he didn't want to get anyone in trouble. "It was a mistake," he told me.

"A mistake?" I said. "Nobody gives away a million bucks by mistake!"

Paul was silent. When I persisted, he said: "You don't think I'd do something like that on my own, do you?"

"What do you mean by that?" I asked. "Do you mean to tell me that somebody told you to do it?"

Paul replied: "Well, no, but the chairman sort of winked at it and said: 'That's how things are done over there.' "

Now, it's true that American corporations doing business in Third World countries sometimes offered bribes. But as far as I knew, a thing like that could never happen at Ford.

As soon as the press got wind of the attempted bribe, a full-scale cover-up went into operation within the company. It was at least as impressive as anything that went on during Watergate. There was an internal purging of the files. There were even special meetings to coordinate excuses on why we did it.

We had no choice but to fire Paul Lorenz, and, as usual, I was assigned the task of doing it. "I'll go quietly if there's no stigma on my record," he told me. "But I'm taking the rap for this. You know I wouldn't have done it without approval from the highest levels." I knew Paul well and I believed he was telling the truth.

A few days later, Henry made a confession of sorts. "I think I might have led Lorenz to believe that the payoff was all right," he said to me. "Maybe I led the poor bastard astray."

A full year and a half later, I was looking over the bonus sheet. To my shock, I saw that Henry had decided to give Paul Lorenz $100,000.

"I fired the guy," I said to Henry. "How can *you* give him a hundred grand as a bonus?"

"Well," said Henry, "he wasn't a bad fellow." It was almost like Watergate all over again. Lorenz took the rap, and the boss was taking care of him.

Here, too, the press was very easy on Henry. And so were the courts. A couple of years later, I was called down to the Justice Department to give a deposition on the matter. Henry never gave one. I don't know how he got away with it.

During that same winter, we announced our fourth-quarter losses for 1974, which came to $12 million. As losses go, this was a small one. Compared to what the auto industry went through between 1979 and 1982, a loss of $12 million might have been a cause for celebration.

Still, this was the first time since 1946 that the Ford Motor Company had experienced a losing quarter. So in addition to his failing health and his crumbling marriage, Henry had one more thing to worry about. As a result, he became more paranoid than ever.

In those days my secretary was a terrific woman named Betty Martin. If it weren't for the chauvinism built into the system, Betty would have been a vice-president—she was better than most of the guys who worked for me.

Betty always knew when something fishy was going on. One day she came to me and said: "I've just learned that every time you make a call on the company credit card, a record of it goes to Mr. Ford's office."

A couple of weeks later she told me: "Your desk is always pretty messy, so sometimes before I go home I try to organize it for you. I always remember exactly where I put everything, but the next morning, everything's moved around. It happens a lot, and I thought you should know about it. I don't think the cleaning ladies would touch it."

I went home and said to Mary: "Now I'm worried." Betty Martin was a no-nonsense woman. She hated gossip. She wouldn't have told me these stories if she didn't think they were important. Something bad was in the air, and, as usual, the secretaries were the first to know.

After that, things got stranger and stranger. On April 10, at our monthly board meeting, we responded to our recent losses by cutting our quarterly dividend by twenty cents. That alone saved us $75 million a year.

But that same day Henry raised the directors' fees from $40,000 to $47,000 a year. That's what I call neutralizing the board.

Later that month we announced our first-quarter losses of $11 million after taxes, which meant that we now had two losing quarters in a row.

Henry was starting to come apart at the seams. On July 11, he went public with his madness. That day he called a meeting of the top five hundred managers. He gave no advance indication—not even to me—as to the purpose of this extraordinary gathering.

When everyone had assembled in the auditorium, Henry proceeded to give a speech in which he announced: "I am the captain of this ship." Our management, he said, was going about things all wrong. I was the top manager, so there was no question about whom he had in mind. It was an unprecedented meeting. Henry was rambling and often incoherent. People walked out of there asking each other: "Hey, what was *that* all about?"

After this meeting, we all started to wonder if Henry was losing his mind. Everybody got nervous. The whole company was frozen. Nobody was doing a thing. Instead, people were busy trying to figure out what Henry was up to—and whose side to take.

Although the press was mostly unaware of these squabbles, our dealers were getting the distinct impression that something was rotten in Denmark. On February 10, 1976, there was a meeting of Ford Division dealers in Las Vegas. The minutes read: "There appears to be too much politics within the leadership of Ford Motor Company and it is blunting the effectiveness of the leaders. . . . Henry Ford II is not at this time offering the type of quality leadership that his dealers expect from him."

The dealers also expressed their concern about the lack of new products from Ford and the fact that they now felt in a "catch-up" position with respect to GM.

During my struggles with Henry, the dealers made it very clear that they sided with me. This only made matters worse. Every statement of support from the dealers was more ammunition for Henry. The Ford Motor Company was not a democracy, so the very fact of my popularity among the troops was enough to convince him I was dangerous.

But all these events were small potatoes compared to the really big news of that year.

In the fall of 1975, Henry called in Paul Bergmoser and grilled him about doing business with Bill Fugazy, who ran a limousine and travel company in New York and arranged our dealer incentive programs.

"Aren't you afraid of Fugazy?" Henry asked. "Aren't you scared of ending up in the East River with a pair of cement boots?"

Shortly after that, Henry called me in. "I know Fugazy's a good friend of yours," he said. "But I'm starting a full investigation of him."

"What's the problem?" I asked.

"I think he's mixed up with the Mafia," said Henry.

"Don't be ridiculous," I said. "His grandfather started the travel business in 1870. Besides, I've had dinner with Bill and Cardinal Spellman. He's connected to all the right people."

"I don't know about that," said Henry. "He's got a limousine company. Limousine and trucking companies are always Mafia fronts."

"Are you kidding?" I said. "If he's involved with the Mafia, why is he losing so much money?" That line didn't seem to register, so I took another tack. I reminded Henry that it was Bill Fugazy who had arranged for Pope Paul to ride in a Lincoln instead of a Cadillac when the Pope came to New York.

But Henry was adamant. The next thing I knew, Fugazy told me files had been removed from his office without his knowledge. He was convinced his telephones were tapped, too, but nothing incriminating was ever found.

Very soon it became clear that the Fugazy affair was really a cover. The real subject of Henry's probe wasn't Bill Fugazy at all. It was Lee Iacocca.

The investigation, which ended up costing the company close to $2 million, began in August 1975. Inspired by Watergate, Henry

even appointed a special prosecutor—Theodore Souris, a former justice of the Michigan Supreme Court.

The investigation began by focusing on a Ford dealer meeting in
Las Vegas. Wendell Coleman, head of our San Diego branch sales
office, was in charge of expense accounts for the Las Vegas meeting.
He was called in for an interrogation in which they verbally beat the
hell out of him. He was so outraged by what happened that he wrote
down a full account and sent it to me.

Coleman was asked to come to World Headquarters on December 3, 1975, where he was "interviewed" by two men from the finance staff. They began by advising him of his rights. They then told
him that this was not a Ford Division audit review but rather a review
done at the request of World Headquarters, and they asked him not to
discuss the interview with anyone else in the company.

The interview began with a detailed review of several Ford dealer
dinners in Las Vegas. Coleman was asked whether there were any
women in the party of executives at one fancy restaurant. He was
specifically asked if there were any women with me. Then they grilled
him on why he'd given a generous tip to the maître d', whether
Fugazy had been part of our group, if certain executives had done any
gambling, and if Coleman had supplied them with money for that
purpose.

"It was a witch-hunt," Coleman told me. "They were looking for
something—anything—gambling, girls, whatever." When Coleman
objected to the line of questioning, he was asked outright: "Did you at
any time give money to Iacocca to gamble with?"

"No."

"Did any executives ask for money to gamble with?"

"No."

Coleman had the impression that the investigators believed he
stood around handing out wads of cash to the top officers of the
company.

Under the guise of an audit of the travel and expense accounts of
top executives, Henry conducted nothing less than a full-scale investigation of both my business and my personal life. The "audit" consisted of something like fifty-five interviews, which were conducted
not only with Ford executives but also with many of our suppliers,
such as U.S. Steel and Budd, as well as our advertising agencies.

Despite an incredible effort, the investigation failed to turn up a
single damaging item about me or my people.

A full report was made to Franklin Murphy, who came to see me and said: "You have nothing to worry about. The whole thing is over."

I was outraged. "Why didn't any of you guys on the board get involved in this while it was going on?" I asked.

"Forget about it," said Frank. "You know Henry. Boys will be boys. Anyway, he came in with a cannon and went out with a peashooter."

After spending $2 million and coming up with nothing, a normal person might have apologized. A normal person might have shown a little remorse. A normal person might have said: "Well, I checked out my president and some of my vice-presidents, and they're as clean as a whistle. And I'm proud of them because that investigation was relentless."

It sure was. During those months, we found ourselves leaving the building to make phone calls. Henry had gone to Japan, and he was a real nut about the new, high-powered electronic gadgets he saw over there. We were all afraid our offices were tapped. Bill Bourke, one of our vice-presidents, told us that he was with Henry when he bought a $10,000 device that could pick up conversations from another building. Knowing Henry, nobody doubted it was true.

The impact of all this on our top management is hard to believe. We started to pull the drapes and talk in whispers. Ben Bidwell, who later became president of Hertz before joining me at Chrysler, used to say he was even afraid to walk in the halls. Grown men were quaking in their boots, afraid the king would condemn them to death.

It was incredible. One man with inherited wealth was making a shambles of everything, launching a company on three years of hell just because he felt like it. He was playing with people's lives. Guys were drinking too much. Their families were falling apart. And nobody could do a thing about it. This juggernaut was running amok.

That was the atmosphere in the Glass House in 1975.

And that was when I should have quit.

Certainly Henry must have expected me to leave. Originally, he had probably figured: "I'll find something on the guy. He's going on all these trips, he's living off the fat of the land. If I dig hard enough, I'm bound to hit pay dirt."

But he never did. When the investigation was finally done, my friends said: "Thank God it's over."

"No," I said. "Henry came up empty. He looks like a fool. Now our real troubles begin."

XI

THE SHOWDOWN

I often ask myself why I didn't quit at the end of 1975. Why did I accept the fate Henry was dishing out? How could I let a guy take my destiny and pummel it?

Looking back, I don't know how I lived through those years. My life was so crazy that I started writing everything down. Mary always said: "Keep track of this stuff. Someday you might want to write a book. Nobody would believe what we're going through."

So why didn't I just take a walk?

First, like anybody who's in a bad situation, I hoped that things would get better. Maybe Henry would come to his senses. Or the board would get its back up.

Another scenario I imagined was that his brother Bill, who owned twice as much stock as Henry, would say one day: "Look, my brother's gone nuts. We've got to replace him." I know that the idea had certainly crossed Bill's mind. But he never acted on it.

Why did I stay? In part because I couldn't imagine working anywhere else. I had spent my whole adult life at Ford, and that's where I wanted to be. The Mustang, the Mark III, and the Fiesta were my babies. I also had a lot of allies. The suppliers kept getting big orders. The dealers said: "We've never done this well." The managers were making huge bonuses. Unless I was some kind of swami who had a magic hold on all these people, I have to conclude that my popularity was due to my performance. Despite my troubles with Henry, I got a lot of satisfaction from my success.

I never expected a showdown, but if it came to that, I was ready. I knew how valuable I was to the company. In terms of everything

"Hal," I said, "I know this sounds ridiculous, but you can't sit next to me anymore." That was as far as I was willing to go. Hal was easily the most valuable player on the team, and there was no way on earth that I was going to bench him.

Eventually the only thing I could do to save Hal was to move him completely out of Henry's line of vision. I assigned him to a number of projects in Europe, and he soon became a regular transatlantic commuter. No matter what the problem was, Hal would go in and get the job done. The Fiesta was his greatest coup, but almost everything he touched turned to gold.

Shortly thereafter Henry called me and ordered me to fire Hal Sperlich.

"Henry," I said, "you gotta be kidding. He's the best we've got."

"Fire him now," said Henry.

It was the middle of the afternoon. I was about to leave the office to catch a flight to New York. I asked Henry if it could wait until I returned.

"If you don't can him right now," Henry replied, "you'll go out the door with him."

I knew it was hopeless. Still, I tried to reason with him. "Sperlich did the Mustang," I told Henry. "He made us millions."

"Don't give me any bullshit," said Henry. "I don't like him. You're not entitled to ask why. It's just a feeling I have."

Hal took it very hard. Although both of us could see it coming, you always live in the hope that if you do your job well, justice will prevail. Hal genuinely believed that his talent was enough to keep him at Ford, even if the boss didn't like him. But he forgot that we worked in a dictatorship.

"This is a chickenshit outfit," I told Sperlich. "And I should probably be getting out with you. I'm higher up than you are, but I have to put up with the same garbage. Maybe Henry's doing you a favor," I said. "In a more democratic environment, your talent will be recognized and rewarded. It's hard to believe right now, but you might look back on this day and be grateful that Henry kicked you out."

I guess I was prophetic. Shortly after Hal was fired, the president of Chrysler took him to lunch. Early in 1977, Hal started working at Chrysler. He immediately took a leading role in the planning of their small cars, where he did everything he had wanted to accomplish at Ford.

Less than two years later, Hal and I were working together again.

Today he's president of Chrysler. And in a delicious turn of events, his front-wheel-drive cars, especially the new T115 minivans—the cars that Henry never let him do at Ford—are inexorably eating into Ford's share of the market.

At the beginning of 1977, Henry declared war. He brought in McKinsey & Company, the management-consultant people, to reorganize our top administration. When the project was over, an executive high in the company left a little note on my desk that said, in effect: "Hang in there, Lee. But it won't be easy. Your boss is an absolute total dictator and I don't know how you guys put up with it."

After months of study and a couple of million dollars in fees, McKinsey issued its recommendation. The plan called for a troika—a three-member office of the chief executive—to replace the standard structure of chairman and president.

The new arrangement was formally established in April. Henry, of course, remained as chairman and chief executive officer. Phil Caldwell was named vice-chairman, while I continued as president.

We each had our own areas of responsibility, but the key change— and the obvious reason for the new arrangement—was spelled out in a memo issued by Henry, which specified that "The Vice Chairman is the Chief Executive Officer in the absence of the Chairman." In other words, if Henry was first among equals, Phil Caldwell was now second.

Making Caldwell number two brought my fight with Henry out in the open. Until then, it had been guerrilla tactics. But now Henry was getting bolder. The entire management shift was no more than an ornate and expensive way to defuse my power in a socially acceptable manner. Without having to confront me directly, Henry had succeeded in installing Caldwell above me.

It was a real crack in the face. Every time there was a dinner, Henry hosted table one, Caldwell hosted table two, and I was shoved down to three. It was public humiliation, like the guy in the stockade in the center of town.

He tore me up inside. He tore up my wife and my kids. They knew I was under great pressure, but I didn't tell them all the details. I didn't want them to go crazy. I was killing myself but I wouldn't yield. It might have been pride, it might have been stupidity, but I was not going to crawl out of there with my tail between my legs.

The office of the chief executive was a three-headed monster. It was ridiculous that Caldwell, who used to work for me, was suddenly above me for no apparent reason except malice. Privately, I told Henry that his new plan was a big mistake. But in typical fashion, he tried to reassure me with platitudes. "Don't worry," he said. "It will all work out in the end."

Although I was boiling inside, in public I defended the new structure. I reassured all the people who worked for me that the new arrangement was perfectly fine.

Not surprisingly, the office of the chief executive didn't last very long. In June of 1978, fourteen months after it was established, Henry announced another shift in top management. Instead of three members, our little team would now have four. The new arrival was William Clay Ford, Henry's younger brother. Bill was brought in to maintain a Ford family presence in the event of Henry's illness or death.

Now I had dropped to fourth in the pecking order. Moreover, I was reporting not to Henry but to Phil Caldwell, who was named deputy chief executive officer. To make the humiliation complete, Henry didn't even bother to tell me about this new restructuring until the day before it was announced.

When he finally gave me the news, I said: "I think you're making a mistake."

"That's my decision and the board's," he snapped.

It was salami-slicing time—one slice at a time. I was getting cut up. Each day I found another part of my body missing. I put out the word that I wasn't going to take it.

Four days later, on June 12, Henry met with our nine outside board members and told them he was about to fire me. This time the board drew the line. They said: "No, Henry, you're doing this wrong, let's cool it. We'll talk to Lee. We'll work things out. You go in and apologize to him."

"I lost my board today," he told Franklin Murphy.

The next day Henry came to my office for only the third time in eight years. "Let's bury the hatchet," he said.

The board had decided that I should get together with some of its members to try to iron out the problems. Over the next couple of weeks, I met separately with Joseph Cullman, chairman of Philip Morris in New York, and George Bennett, president of the State Street Investment Corporation in Boston. There was nothing secret about these meetings. It was their idea. I flew to see each of them on the company plane and I submitted expense accounts, so they were all a matter of record.

The false peace lasted one month. On the evening of July 12, 1978, Henry had dinner with the outside board members, as he did every month on the eve of the board meeting. Again he announced that he was going to fire me. Now he claimed I was ganging up on him by going to the outside directors behind his back—even though they had asked for the meeting with me. He also said that the personal chemistry between the two of us had never been right. It seems to have taken Henry Ford thirty-two years to decide he didn't get along with me.

This time, too, several of the board members challenged him. They cited my loyalty and my value to the company. They asked Henry to reinstate me to my former position as number two man.

Henry was livid. He wasn't used to backtalk from the board. "It's him or me," he growled. "You have twenty minutes to make up your minds." Then he stormed out of the room.

Until this point he had not dared to fire the guy who was making him all this money, who was the father of the Mustang and the Mark and the Fiesta, and who was so popular in the company. I think he had doubts as to whether he could get away with it.

But finally, in frustration, he just blew his stack. "It's taken three whole years," he must have been thinking, "and this bastard's still here!" When he couldn't get me to quit, he finally decided to move in and occupy the land. He could always justify it later.

That same night I received a telephone call from Keith Crain. Crain was the publisher of *Automotive News*, the trade weekly of the car industry. "Say it isn't so," he said.

I had no doubt as to what he meant. Crain was a close friend of Henry's son, Edsel, and my guess is that Henry had instructed Edsel to leak the story to him. That way, I could learn about my own firing indirectly, through the press.

It was classic Henry. He wanted the news of my firing to reach me through a third party. Henry was a pro at turning the screws. This move also ensured that the king wouldn't have to get his hands dirty with messy affairs of state.

The next morning I went to work as usual. At the office there was no indication anything was wrong. By lunchtime I was beginning to wonder whether Keith Crain had been misinformed. But just before three o'clock, Henry's secretary summoned me to his office. "This is it," I thought.

When I walked into the inner sanctum, Henry and his brother Bill were sitting at a marble conference table with an "I smell shit" look on their faces. They were tight and nervous. In a strange way I was relaxed. I had already been tipped off. I knew what was about to happen. The meeting was just to make it official.

I hadn't expected Bill to be there for the firing, but it made good sense. His presence was a way of letting me know that this was not just Henry's decision but the family's. Bill was the company's biggest individual shareholder, so his being there carried a political message as well. If Bill went along with his brother's decision, I would have no recourse.

Henry also wanted a witness. Normally, he delegated his dirty work by getting other people—especially me—to do his firings for him. But this time he was on his own. Having Bill there by his side probably made it easier for him to let me go.

The fact that Bill was there also made *me* feel better. He was a great fan of mine as well as a good friend. He had already promised me that when push came to shove—as we both knew it would—he would fight for me. I knew I couldn't totally count on his support, because Bill had never stood up to Henry in his life. Still, I held out some hope that he would intervene.

As I took my seat at the table, Henry hemmed and hawed. He had never fired anyone, and he didn't know how to begin. "There comes a time when I have to do things my way," he finally said. "I've decided to reorganize the company. This is one of those things that you hate to do, but you have to do it anyway. It's been a nice association"—I looked at him in disbelief—"but I think you should leave. It's best for the company."

At no point during our entire forty-five-minute meeting did he ever use the word "fired."

"What's this all about?" I asked.

But Henry couldn't give me a reason. "It's personal," he said, "and I can't tell you any more. It's just one of those things."

But I persisted. I wanted to force him to give me a reason because I knew he didn't have a good one. Finally, he just shrugged his shoulders and said: "Well, sometimes you just don't like somebody."

I had only one card left to play. "What about Bill over here?" I said. "I'd like to know what he thinks."

"I've already made the decision," said Henry.

I was disappointed but not really surprised. Blood is thicker than water, and Bill was part of the dynasty.

"I do have certain rights," I said, "and I hope there won't be any quarrel over that." I was concerned about my pension and my deferred compensation.

"We can work that out," said Henry. We agreed that the record would show I was resigning from the company effective October 15, 1978—my fifty-fourth birthday. Had I left any earlier, I would have forfeited a lot of benefits.

Up to this point, our conversation had been remarkably calm. Then I took over. For Henry's benefit, I recited a list of my accomplishments on behalf of the Ford Motor Company. I reminded Henry that we had just completed the two best years in our history. I wanted him to know exactly what he was throwing away.

When I finished my speech, I said: "Look at me." Until this point he had not been able to look me in the eye. My voice was rising now as I realized that this would be our final conversation.

"Your timing stinks," I said. "We've just made a billion eight for the second year in a row. That's three and a half billion in the past two years. But mark my words, Henry. You may never see a billion eight again. And do you know why? Because you don't know how the fuck we made it in the first place!"

It was true. Henry was an old pro at spending money, but he never understood how it all came in. He just sat in his ivory tower and said: "My God, we're making money!" He was there every day to throw his weight around, but he never knew what made the place tick.

Near the end of the meeting, Bill made an honest effort to change his brother's mind. But it was too little, too late. As we left Henry's office, Bill had tears running down his face. "This shouldn't have happened," he kept saying. "He's ruthless."

Then he composed himself. "You were so cool in there," he said. "You've been with us thirty-two years, and he didn't even give you a reason. You really laid him out. Nobody in his life ever took him on the way you just did. I'm surprised he held still for it."

"Thanks, Bill," I said. "But I'm dead, and you and he are still alive!"

Bill is a good man, but it's always been the Fords against the world. Still, he and I remained friends. I know that he genuinely wanted me to continue as president—just as he genuinely believed there was nothing he could do about it.

When I returned to my office, I began getting phone calls of inquiry from some of my friends and colleagues. Apparently, word of my firing had already spread. Before the day was over, Henry issued a cryptic memo to top executives that said simply: "Effective immediately you will report to Philip Caldwell."

Some people received that memo in their office. But most found it waiting on the front seat of their cars in the executive garage. Somebody told me later that Henry himself had come down and put them there. That was probably the only way he could know for sure that the deed was finally done.

Leaving the office that afternoon, I felt a great sense of relief. "Thank God the bullshit is over," I said to myself in the car. If I had to get fired, at least my timing was good. We had just finished the best six months in our history.

When I got home, I received a call from Lia, my younger daughter, who was at tennis camp—her first time away from home. She had heard about the firing on the radio, and she was in tears.

When I look back on that awful week, what I remember most clearly is Lia crying on the telephone. I hate Henry for what he did to me. But I hate him even more for the way he did it. There had been no opportunity to sit down and talk to my kids before the whole world knew. I'll never forgive him for that.

Lia wasn't only sad. She was also angry that I hadn't told her in advance that I was about to be fired. She couldn't believe I hadn't known it was about to happen.

"How could you not know?" she asked. "You're the president of this big company. You always know what's going on!"

"Not this time, honey."

She had a very hard week. I think there were kids who took some sadistic pleasure that the president's daughter, who always had the best of everything, was finally getting her comeuppance.

It soon became clear that Henry had made his decision to fire me on impulse, even if it was inevitable in the long run. That same week, the company had mailed out an advance press kit for the 1979 Mustang. Inside was a photograph of me standing in front of the new car. But when the Mustang was introduced a few weeks later at the Dearborn Hyatt Regency, it was Bill Bourke who represented the company.

They say that the bigger you are, the harder you fall. Well, I fell a great distance that week. I instantly identified with every person I had ever fired.

When I moved to Chrysler a few months later, I had to lay off hundreds of executives in order to keep the company alive. I tried my best to do it with some degree of sensitivity. For the first time in my life, I learned how terrible it felt to be let go.

After I was fired, it was as if I ceased to exist. Phrases such as "father of the Mustang" could no longer be used. People who had worked for me, my colleagues and friends, were afraid to see me. Yesterday I had been a hero. Today I was somebody to be avoided at all costs.

Everybody knew that Henry was prepared to carry out a major purge of Iacocca supporters. Anyone who failed to break off complete diplomatic and social relations with me risked being fired.

My former friends stopped calling me because my phone might be tapped. They would notice me at an auto show and look the other way. The really courageous ones would come up and give me a quick handshake. Then they'd get out of sight before the photographer from the *Detroit Free Press* could capture the moment. After all, Henry might see the picture in the paper. And then he might execute the offender for being seen in public with the pariah.

The week I was fired, Walter Murphy, who had been my close associate and executive director of the company's worldwide public relations staff for twenty years, received a phone call from Henry in the middle of the night.

"Do you love Iacocca?" Henry wanted to know.

"Sure," said Walter.

"Then you're fired," said Henry.

Henry rescinded the order the next day, but it shows you how crazy he got.

Several months later, Fred and Burns Cody, two old friends of mine, gave a party for me. Only a couple of Ford guys showed up, and only one of the officers—Ben Bidwell. He took a hell of a chance. The next day, when Bidwell went to work, he was called on the carpet. "We want to know who was at that party," they said to him.

It didn't stop. The company masseur, a great friend of mine, kept coming to my house for a year or two. Then one Sunday he didn't show. He said he was tied up, and I never saw him again. Somebody must have put out the word that he was seen coming to my house to give me a rubdown, and he couldn't afford to lose his job. Almost four years after I was fired, the chief stewardess of the company fleet got moved out and demoted because she was still friendly with my wife and kids.

For me, the pain continued long after the deed was done. One of my best friends in the company had been close to my family for twenty-five years. We had played poker together every Friday night. Our families went on vacations together. But after I was fired, he never even called. And when Mary died in 1983, he didn't even come to her funeral.

My father always used to say that when you die, if you've got five real friends, you've had a great life. I found out in a hurry what he meant.

It was a bitter lesson. You can be friends with someone for decades. You can share all the good times and bad with him. You can try to protect him when the going gets rough. And then you have some rough luck yourself and you never hear from the guy again.

It really makes you ask yourself the big questions. If I could do it over, could I have protected my family better? The pressure on them was awful. You watch your wife get sicker—Mary had her first heart attack less than three months after I was fired—and you wonder. A cruel man and cruel fate intervene and change your life.

I was hurting pretty bad after the firing, and I could have used a phone call from somebody who said: "Let's have coffee together, I feel terrible about what happened." But most of my company friends deserted me. It was the greatest shock of my life.

To some extent, I can understand their attitude. It wasn't their fault that the corporation was a dictatorship. Their jobs really *were* on the line if they continued to associate with me. They had their mortgages and their kids to worry about.

But what about the board? These guys were the illustrious guardians of the Ford Motor Company. They were supposed to constitute the system of checks and balances to prevent the flagrant abuse of power by top management. But it seemed to me their attitude was: "As long as we're taken care of, we'll follow the leader."

When Henry ordered the board to choose between himself and me, why did they let him fire the guy they had such great faith in? They may not have been able to prevent it, but at least some of them could have resigned in protest. Nobody did. Not one person said: "This is a disgrace. This guy is making us a couple of billion a year, and you're firing him? Then I'm leaving, too."

That's one mystery I want to unravel before I die: How can those board members sleep at night? Why didn't Joe Cullman and George Bennett and Frank Murphy and Carter Burgess really stand up to Henry Ford? To this day, I can't figure out how the board members can defend their decision, to themselves or to anyone else.

After I left the company, the only ones I ever heard a word from were Joe Cullman, Marian Heiskell, and George Bennett. The day I signed on with Chrysler, Marian called to wish me well. She was a real lady.

I stayed on good terms with George Bennett of State Street Investment. He said: "You know, if I'd had any guts I should have quit with you. But I handle a pension fund for Ford and I'd lose it in an instant if I followed you to Chrysler."

After Mary died, I got a letter from Bill Ford and a note from Franklin Murphy. But that was it. For all the years of our working together, that was the first and last I ever heard from the board during my time of grief.

In the annual meeting that followed my firing, Roy Cohn stood up to Henry and asked: "By firing Iacocca, how did you help the stockholders?"

But Henry just smiled and replied: "Well, the board supported me, and that's privileged information."

The firing got a lot of attention in the outside world. Walter Cronkite reported the details on *The CBS Evening News*, commenting that "it all sounds like something from one of those enormous novels about the automobile business." *The New York Times*, in a front-page story, called the firing "one of the most dramatic shakeups in the history of the Ford Motor Company." Given our turbulent history, that was saying a great deal.

I was especially pleased with an editorial in *Automotive News*. It mentioned my $1 million annual income and said that "by all standards, he earned every penny." Without directly criticizing Henry, the editorial said: "The best ballplayer in the business is now a free agent."

A number of editorial writers and columnists found the firing disturbing—and difficult to believe. Jack Egan, writing in the financial pages of the *Washington Post*, wrote that the way it all happened "raises questions about how much an enterprise as large as Ford Motor is run like a private duchy by the whim of one man."

In Warren, Rhode Island, the local paper made a similar point. Quoting a *Wall Street Journal* story that explained my firing by saying I "flew too close to Air Force One," a columnist observed: "That's a little scary when you think that Ford is so big in America that what Ford does affects everybody. And what goes on at Ford is apparently under the control of one arrogant old man who isn't responsible to anybody. He simply does as he pleases."

Nicholas Von Hoffman, the syndicated columnist, went even further. Calling Henry a "60-year-old adolescent," he concluded: "If a guy like Iacocca's job isn't safe, is yours?"

XII

THE DAY AFTER

As soon as they heard the news, the Ford dealers were up in arms. Ed Mullane, a dealer in Bergenfield, New Jersey, who was president of the twelve-hundred-member Ford Dealer Alliance, was especially upset.

Mullane had already figured out I was in trouble. On his own, he had written a letter supporting me to Henry and all of the directors. Henry wrote back telling him to mind his own business. Once I went by Henry's office and heard him yelling on the phone: "Iacocca went to see Mullane, the son-of-a-bitch, and put him up to this." Of course I never did.

After the firing, Mullane led a campaign to get me back and to have a dealer named to the board of directors. He calculated that the dealers had a combined investment of close to $10 billion in their various franchises and that I represented the best way to protect that investment. Later that summer, he actually tried to bring about an organized protest on the part of dealers who were also stockholders in the company, but the plan fizzled.

Although Mullane was unsuccessful in his efforts to have me reinstated, there were indications that the company was worried about its dealer base in the wake of my departure. The day after I was fired, Henry sent off a letter to every Ford dealer in the country, trying to reassure them all that they wouldn't be neglected:

"The Company has a strong and experienced management team. Our North American Automotive Operations are headed by talented executives who are well known to you and who are fully attuned to your needs and the needs of the retail market." Of course, if that were really true, there would have been no need for the letter.

I received a great many phone calls and letters of support from our dealers. Their concern and good wishes meant a lot to me. In the press I'm often described as "demanding," "tough-assed," or lacking in compassion. But if that were so, I don't think the dealers would have rallied on my behalf. We had our share of disagreements, but I always treated them fairly. While Henry was running with the jet set and raising hell, I was paying attention to them as people. I also helped quite a few of them become millionaires.

Meanwhile, back at the office, Henry had appointed Bill Ford and Carter Burgess, a board member, to decide upon my compensation. I told them how much I had coming to me, but they were bastards to the bitter end. To get what I deserved, I hired Edward Bennett Williams, the best lawyer I knew. In the end, I got about 75 percent of what I was entitled to.

Looking back on this episode, what sticks in my craw is Carter Burgess and Henry Nolte, Ford's chief counsel, mouthing platitudes about how they wanted to be fair but couldn't set any precedents on financial settlements because of "stockholder interests." Bill Ford, on the other hand, just sat there and bit his lip.

I did get a lot of letters of support from fellow employees. These letters were all written by hand, of course, so that there would be no record they had been sent. There were also letters and phone calls from headhunters eager to help me find a new job.

I think that morning of exile in the parts depot had a major influence on my decision, two weeks later, to accept the presidency of Chrysler. Had it not been for the humiliation of the warehouse, I might have taken some time off, played a little golf, or gone away on a vacation with my family.

But I was so enraged by what had happened that it's a good thing I found myself a new job right away. Otherwise, I might have burned myself out, just stewing in my own anger.

A curious sidelight to the firing was that I could now invite Pete and Connie Estes to our house for dinner. Pete, who lived a couple of doors away, was president of General Motors. In all the years we knew each other, we had never been together socially.

For as long as I was working for Ford, we both had to obey the unwritten rule that if a Ford and a GM guy were seen playing tennis or golf together, it was a sure sign they were price-fixing or otherwise plotting the overthrow of our free enterprise system. GM executives were especially careful, because their company was always under the threat of being broken up for being a monopoly. As a result, those of us in positions of power at the Big Three rarely even said hello to our counterparts.

This change was a special bonus for Mary, because she liked Connie Estes and now they wouldn't have to socialize on the sly. It sounds funny, but that was the code of conduct in Grosse Pointe and Bloomfield Hills in the 1970s.

My newly found friendship with Pete Estes was all too brief. The moment I signed on with Chrysler, we had to become strangers again.

Not long after I was dismissed, a story ran in one of the Detroit papers in which a "family spokesman" from Ford was quoted as saying that I had been fired because I "lacked grace," was too "pushy," and that "the son of an Italian immigrant born in Allentown, Pennsylvania, is a long way from Grosse Pointe."

That was an awful slur, but it wasn't really surprising. To the Fords I would always be an outsider. Hell, even Henry's wife, Christina, was always an outsider. Everyone in the family called her "The Pizza Queen."

Given how Henry felt about Italians, the comments were par for the course. For the past few years he had been convinced I was in the Mafia. I guess *The Godfather* was enough to persuade him that all Italians were linked to organized crime.

He would have *really* trembled if he had known about an unexpected phone call I received after those anonymous words appeared in the paper. A guy with an Italian accent called me at home and said: "If what we're reading in the papers is true, we want to do something about that no-good SOB. He destroyed the honor of your family. I'm gonna give you a number to call. Whenever you tell us, we'll break his arms and legs for you. It will make us feel better. And it will certainly make *you* feel better."

"No, thanks," I said, "that's really not my style. If you guys did it, I wouldn't get any satisfaction out of it. If I'm going to get violent, I'd want to break his legs *myself*."

During the 1975 investigation, Henry had continually implied that I had Mafia connections. To the best of my knowledge, I had never met a Mafia guy in my life. But now Henry had created a self-fulfilling prophecy. Suddenly I had access to just about the only people in the world who could really throw the fear of God into him.

It's not that I believe in turning the other cheek. Henry Ford destroyed a lot of lives. But I got revenge without resorting to violence.

Because of my pension, he still pays me a lot of money to go to work every morning to see if I can knock his block off. It must drive him crazy.

After the initial shock of the firing wore off, I started to think about what had happened between Henry and me. In some respects, it doesn't matter much whether you're the president of the company or the janitor. Being fired is still a terrible blow, and you immediately start to wonder: what did I do wrong?

Certainly I never had any illusions about becoming number one. I made my peace with that very early. If I had wanted to be the CEO of a company, I had plenty of opportunities to go elsewhere. But as long as I remained at Ford, I knew that a member of the family would always be at the head of the company, and I accepted that. If being a CEO had been one of my undying ambitions, I would have left long ago. But until 1975 I was very happy where I was.

I was fired for being a threat to the boss. Henry was infamous for dropping his number two men under unpleasant circumstances. To him, it was always the uprising of the peasants against their lord and master. Still, I had always clung to the idea that I was different, that somehow I was smarter or luckier than the rest. I didn't think it would ever happen to me.

I should have thought a little more about the company's history. I *knew* that Ernie Breech was put out to pasture in Slobbovia, where I would follow him one day. I *knew* that Tex Thornton and McNamara couldn't wait to get out after they had come in as Whiz Kids. I *knew* that Beacham said every day: This guy's a nut and you better get ready for rainy days. Arjay Miller, Bunkie Knudsen, and even Henry's good friend John Bugas ended up the same way. All I had to do was review history and my autobiography was staring me in the face.

Then there was Henry's illness. He was convinced that if anything happened to him, I would somehow manipulate the family and take over the company. "When I got angina in January 1976," he told a reporter from *Fortune*, "I suddenly discovered I wasn't going to live forever. I asked myself, 'Where does the Ford Motor Company end up without me?' I came to the conclusion that Iacocca could not succeed me as chairman." That evil man has never explained that line to me, to his board, and probably not even to himself.

The Fords are one of America's last great family dynasties. In any dynasty, the first instinct is self-protection. Anything, *anything—*

good, bad, or indifferent—that might affect the dynasty becomes a potential problem in the mind of the man who heads it.

Henry has never hidden his intention of having his son, Edsel, succeed him, and he believed that I stood in the way of those plans. As a friend of mine likes to say, "Lee, you weren't touched by the first Edsel fiasco. But you sure as hell got creamed by the second one!"

I saw Henry only once after I was fired. Four and a half years later, Mary and I were invited by Katharine Graham to one of the fiftieth-anniversary parties for *Newsweek*, which were held in several cities across the country. In Detroit, ironically for me, the celebration took place in the ballroom of the Renaissance Center.

This was a few months before Mary's death. She wasn't feeling very well, so I was at her side the whole evening. We were sitting at a table with Bill Bonds, our premier newscaster in Detroit and a great guy. At one point, while Mary and Bill were talking, I looked over and noticed Henry and his wife coming through the receiving line.

"Uh-oh," I said. Mary turned around. "Uh-oh," she said. This was a moment I had often thought about. I'm a pretty serene guy, but I had always wondered what would happen if I ever saw Henry after I'd had a couple of drinks. I wondered if I would flip out. I had fantasized for so long about kicking him where it hurts, I really wasn't sure I could handle it.

Our eyes met. I nodded, and I knew that he had three choices. The first was to nod and say hello, and then get lost in the crowd. That would be holding his ground.

His second alternative was to come over and say a few words. We could shake hands, and he could even put his arm around me. This would be letting bygones be bygones. It would be the decent thing to do, which meant that it would be expecting too much.

His third option was to run like hell. And that's what he did. He grabbed his wife, Kathy, and he *ran*.

And that was the last I ever saw of Henry Ford.

A lot has happened since July 13, 1978. The scars left by Henry Ford, especially on my family, will be lasting, because the wounds were deep. But the events of recent years have had a healing effect. So you move on.

THE CHRYSLER STORY

XIII

COURTED BY CHRYSLER

If I'd had the slightest idea of what lay ahead for me when I joined up with Chrysler, I wouldn't have gone over there for all the money in the world. It's a good thing God doesn't let you look a year or two into the future, or you might be sorely tempted to shoot yourself. But He's a charitable Lord: He only lets you see one day at a time. When times get tough, there's no choice except to take a deep breath, carry on, and do the best you can.

As soon as the firing was announced, I was approached by a number of companies in other industries, including International Paper and Lockheed. Charles Tandy, who owned Radio Shack, asked me to come and work for him. Three or four business schools, including NYU, wanted me as their dean. Some of these offers were very tempting, but I had trouble taking them seriously. I had always worked in the car business, and that's where I wanted to stay. As far as I was concerned, it didn't make much sense to be changing careers at this point in my life.

At fifty-four, I was too young to retire but too old to start working in a completely new business. Besides, cars were in my blood.

I've never gone along with the idea that all business skills are interchangeable, that the president of Ford could be running any other large corporation just as well. To me, it's like a guy who plays the saxophone in a band. One day the conductor says to him: "You're a good musician. Why don't you switch over to the piano?" He says:

"Wait a minute, I've been playing the sax for twenty years! I don't know beans about the piano."

I did have one offer from a car company. Renault, over in France, was interested in hiring me as a worldwide automotive consultant. But I'm not the consultant type. I flourish where the action is. I like hands-on responsibility. If it works, give me the credit. If it doesn't, I'll take the rap.

Besides, the entrepreneur in me was getting restless. During this interim period in the summer of 1978, I got obsessed with an idea I called Global Motors. This plan was a biggie, not exactly the sort of project you could do overnight. My dream was to put together a consortium of car companies in Europe, Japan, and the United States. Together, we'd create a major force that could challenge the dominance of General Motors. I envisaged myself as the new Alfred Sloan, the man who reorganized GM between the wars—and, in my opinion, the greatest genius ever in the auto business.

The partners I had in mind for Global Motors were Volkswagen, Mitsubishi, and Chrysler, although the plan could also work with a different partner, such as Fiat, Renault, Nissan, or Honda. But Chrysler was the logical American choice. GM was too big to join up with anybody else, or so I thought at the time. Ford was out of the question—for obvious reasons.

Chrysler, however, could provide a solid engineering base for Global Motors. Engineering may have been Chrysler's only strength, but it was a vital one.

I asked a friend of mine—Billy Salomon of Salomon Brothers, the New York investment bankers—to do some research about what such a merger might involve. In the process I learned a great deal about several car companies, including Chrysler. To be more precise, I learned a great deal about their balance sheets. But as I would soon find out, there's a hell of a difference between what a company looks like on paper and how it actually operates.

According to Salomon Brothers, the biggest obstacle to Global Motors was the American antitrust laws. What a difference five years makes! At the moment, the White House is embracing a cooperative venture between General Motors and Toyota, the two biggest auto companies in the world. Back in 1978, even a merger between Chrysler and American Motors would have been impossible. It goes to show you how the world changes.

*   *   *

Ever since I was fired from Ford, there were rumors around town that I might be headed for Chrysler. I was available, Chrysler was in trouble, so people put two and two together. The first overture came through Claude Kirk, the ex-governor of Florida and a personal friend of mine, who asked me if I'd have lunch in New York with Dick Dilworth and Louis Warren, two of Chrysler's board members. Dilworth ran the financial empire of the Rockefeller family, and Warren was a Wall Street lawyer who had been associated with Chrysler for thirty-five years. I agreed to the meeting. For some reason, I still remember what we ate for lunch: raw clams on the half shell. They were so good I ate two dozen of them.

This was a getting-to-know-you meeting rather than anything official, and our conversation remained pretty general. Dilworth and Warren made it clear that they were talking to me as private individuals, not official representatives of the company. They did speak with deep concern about the auto business—and especially about Chrysler. But for the most part, it was only an exploratory discussion, more social than business.

Meanwhile, I had remained in touch with George Bennett. I soon learned that he had been my one real friend on the Ford board. Besides serving there, George was also on the board of Hewlett-Packard. And Bill Hewlett, the cofounder of that company and a likeable genius, was a member of the Chrysler board. Hewlett knew that Bennett and I were friends, and when they talked, George had the honesty to tell him how valuable I had been at Ford.

A little later I got a call from John Riccardo, chairman of the board of Chrysler. He and Dick Dilworth wanted to meet me down at the Hotel Pontchartrain, just a few blocks from Henry's Renaissance Center. The purpose of the meeting was to talk in general terms about the possibility of my coming to Chrysler.

We kept the meeting as quiet as possible. I drove my own car and entered the hotel through a side door. Even Gene Cafiero, the president of Chrysler, was kept in the dark. Riccardo and Cafiero had been feuding so openly that the whole town knew about it.

At the meeting, both Dilworth and Riccardo were still pretty vague. "We're thinking of making a change," Riccardo said. "Things aren't going right."

That was about as specific as they wanted to get. Both of them were trying to offer me a job without actually coming out and saying it. That sounded like baloney to me, so I put it to them directly: "What are we really here to talk about?"

"About hiring you," Riccardo said. "Would you be interested in coming back into the auto business?"

I told them that before we could talk specifics, I had a number of questions about Chrysler's current situation. I wanted to know exactly what I'd be getting into.

"I don't want to go into this blind," I said. "I need to know how bad things are. I need to know where the company stands. How much cash you have. What your operating plan is for next year. What your future products look like. And especially whether you guys really think you can make it."

Our next two meetings were held at the Northfield Hilton in suburban Detroit. Riccardo painted a bleak picture, but one that I thought could be turned around in a year. I really don't think that John or anyone else at Chrysler was trying to pull the wool over my eyes. One of Chrysler's biggest problems, as I soon learned, was that even its top management didn't have a very good idea of what was going on. They knew Chrysler was bleeding. What they didn't realize—and what I would soon find out—was that it was hemorrhaging.

That fall it sounded like a good, tough challenge. I went home from these meetings and talked things over with Mary. She said: "You won't be happy doing anything except cars. And you're too young to sit around the house. Let's give that bastard Henry a shot he'll always remember." She was feisty that way. I also talked it over with my kids. Their attitude was: "If it makes you happy, go for it!"

The only remaining question was whether Chrysler could afford me—and I don't just mean financially. What I wanted now was to be my own man. At this point in my life, I had no interest in working for somebody else. I had been number two for too long. If I took the Chrysler job, I had to be *número uno* within a year or so—or no dice!

That was my going-in price to even discuss coming to Chrysler. It wasn't just my experience with Henry, although that was part of it. It was also that I needed a completely free hand to be able to turn the company around. I already knew that my way of doing things was totally different from theirs. Unless I had full authority to put my management style and my policies into effect, going over to Chrysler would be a major exercise in frustration.

I had the impression that Riccardo wanted me to be president and chief operating officer, with himself as chairman and chief executive officer. But when I told him what I wanted, I found out I was wrong. "Listen," he said. "I'm not going to stay in this job much longer. There's only room for one boss here. If you come with us, you'll be it. Otherwise, we wouldn't have gone to all the trouble of setting up these meetings."

It was sad in a way, because he hadn't even been pushed by Chrysler's board of directors to approach me. He did it on his own. He obviously realized that the company was in deep trouble and that he wasn't going to be able to nurse it back to health. He would get rid of Cafiero to bring me in, knowing full well that if I joined, his own days as chairman were numbered. We agreed that I would come in as president but would become chairman and CEO on January 1, 1980. As it turned out, Riccardo resigned a few months early, and I became the boss in September of 1979.

John Riccardo and his wife, Thelma, were two of the finest people I've ever met. Unfortunately, the crisis at Chrysler was so severe that I never really got to know them. But one thing was perfectly clear: John was sacrificing himself to save the company. He was over his head and he knew it. Although it meant the end of his own career, he bent over backward to make sure that the transition would go as smoothly as possible. He blew himself out of the water to bring Chrysler back to life. And that is the test of a real hero.

The next step in the hiring process was a meeting with Chrysler's compensation committee in the Chrysler suite at the Waldorf Towers in New York. This time, by way of discretion, I took the elevator up to the thirty-fourth floor, where Ford had its suite, and then walked up two flights to the Chrysler suite. Riccardo followed in a separate elevator.

We had to be that careful. If Iacocca, who was still in the news because he was just fired from Ford, was seen talking to Riccardo and the Chrysler board, the press would jump the gun and I'd find myself hired before we had come to any decision. But the story never did leak out. There was some light speculation in *New York* magazine a week before the announcement, but generally the security was first-rate.

The announcement that I would be joining Chrysler in November must have been a real jolt to Henry Ford. Normally in these situations, the man who's fired takes his pension and goes off quietly to Florida, never to be heard from again. But I stayed within the walls of the city, and that really got to him. When word got out that I was going to Chrysler, I heard from good sources that Henry was getting sloshed every night. He was always a big drinker, but I'm told that he really got bad during this period. Rumor had it that he was putting away two bottles of Château Lafite-Rothschild a night. At $120 a bottle, that's an expensive nightcap! But based on past experience, I imagine the Ford stockholders were still picking up the tab.

When Henry fired me, my settlement with Ford included severance pay of $1.5 million. But there was one important catch—Ford's very restrictive contract included a competitive clause which stipulated that if I worked for another car company I would forfeit the money.

"Don't worry about that," Riccardo told me. "We'll make you whole." When my appointment to Chrysler was made public, the press made a big fuss about how I had been given a bonus of $1.5 million just for signing up with Chrysler. In reality, I didn't get a nickel for signing. I had earned that money over many years at Ford, through deferred compensation as well as retirement and pension benefits. Chrysler was simply matching it. In effect, they were buying out my contract.

At Ford, my official salary had been $360,000, although in good years my bonuses raised that total to as much as $1 million. I knew that Chrysler couldn't afford to pay me more than that, so I told the committee that I'd accept the same salary I was earning when I was fired.

Unfortunately, Riccardo's own salary at the time was only $340,000. This made things a little awkward, because I was starting out as the president, and he was still the chairman. It wouldn't look right if I was earning more than he was. The board solved the problem by granting Riccardo an immediate raise of $20,000, which made us even.

I've never had any qualms about getting a high salary. I'm not a big spender, but I appreciate the achievement a high salary represents. Why does a guy want to be president? Does he enjoy it? Maybe, but it can make him old and tired. So why does he work so hard? So he can say: "Hey, I made it to the top. I accomplished something."

My father always said: "Be careful about money. When you have five thousand, you'll want ten. And when you have ten, you'll want twenty." He was right. No matter what you have, it's never enough.

Still, I'm an entrepreneur at heart. At Ford, I used to watch with some envy as the car dealers made the really big bucks. It's not that I wasn't earning a good living. For a couple of years in the 1970s, Henry Ford and I were listed as the two highest-paid businessmen in America. My mother and father thought that was terrific, a real badge of honor.

Yet I know guys in real estate in New York who can make that much money in a single day. But unlike the big dealmakers, my income is public knowledge. I get more mail and more requests for money than I can handle. Which brings me to another of my father's favorite sayings. "You think *making* money is hard? Wait until you try giving it away!" It's true. Everybody writes me and wants me to share the wealth. Every college, every hospital, every good cause on the face of the earth. Seems it's a full-time job to do it right.

When I worked at Ford, I barely knew that Chrysler existed. It was GM that we followed and nobody else. We never thought much about Chrysler. Their products didn't even show up on the monthly sales sheets that measured how well our cars were doing against the competition.

I can think of only two occasions at Ford when we were forced to pay attention to Chrysler. The first was over the logo. In the early 1960s, Lynn Townsend, Chrysler's chairman, made an extended trip to visit Chrysler dealers across the country. When he came back, he told one of his colleagues that he had been amazed by the number of Howard Johnson outlets in the United States. He was even more amazed when his colleague replied that there were actually more Chrysler dealerships in America than there were Howard Johnsons.

Townsend started to think about the bright orange roofs that identify Hojos. He decided that to increase their visibility Chrysler dealerships ought to have a symbol, too. The company commissioned a New York firm to create a logo for Chrysler. Before long, the white pentastar on a blue background was popping up all over.

The Chrysler logo was so successful that within a year we at Ford were forced to respond. We already had our famous blue oval. Now we started putting it up on the dealers' signs. But we blew it. Chrysler used the pentastar with the dealer's name under it. GM put the dealer's name right in the sign. Ford Division dealers had the oval in Ford script and then another "Ford" next to it in block letters, but there was no place for the dealer's name in that sign. It prompted many a dealer to complain that if Henry Ford could use his name twice, the dealer was at least entitled to use his name once.

The other time we followed Chrysler was on their extended warranty in 1962. Until then, Ford had the best warranty in the business—twelve months or twelve thousand miles. At the time we didn't pay much attention to Chrysler's decision to take the warranty all the way up to five years or fifty thousand miles. But within about three years, Chrysler's market share had gone up so much that we at Ford had to come up with a similar program.

The so-called warranty wars among the Big Three automakers lasted for about five years. Eventually we all discontinued the plans because they were too expensive. In those days, our cars weren't really good enough for us to back them for half a decade.

Then there was Chrysler's great reputation for engineering. The engineers at Chrysler have always been a cut above their counterparts at Ford and GM. I assumed it was because of the Chrysler Engineering Institute, and I was always after Henry to set one up, although he never did. Over the years we stole a few of their best people. In 1962, I had raided Chrysler and brought over a dozen of their top engineers. Several of them rose to the highest ranks at Ford.

But ever since Ford had surpassed Chrysler in the early 1950s, all our attention was directed toward General Motors. I was and still am a devoted GM-watcher. They're like a country unto themselves, and I envy their tremendous brute power.

Still, I was familiar with the history of the auto industry, and I knew a little about the origins of the Chrysler Corporation and the man who founded it. When the car business started, there was just one key figure: Henry Ford. With all his quirks and his idiosyncrasies— and with all his bigotry—the original Henry Ford was an inventive genius. He started by tinkering with cars and eventually he learned how to mass-produce them.

Henry Ford often gets credit for the assembly line, but actually that was the creation of others. Where the old man was truly innovative was in coming up with the $5.00 day in 1914. Five bucks was more than double what workers had been making, and the publicity from this announcement was overwhelming.

What the public hasn't always realized was that Ford didn't make his offer to the workers out of any great generosity or compassion. It wasn't their standard of living he cared about. Henry Ford never hid his real reason for the $5.00 day: he wanted his workers to earn enough so that they could eventually buy their own cars. In other words, Henry Ford was creating a middle class. He realized that the industry—and therefore the Ford Motor Company—could only be truly successful if its cars appealed to the workingman as well as the wealthy.

The next major figure in the industry was Walter P. Chrysler. He was an innovator in engines, transmissions, and mechanical components, and his company has been strong in those areas ever since. Walter P. left General Motors in 1920, when the chairman, William Durant, wouldn't give him the freedom to run the Buick Division the way he wanted. This guy was my kind of maverick!

I have a special interest in the next part of the story. Three years later, Walter Chrysler comes out of retirement to reorganize the Maxwell and Chalmers Motor Car Companies, which are dying. So what does he do? He brings out new models and promotes them aggressively. *He even appears in some of the advertising!* By 1925, he has reorganized a joke of a company into the Chrysler Corporation.

But he didn't stop there. In 1928, he bought out Dodge and Plymouth. His own company was now one of the big boys, and it has remained there ever since. When Walter Chrysler died in 1940, the company had surpassed Ford and was second only to General Motors, with 25 percent of the domestic market. Oh, how I'd love to repeat his achievement! To get 25 percent of the market and knock off Ford? I'd give my eyeteeth.

Although they were having a hell of a tough time by the late 1970s, Chrysler did have that long tradition of design and engineering innovation you could build on. Frederick Zeder, Chrysler's chief engineer during the 1930s, was the first man to figure out how to get the vibrations out of cars. His solution? He mounted their engines on a rubber base. Zeder also invented the high-compression engine, the oil filter, and the air filter.

I learned that Chrysler engineers in Michigan had designed the world's most sophisticated tank. Their engineers in Alabama designed the world's first electronic ignition for cars. Chrysler people designed the first lock-up torque converter for greater fuel efficiency, the first modern electronic voltage regulator, the first hydraulic brakes, and the first under-the-hood computer. I already knew that Chrysler had the best engines and transmissions in the business.

So there was no question that Chrysler had a respectable past. I was also convinced it had a future. The company already had a solid dealer organization, as well as engineers second to none. The only trouble was that they weren't given the resources to build good products.

I was equally confident of my own abilities. I knew the car business, and I knew I was good at it. In my heart I honestly believed that the place would be humming within a couple of years.

But the opposite happened. Everything collapsed. We had the Iranian crisis, and then we had the energy crisis. In 1978, nobody could have imagined that by the next spring there would be havoc in Iran and the price of gas would suddenly double. Then, to top it off, came the biggest recession in fifty years.

All this took place only a few months after I had signed on at Chrysler. It made me wonder whether my destiny had caught up with me. Maybe when God—the real God, not Henry—had me fired from Ford, He was trying to tell me something. Maybe I had been fired at the perfect time, right before everything fell apart, and I was just too stupid to accept my good fortune.

For a variety of reasons, Chrysler turned out to be a hell of a lot more than I bargained for. But once I was in, once I had decided what it was I wanted to do, I never thought seriously of leaving.

Of course, that's not always the best policy. People sometimes die with that attitude. They get swamped and overtaken by events, and they're still holding on as the waters rise up above them. When I signed on for my new job, I couldn't imagine that anything in the automobile business could be *that* bad. I was wrong. In retrospect, I have to admit there were several times at Chrysler when I came close to drowning.

XIV

ABOARD A
SINKING SHIP

On November 2, 1978, the *Detroit Free Press* carried two headlines: CHRYSLER LOSSES ARE WORST EVER, and LEE IACOCCA JOINS CHRYSLER. Great timing! The day I came aboard, the company had announced a third-quarter loss of almost $160 million, the worst deficit in its history. "Oh, well," I thought, "from here things can only get better." Despite the huge losses, Chrysler's stock closed up three eighths that day, which I took as a vote of confidence in my new administration. Ha, ha!

On my first day on the job, I had a little trouble getting to the office. To be honest, I wasn't exactly sure where it *was*. I knew that Chrysler headquarters were in Highland Park, just off the Davison Expressway. But beyond that I had to ask for directions. I didn't even know what ramp to get off.

I had been to Chrysler only once, when I was president of Ford. But in those days I had a driver, and I didn't pay much attention to the route we followed. Every three years, the heads of the Big Three used to get together for what we called summit meetings, to prepare a joint strategy for labor negotiations. Henry Ford and I had gone to one of those meetings over in Highland Park. We were joined there by Lynn Townsend and John Riccardo of Chrysler as well as by the GM people and all the lawyers.

By the way, the union would get uptight about these meetings. They were sure that we were conspiring against them. Little did they know that these talks were always an exercise in total futility. As the marginal producer, Chrysler could never afford the possibility of a strike, so all our tough talk about dealing with the union came to naught.

When I got there that morning, Riccardo showed me around the place and introduced me to some of the officers. There was a meeting with a few of the top people, and, as usual, I lit up a cigar. Riccardo turned to his group and said: "You guys know I've always had a fetish about no cigar smoking in meetings. As of this morning, we've just rescinded that rule." I took it as a good omen. From everything I had heard about Chrysler, rescinding some of the house rules sounded like a super idea.

Before the day was over, I noticed a couple of seemingly insignificant details that gave me pause. The first was that the office of the president, where Cafiero worked, was being used as a thoroughfare to get from one office to another. I watched in amazement as executives with coffee cups in their hands kept opening the door and walking right through the president's office. Right away I knew the place was in a state of anarchy. Chrysler needed a dose of order and discipline—and quick.

Then there was the fact that Riccardo's secretary seemed to be spending a lot of time taking personal calls on her own private phone! When the secretaries are goofing off, you know the place has dry rot. During the first couple of weeks in a new job, you look for telltale signs. You want to know what kind of fraternity you've joined. These are the signs I remember, and what they told me about Chrysler made me apprehensive about what I was getting myself into.

It turned out that my worries were justified. I soon stumbled upon my first major revelation: Chrysler didn't really function like a company at all. Chrysler in 1978 was like Italy in the 1860s—the company consisted of a cluster of little duchies, each one run by a prima donna. It was a bunch of mini-empires, with nobody giving a damn about what anyone else was doing.

What I found at Chrysler were thirty-five vice-presidents, each with his own turf. There was no real committee setup, no cement in the organizational chart, no system of meetings to get people talking to each other. I couldn't believe, for example, that the guy running the engineering department wasn't in constant touch with his counterpart in manufacturing. But that's how it was. Everybody worked independently. I took one look at that system and I almost threw up. That's when I knew I was in really deep trouble.

Apparently these guys didn't believe in Newton's third law of motion—that for every action there's an equal and opposite reaction. Instead, they were all working in a vacuum. It was so bad that even this description doesn't begin to do it justice.

I'd call in a guy from engineering, and he'd stand there dumbfounded when I'd explain to him that we had a design problem or some other hitch in the engineering-manufacturing relationship. He might have the ability to invent a brilliant piece of engineering that would save us a lot of money. He might come up with a terrific new design. There was only one problem: he didn't know that the manufacturing people couldn't build it. Why? Because he had never talked to them about it.

Nobody at Chrysler seemed to understand that interaction among the different functions in a company is absolutely critical. People in engineering and manufacturing almost have to be sleeping together. These guys weren't even flirting!

Another example: sales and manufacturing were under the same vice-president. This was inconceivable to me because these were huge and primarily separate functions. To make matters worse, there was virtually no contact between the two areas. The manufacturing guys would build cars without ever checking with the sales guys. They just built them, stuck them in a yard, and then hoped that somebody would take them out of there. We ended up with a huge inventory and a financial nightmare.

The contrast between Chrysler's structure and Ford's was simply amazing. Nobody at Chrysler seemed to realize that you just can't run a big corporation without calling some pregame sessions to do blackboard work. Every member of the team has to understand what his job is and exactly how it fits in with every other job.

But instead of tying the loose ends together and looking at the larger picture, Riccardo and Bill McGagh, the treasurer, had to spend their time visiting all the banks that had lent Chrysler money. They were continually running from one bank to the next just to keep the outstanding loans intact. That meant they were dealing with the day-to-day crises, always focusing on next month instead of next year.

A couple of months after I arrived, something hit me like a ton of bricks. We were running out of cash! Before I came to Chrysler, I had been vaguely aware of a number of problems there, ranging from poor management techniques to skimping on research and development. But the one area where I had some degree of confidence was financial controls. After all, everybody in Detroit knew that Chrysler was run by financial men. We all assumed, therefore, that financial controls were given top priority.

But I soon discovered to my horror that Lynn Townsend (who had retired a couple of years earlier) and John Riccardo were basically a couple of accountants from the Detroit auditing firm of Touche Ross. What's more, they hadn't brought in any serious financial analysts. Their attitude seemed to be: "We'll handle that stuff ourselves." But there was no way they could do that in a company the size of Chrysler.

Gradually I was finding that Chrysler had no overall system of financial controls. To make matters worse, nobody in the whole place seemed to fully understand what was going on when it came to financial planning and projecting. Even the most rudimentary questions were impossible for them to answer. But never mind the answers: these guys didn't even know the questions!

At Ford, as soon as I became president I had asked for a list of all the plants, marked with the rate of return on investment for each one. But talking this way at Chrysler, I might as well have been speaking a foreign language. I couldn't find out *anything*.

This was probably the greatest jolt I've ever had in my business career. When I thought about it, I was bereft. (That's a euphemism for feeling lower than whale shit!) I already knew about the lousy cars. I was well aware of the bad morale and the deteriorating factories. But I simply had no idea that I wouldn't even be able to get hold of the right numbers so that we could begin to attack some of Chrysler's basic problems.

Lynn Townsend always enjoyed a good reputation as a financial man, but I think his decisions, like those of many businessmen, had more to do with the next quarter's profits than with the long-range good of the company. For years, Chrysler had been run by men who didn't really like the car business. And now the chickens were coming home to roost.

As a result, the company had begun to play follow the leader. As the smallest of the Big Three, Chrysler could have and should have been the industry front-runner when it came to developing new cars. But engineering, which had always been Chrysler's ace in the hole, became a low priority under Lynn Townsend. When profits started to fall, it was engineering and product development that paid the price.

Instead of concentrating on good cars, Lynn Townsend and his group started to expand overseas. In their zeal to become an international company, they bought European firms that were dead on their feet—companies that were dogs, such as Simca in France and Rootes in England. They were babes in the woods when it came to international operations. I began to think there were Chrysler people who didn't even know that the British drove on the left-hand side of the street!

Lynn Townsend was always popular with the stockholders, and as one of them, he himself became rich. But I don't think he ever really understood the fundamental business of the company. At one point during his administration, Chrysler was actually running marginal or losing operations on every continent except Antarctica.

Townsend did do some good things at Chrysler, such as establishing Chrysler Financial, a subsidiary that was designed to provide credit for both the dealers and the retail customers. Today Chrysler Financial is a model of its kind. So Townsend certainly doesn't deserve all the blame for Chrysler's weak position. I often wondered: where was the board when all of this was going on?

When I went to my first board meeting, I began to understand the problem. Chrysler's board of directors had even less information than their counterparts at Ford—and that's saying a mouthful. There were no slides and no financial reviews. Riccardo was giving a little pitch from the back of an envelope. This was hardly the way to be running the tenth largest corporation in the country.

When I became chairman, I moved in on the board members very gradually. I wasn't crazy enough to point my finger at a group that had just hired me and tell them: "It's your fault." But once or twice I did ask the board, as politely as I could: "How did management ever get their plans past such a distinguished group of businessmen? Didn't you guys get any information?"

Within the ranks, Chrysler's problems were not confined to top management. All through the company, people were scared and despondent. Nobody was doing anything right. I had never seen anything like it. The vice-presidents were all square pegs in round holes. Townsend and his people had taken guys who had performed well enough in one area and had moved them around at will. Their attitude was that a guy with talent could climb any mountain. After a few years of being shuffled around, everybody at Chrysler was doing something he wasn't trained for. And believe me, it showed.

The guy who ran parts and service in South America had been brought in as controller and he hated it. When I had to let him go, he was actually relieved. The guy who used to run the European operations had been shipped over here and been made vice-president of purchasing, although he'd never been in purchasing in his life. It was pathetic.

I felt terrible, because in their own environment these guys might have been great. They tried to explain their predicament by saying: "Hey, I never asked for this job. You're asking questions of a controller, and I don't know the answers. What I know about is parts and service. I'm really a catcher, but these guys have me playing shortstop. Hell, I don't know how to play shortstop. I could learn, but I need more time."

They all knew that I was coming in to clean house, and each one was afraid he was going to be the target. They had no certainty in their lives. They were living in fear—and for good reason. Over a three-year period I had to fire thirty-three out of the thirty-five vice-presidents. That's one a month!

In a few cases, I tried to resurrect some of the executives. But it didn't work—they just couldn't cut it. Charlie Beacham used to say that once a guy is over twenty-one, you'll never really change his style or his habits. You may think you can, but his self-image is locked in. Nobody is ever humble enough to learn after he's grown up.

Unfortunately, Beacham was right—as usual. When Paul Bergmoser came in, I remember saying to him: "Try to save some of these guys." He worked with them for six months. "It's impossible," he then told me. "These people have learned the Chrysler way of running their own show. They will never adjust. It's too late."

Problems always lead to other problems. When you have a guy who isn't very sure of himself on the job, the very last thing he wants is a guy backing him up who *is* sure of himself. He figures: "If the next guy is too good, he'll show me up—and eventually replace me." As a result, one incompetent manager brings along another. And all of them hide behind the overall weakness in the system.

Don't get me wrong. I don't mean that if somebody went to school to study accounting, he has to be dubbed an accountant for the rest of his career, no matter what his other skills may be. My point is simply that each guy has to have a management development plan early in his career. He has to be given enough time on a job to prove that he really learned that particular area.

You don't want to overdo specialization, because if you carry it to extremes, you'll never have general managers. Still, not everybody should be trained for general management.

*   *   *

All of Chrysler's problems really boiled down to the same thing: nobody knew who was on first. There was no team, only a collection of independent players, many of whom hadn't yet mastered their positions.

Now, it's one thing to say all that and to understand in theoretical terms what it means. Believe me, it's quite another matter to see it unfold in front of you in living color. It's pretty scary to witness one of the world's largest corporations, playing for billions of dollars, going down the tubes without anybody being able to stop it. This was a tremendous shock to me. And each day brought more bad news.

The only parallel I could think of was the situation that Henry Ford II had faced thirty-two years earlier. When young Henry came out of the Navy to join his grandfather's company, it was in ruins. In one department, so the story goes, expenses were estimated by weighing the invoices.

The Ford Motor Company had become a disaster because the old man ran it so poorly. He knew nothing about sound business practices. In those days, companies were routinely run by swashbuckling entrepreneurs rather than planners and managers.

But Chrysler was even worse. Chrysler couldn't blame its condition on its founder, who came from another era. The Chrysler fiasco had occurred after thirty years of postwar, scientific management. That in 1978 a huge company could still be run like a small grocery store was incomprehensible.

These problems didn't develop overnight. In Detroit auto circles, Chrysler's reputation had been sinking for years. The place had become known as a last resort: if somebody couldn't hack it elsewhere, he could always go to Chrysler. Chrysler executives had a better reputation for their golfing abilities than for any expertise with cars.

Not surprisingly, morale in Highland Park was very low. And if morale is low, the place becomes a sieve. All kinds of secrets start flowing out. When guys are upset and worried about going bankrupt and losing their jobs, then you've tripled your chances for leaks.

Industrial spying in the auto business is something that the press enjoys talking about—and occasionally indulging in. Spying had sometimes been a problem at Ford. One day in the early 1970s, a friend of mine from Chrysler showed me a packet of confidential materials from Ford that one of his people had purchased from one of ours. I showed the papers to Henry, who got very upset. He tried to put in a system to see how deep this spying and industrial espionage really went and to determine what, if anything, we could do about it.

But it's almost impossible to counter that stuff. We started installing shredding machines and giving out numbered copies of certain
reports: 1 was Henry, 2 was Iacocca, and so on. Even then, there
would be leaks. You could call in the twelve guys who had access to
the report and say: "Somebody in this room is lying," but it wouldn't
get you anywhere. I tried it a couple of times, but I never plugged
those holes.

I've known a few cases where a company has gone to great
lengths to get early photographs, grainy as they are, of somebody else's
future cars. But generally, such pictures aren't very useful to the
competition. For example, I've always assumed that General Motors
had pictures of the Mustang two years before the car went on sale.
But what did they really know? They wouldn't want to copy it until it
hit the market, when they could see for themselves how well it was
doing.

On the other hand, there are times when you might have some
engineering work going on that's pretty exclusive. Or maybe you've
had a breakthrough to get better fuel economy. Before you know it,
the other guy's already got your results in his hands. These are the
ones that really hurt.

At Chrysler, bad morale and security leaks were showing up on
the balance sheets. They were the reasons why the company was
doing so poorly while the rest of the auto industry was ending its best
year in history. GM and Ford were reporting record sales and profits
in 1978. GM alone sold close to 5.4 million cars, while Ford sold 2.6
million. Chrysler, as usual, was a distant third, with less than 1.2
million. More important, our share of the American car market had
dropped from 12.2 percent to 11.1 percent within a single year—a
tremendous decline. Our share of the truck market had dropped just
as badly, from 12.9 percent to 11.8 percent.

Even worse, Chrysler had lost 7 percent in owner loyalty during
the past two years. When I arrived on the scene, our owner loyalty
rate was down to 36 percent. By comparison, Ford was at 53 percent,
and that was a huge drop for them. GM was always pretty steady at
around 70 percent.

We were already having trouble getting people to consider our
products. Now the research was telling us that almost two thirds of the
people we did attract were unhappy with us. They didn't expect to
return and buy another Chrysler product.

Another point troubling me about our sales figures was that
Chrysler had long been known as an older guy's car. When I came

aboard, the median age for Dodge and Plymouth buyers was higher than that of Buick, Oldsmobile, Pontiac, or even Mercury customers. Our surveys continued to show that Chrysler owners were more likely to be blue-collar, older, less educated, and more concentrated in the northeastern and the midwestern industrial states than those who bought competing brands.

The demographics made clear what I already knew: Chrysler products were perceived as staid and a little boring. We needed some innovative cars in a hurry. If you stand still in this business, you get run over very quickly.

Fortunately, I wouldn't be starting from scratch. Chrysler had a long tradition of innovation, a tradition I was eager to continue. Not too many years earlier, a lot of young people had wanted a Chrysler because it was a hot item. Chrysler had Chargers and Dusters that ran down Main Street quicker than anybody's. Racing cars like high-winged Dodge Daytonas, the Chrysler 300 series, the Satellites and Barracudas were the ones that were clustered around drive-ins and hamburger stands from Maine to California.

Chrysler was also responsible for the ultimate street racer of them all, the Road Runner, with its 426-cubic-inch "Hemi" engine. This was a classic of the late 1960s—loud, fast, and almost as powerful as a locomotive. Every evening these muscle cars would race up and down Detroit's Woodward Avenue, where they were occasionally joined by professional engineers and car executives on their way back to the suburbs.

Yet now Chrysler was weak in the sunbelt, with its younger and more affluent drivers. We were especially weak in California—and that's the place that really counts. Although the car industry was born in Michigan, it came of age in California. California gave us our first vast system of freeways. It was the entry point for the youth market—with muscle cars and four on the floor and exotic wheel covers and live-in vans and crazy cars and various other permutations of the basic automobile that began in a factory in Michigan.

California has also contributed some things that we in Michigan aren't too happy about. One is the import boom. Californians buy more imported cars than the residents of any other state. Second, they've given us some supercharged emission standards that have almost transformed California itself into a foreign country.

It's been said many times before, but it's worth saying again: California is really the mirror into the future. Sometimes we don't like everything we see when we gaze into that mirror, but we'd be crazy if we didn't take a good, hard look.

We needed to succeed in California, but before we could do that, we had to change the product.

It wasn't only the style of Chrysler products that had a bad reputation. The company had also run into big problems with quality. Among the worst examples were the Aspen and Volaré, the successors to the highly acclaimed Dart and Valiant. The Dart and the Valiant ran forever, and they never should have been dropped. Instead they had been replaced by cars that often started to come apart after only a year or two.

Aspen and Volaré were introduced in 1975, but they should have been delayed a full six months. The company was hungry for cash, and this time Chrysler didn't honor the normal cycle of designing, testing, and building an automobile. The customers who bought Aspens and Volarés in 1975 were actually acting as Chrysler's development engineers. When these cars first came out, they were still in the development phase.

Looking back over the past twenty years or so, I can't think of any cars that caused more disappointment among customers than the Aspen and the Volaré. The Edsel was a different case: people just didn't want it. But with these cars, customers bought them in large numbers and got fooled. They went for the styling, especially the wagon, which Ford and GM didn't have in 1976.

But the Aspen and the Volaré simply weren't well made. The engines would stall when you stepped on the gas. The brakes would fail. The hoods would fly open. Customers complained, and more than three and a half million cars were brought back to the dealers for free repairs—free to the customer, that is. Chrysler had to foot the bill.

But then even cars that were mechanically sound started rusting. The Volaré's rusted fender program cost us $109 million—in 1980, when we could ill afford it. The fenders had rusted through because somebody wasn't paying enough attention to the process of rustproofing them. We weren't asked to recall them, but we had an obligation to our customers to fix them. Even though we stood behind them, the resale value of these cars plummeted, which hurt Chrysler's image badly.

Ford had gone through a similar problem. In 1957, we had come up with a beautiful car, the Fairlane 500, a styling gem that sold like hotcakes. But like the Volaré, it was poorly made. Francis Emerson, my fleet manager in Philadelphia, had one of the first four-doors to

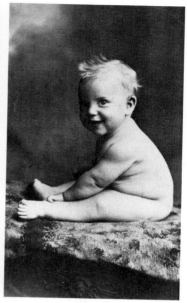

Barely nine months old.

Just married: my parents, Nicola and Antoinette
Iacocca, in 1923.

In pre-Depression finery, 1926.

With my sister, Delma, in 1927.

Learning to drive, 1929.

With my father, 1934.

High jinks at Lehigh, 1942 *(second from left)*.

Big man on campus: Princeton, 1945.

My first paycheck from Ford—after taxes!

Mary, 1948.

With Henny Youngman (*center*) and
Murray Kester (*right*), 1953.

Egg on my face for selling safety in '56.

New Ford president Robert McNamara (*left*) with Henry Ford II in 1960.

With Charlie Beacham in Phoenix, 1961.

Father of the Mustang.

While New York City slept, a 1966 Mustang was flying high on top of the
Empire State Building.

Presenting the first 1974 Mustang
to Mr. Honda at his home
in Tokyo.

President of Ford,
1974.

1975:
the beginning of the end.

A collector's item: the car made it, but I didn't. 1979.

The day after.

Chrysler Names Lee Iacocca as New President

DETROIT (AP) — Chrysler Corp. today reported the biggest loss for any quarter in its history.

How's that for timing?

The savior: Chrysler's first K–Car, 1980.

Would you buy a used car from this man? My first commercial, 1981.

With Detroit's Mayor Coleman Young and comedian Bill Cosby.

Life's little rewards.

I'll drink to that!
The payback:
August 15, 1983.

With Jerry Greenwald (*center*) and Hal Sperlich (*right*).

With the President in St. Louis, 1983.

And if drafted,
I shall not run.

The success car of the 80s.

With Kathi, 1964.

The family, 1973.

December 10, 1970: my parents and Mary celebrating my election to the presidency of Ford.

In costume for my 50th birthday.

Kathi (*right*) and Lia, 1981.

Our surprise 25th wedding anniversary party.

The Three Musketeers: with my friends Bill Fugazy (*left*)
and Vic Damone.

show to the managers of the major fleet accounts. The car was so poorly constructed that the rear doors would pop open when he hit a hard bump in the road. He licked the problem by tying the doors together from the inside with a clothesline. "I'm having a hell of a wild time demonstrating this car," he used to tell me. "They like the styling, but I can't let them get in the back seat!"

In those days, the typical Ford customer used to trade in his car every three years. Unfortunately, in 1960 we came up with another clinker, and I thought: "Now we've really got problems. A guy will tolerate one lemon. But what about the '57 customer who bought a new car because he liked the style and then found out the car was lousy? If he stuck with us and bought a '60 Ford, he got burned twice in a row. That guy will never come back. He probably went over to GM or the imports."

The '75 Volaré was in that same category. Of course, GM has had its fiascos, too, like the Corvair. Here I find myself in rare agreement with Ralph Nader: the Corvair really was unsafe. The Vega, with its pancake aluminum engine, was another disaster. The Vega and the Corvair were both terrible cars, but GM is so big and powerful that it can withstand a disaster or two without suffering any major damage. Little Chrysler couldn't afford any.

I can't talk about bad cars without a few words on the Ford Pinto. We brought out the Pinto in 1971. We needed a subcompact, and this was the best one you could buy for under $2,000. A lot of people must have agreed—we sold over four hundred thousand Pintos in the first year alone. This made the car a great success and put it in the category of the Falcon and the Mustang.

Unhappily, the Pinto was involved in a number of accidents where the car burst into flames after a rear-end collision. There were lawsuits—hundreds of them. In 1978, in a major trial in Indiana, the Ford Motor Company was charged with reckless homicide. Ford was acquitted, but the damage to the company was incalculable.

There were two problems with the Pinto. First, the fuel tank was located behind the axle, so if the car got hit hard enough from behind, there was the possibility of a fire.

The Pinto was not the only car with this problem. In those days, *all* small cars had the fuel tank behind the axle. And all small cars were occasionally involved in fires.

But the Pinto also had a filler neck on the fuel tank that sometimes, in a collision, was ripped out on impact. When that happened, raw gas spilled out and frequently ignited.

We resisted making any changes, and that hurt us badly. Even Joan Claybrook, the tough director of the National Highway Traffic Safety Administration and a Nader protégé, said to me one day: "It's a shame you can't do something about the Pinto. It's really no worse than any other small car. You don't have an engineering problem as much as you have a legal and public-relations problem."

Whose fault was it? One obvious answer is that it was the fault of Ford's management—including me. There are plenty of people who would say that the legal and PR pressures involved in such a situation excuse management's stonewalling in the hope the problem will go away. It seems to me, though, that it is fair to hold management to a high standard, and to insist that they do what duty and common sense require, no matter what the pressures.

But there's absolutely no truth to the charge that we tried to save a few bucks and knowingly made a dangerous car. The auto industry has often been arrogant, but it's not that callous. The guys who built the Pinto had kids in college who were driving that car. Believe me, nobody sits down and thinks: "I'm deliberately going to make this car unsafe."

In the end, we voluntarily recalled almost a million and a half Pintos. This was in June 1978, the month before I was fired.

Meanwhile, at Chrysler, my initiation included one more major problem. In my first week on the job, I attended an informal meeting where ten thousand cars were taken out of the production schedule. A week later there was a more formal meeting. This time, *fifty thousand* cars were promptly withdrawn from the first-quarter schedule for 1979.

I was puzzled and distressed. What kind of profit mentality was this—taking cars willy-nilly out of production? I was horrified to discover that we didn't have dealer orders to build these cars, and there was no room to add any more cars to the already bulging factory inventory. This inventory was known as Chrysler's sales bank, which was nothing more than an excuse to keep the plants running when we didn't have dealer orders for the cars.

At regular intervals the Manufacturing Division would tell the Sales Division how many and what types of vehicles they were going to produce. Then it would be up to the Sales Division to try to sell them. This was completely ass backwards in my book. The company had recruited bright young college graduates who were sitting in hotel rooms day after day with their fingers stuck in a telephone, trying to peddle iron out of the sales bank to the dealers. And the system had been operating this way for years.

Most of the excess cars were kept on huge lots in the Detroit area. I'll never forget visiting the Michigan State Fairgrounds, jammed with thousands of unsold Chryslers, Dodges, and Plymouths, vivid evidence of the company's structural weakness. The volume would vary, but the number of cars was usually far and above what we could hope to sell.

In the summer of 1979, when Chrysler first approached the government for help, the sales bank contained eighty thousand unsold vehicles. At one point the number reached as high as a hundred thousand units, representing about $600 million in finished inventory. At a time when our cash was dwindling anyway and interest rates were high, the costs of carrying this inventory were astronomical. But even worse, the cars were just sitting there in the great outdoors and slowly deteriorating.

Building cars had become a gigantic guessing game. It had nothing to do with a customer ordering what he wanted on the car, or a dealer ordering what the customer was likely to ask for. Instead, it was some guy in the zone office saying: "I'll put power steering on this one and automatic transmission on that one. I'll make a thousand blues and a thousand greens." If a customer wanted red, too bad!

Something had to be done about all those cars, so at the end of every month the zone offices used to "move the iron" by running a fire sale. The zone guys used to spend at least one week a month on the phone just trying to move cars out of inventory. And the dealers got used to it. They soon learned that if they waited until the last week of the month, somebody from the zone office would call them and try to package ten cars for a special price. One way or another, the dealers could always get something off the regular wholesale price. At Ford, we had run occasional fire sales when inventories got too large. But here it was a way of life.

Like Pavlov's dogs, the dealers became dependent on these sales. They knew the day was coming, and they waited. They'd hear that bell ring and their hearts would start to beat faster because now they could buy their cars a little cheaper.

I knew that Chrysler would never be profitable unless we got rid of this system—permanently. I also knew it wouldn't be easy. A lot of people in the organization had become accustomed to the sales bank. They counted on it. Some were even addicted to it. When I vowed to wipe it out, they thought I was dreaming. At Chrysler, the sales bank was so big and so much a part of doing business it was hard to imagine life without it.

I talked tough to the dealers. I explained to them that the sales bank was destroying the company. I told them there was no place for a sales bank in our operation, that the phrase should be struck from the corporate vocabulary. I told them that from now on, they—not we—would be carrying the inventory. I also made it clear that we weren't going to build a car unless we had a specific order for it and that both the company and the dealers would benefit from running things right.

But it wasn't enough to improve our procedures in the future. We were still stuck with all those cars in the sales bank right now. As I explained to the dealers: "We can't sell these cars and trucks to Sears or J. C. Penney. You are our only customers, and somehow you're going to have to buy these products from us—and I mean *now*. I can't unbuild them and put the pieces back. And you can't leave me sitting with half a billion dollars tied up in inventory—no matter how it happened—while you selectively order the cars you think you would like to market and to hell with the rest."

It didn't happen overnight, but eventually the dealers took up the slack and we finally cleaned up the sales bank. It was incredibly difficult. Dealer inventories were already large, and interest rates were high. But the dealers did what was necessary, and within a couple of years we were finally running our plants to firm dealer orders.

Under our new system, salespeople sit down with each of our dealers. Together they plan the dealer's order for the next month, and they estimate his needs for the following two months. We get a firm commitment from the dealer, and that becomes our building schedule.

The dealer has to come through on his end, and we keep our part of the bargain. This means that we build the order right, keep the dealer posted, and deliver a quality product on time.

Today the system has integrity. We might go to a dealer and tell him that to participate in a certain rebate program he has to buy a hundred cars. He can then take it or leave it. But there's no way to fool around with that number, and there's no fire sale at the end of the month. As a result, we no longer operate in a daily panic. Today, unless a customer chooses to buy the car out of the dealer's inventory, his purchase is made to order and he can pick it up within a few weeks.

The sales bank was bad enough, but I also learned that Chrysler had been running the world's largest leasing company. Instead of selling cars to Hertz and Avis, we had been leasing them. And every six months we were buying them back. Without protest we became used-car brokers. Our dealers didn't want these cars, so we had to dump them at auctions. The first year I was at Chrysler, I wrote off $88 million in used-car losses!

We chose the alternative: to sell the cars to the rental companies, even if the profit margin was minimal. Let *them* worry about how to get rid of the cars later. Sixty thousand used cars were about the last thing we needed.

The rental companies drive a hard bargain, but especially for Chrysler it's essential to be represented in their fleets. The average Hertz car is out with two or three guys a week, which means I've got two or three product demonstrations of one of my cars that week—to people who may never have driven a Chrysler product before. They get in and they ask: "Who builds this car?" We get a tremendous amount of mail from the rental customers saying: "Why don't you promote this car? Where has it been hiding? I rented a Reliant to drive from Seattle to San Francisco and I was amazed."

The rental cars get us exposure. They attract the youth market, the more affluent crowd, the professional, upscale guy who traditionally hasn't even considered one of our cars. We need much greater penetration in the Southwest and in California, and that's where the rental business is especially important.

Between the sales bank and the rental cars and various other problems, we had to write off $500 million in management mistakes before we could even begin to enjoy the lousy market that was prevailing in those days.

There was so much to do and so little time! I had to eliminate the thirty-five little duchies. I had to bring some cohesion and unity into the company. I had to get rid of the many people who didn't know what they were doing. I had to replace them by finding guys with experience who could move fast. And I had to install a system of financial controls as quickly as possible.

These problems were urgent, and their solutions all pointed in the same direction. I needed a good team of experienced people who could work with me in turning this company around before it completely fell apart. My highest priority was to put that team together before it was too late.

XV

BUILDING THE TEAM

In the end, all business operations can be reduced to three words: people, product, and profits. People come first. Unless you've got a good team, you can't do much with the other two.

When I came to Chrysler, I brought along my notebooks from Ford, where I had tracked the careers of several hundred Ford executives. After I was fired, I had prepared a detailed list of everything I wanted to remove from my office. Those black notebooks were clearly mine, but it could be argued that they belonged to the company. I didn't want to take any chances. Henry and I were not on speaking terms, so I brought the list to Bill Ford and he gave me his permission to take the books home.

I went back to those notebooks as soon as I learned that Chrysler was in urgent need of first-rate financial people. A few months earlier, as president of Ford, I had asked J. Edward Lundy, our top finance man, for a report on the best financial talent in the company. Lundy had been one of the original Whiz Kids, and he, as much as anyone else, was responsible for Ford's excellent financial system.

On the surface, my request was perfectly routine. But in retrospect I wonder if I knew on some unconscious level that I might soon be in a position where this information would be valuable. As it turned out, Lundy's list was a godsend.

I opened the notebooks and started reading down the names. Lundy had ranked everybody A, B, or C. There were about twenty names on the A list, but I wasn't sure I wanted any of them. I respected Lundy, but his priorities and mine were different. The A list consisted of first-rate bean counters. What I was looking for was a little more than that.

Looking through the B list, I noticed the name of Gerald Greenwald. He was only forty-four, but he had already accomplished a great deal. I had met Greenwald on a number of occasions and I liked him. I remembered that he was always trying to get out of finance. Once I had helped him expand his range of skills by sending him over to Paris to take over Richier, a farm and construction equipment company we had bought. The company failed, but that wasn't Greenwald's fault. It was simply a bad operation, and eventually we had to sell it.

Next we had sent Greenwald to Ford of Venezuela. He was an aggressive manager, to the point where Ford's market share in Venezuela for both cars and trucks was higher than any other Ford subsidiary. At the time, gas in Venezuela was fourteen cents a gallon, and I've always kidded Jerry that under those conditions he couldn't miss. In France he had drawn the bad end of the stick. In Venezuela he got the golden end. But the truth is that he showed real business savvy in both jobs—he was obviously more than just a bean counter.

Jerry's background is highly unusual for the auto business. He's Jewish, the son of a chicken farmer from St. Louis. He got himself a good education in economics at Princeton and then came to Ford with the intention of working in labor relations.

"We have a better idea," they told him. Greenwald was assigned a position in a new division—Edsel. Within a few months of that fiasco he was thinking: "I'm just out of school. How could I have been so lucky?"

Jerry has the talent and the know-how of the entrepreneur who can analyze a problem and then move on to solve it. He doesn't talk things to death—he *acts*. He had always wanted to go beyond finance, and it was clear from his work in Venezuela that his talents extended to other areas as well. I wanted Jerry Greenwald because he was a good businessman, period.

In December of 1978, I called Greenwald in Venezuela. Jerry and his wife were out at a party, so I left a message at their house. When they got back, Glenda Greenwald immediately guessed why I'd called. "Don't call him back!" she told her husband. The Greenwalds were living the good life in Caracas, where Jerry was a big fish in a little pond. The prospect of moving to Detroit to work for a failing company could not have been very appealing.

But Jerry did call back, and we decided to meet in Miami. He showed up with a beard. He wasn't at all sure he wanted to come to Chrysler, and he went to great lengths to keep our talks secret.

Our second meeting was in Las Vegas, where I was attending a Chrysler dealer convention. When Jerry arrived at the hotel, he was jolted to find that a Ford meeting was going on at the same time. He spent the entire time up in his room to avoid running into anyone he might know from Ford. We talked all evening. Jerry had an early plane to catch the next morning, and at 5:30 A.M. he called my room and asked, "Are you up?"

"Are you out of your mind?" I replied. He said that he hadn't slept all night and that he needed to ask a few more questions before he could make his decision. I told him to come right over to my room. As I sat there in my bathrobe, he told me about his doubts. "All my life I fought to get out of that bean-counter syndrome at Ford," he said. "And at Chrysler I'd be coming right back into it."

I explained that I needed him to set up the financial controls, but that when that was taken care of, he could move into other operations. As he left my room and started walking down the hall, I called after him: "Wait a minute, Jerry. You may end up as president sooner than you think." He gave me a skeptical look, as though I were trying to give him the hard sell. But I was serious. Within two years, Jerry became the number two man at Chrysler.

After he agreed to make the move, Jerry flew up to Ford headquarters in Dearborn to give them the news. To his surprise, Henry asked to meet with him. Both Henry and Bill Ford knew Jerry was a prize, and they tried to talk him out of going to Chrysler. Jerry explained to Henry that he just couldn't pass up the excitement Chrysler represented—the opportunity to be involved in turning around a big, ailing company. Henry of all people ought to appreciate his motivation, he said, because Henry had faced a similar challenge when he came into his grandfather's company in 1946. That silenced Henry, so apparently the analogy hit home.

One of Greenwald's first responsibilities was to centralize the accounts payable. Coming from Ford, he probably went into shock when he discovered that bills were being paid from about thirty different locations.

In his first few days on the job, he talked at length to the people involved in running the controller's office. Predictably, he learned that they had no idea how to evaluate from a financial perspective what management was doing and that they couldn't project the consequences of our corporate decisions. He had a hell of a time finding anybody who could be identified as having a specific responsibility for anything. They would tell him: "Well, everyone is responsible for controlling costs." Jerry knew very well what that meant—in the final analysis, nobody was.

One of several disaster areas Greenwald uncovered was Chrysler's handling of warranty costs, which were running as high as $350 million a year. Greenwald immediately asked for a list of the top ten warranty problems with somebody's name next to each one, and a specific plan for correcting the deficiencies and reducing the costs. To his dismay, he quickly learned what I already knew. At Chrysler, to get the financial data in order to address a problem, you had to first put in a system to get the data!

Jerry never let me forget he wanted to be more than a controller. After a few months, when I saw how effective he was, I made him an offer: "If you can find somebody else as good as you are, I'll free you up to do other things."

Greenwald promptly brought in Steve Miller, who had been his main financial man in Venezuela. As our chief financial officer, Miller has been a brilliant addition to the team. During our seemingly endless negotiations with hundreds of banks during 1980 and 1981, Miller's work was absolutely critical. Amazingly, both he and Greenwald managed to stay calm and cool through those chaotic times. Chrysler could not have survived without them.

Hal Sperlich was already at Chrysler when I arrived, having come over when Henry fired him in 1977. Having Hal at Chrysler was like finding a tall, cold beer in the middle of a desert. Thank you Henry!

Whenever I added someone to the team, I felt a little guilty. In order to recruit these guys, I'd have to lie to myself. If I had really been honest, I would have told them the truth: "Stay away from this place—you can't imagine how bad it is!" But I couldn't do that. I had to tell them what I desperately hoped was true: that if we got the right group together, we could save the company.

With Sperlich, however, I didn't have this problem. He was at Chrysler a couple of years before I arrived and he knew perfectly well how bad things were. More than once I said to him: "You son of a bitch, why did you let me take this job? Why didn't you warn me?" He too had lied to himself in order to get me to Chrysler.

But I forgave Hal because his experience at Chrysler gave him a big advantage over my new recruits: he already knew the place. Hal was like my advance man. Riccardo could tell me about the balance sheets, but it was Sperlich who really knew the nuts and bolts of the operation.

As a result, he was able to unearth a lot of good people who had been passed over by the previous management. Many of them were down a few layers, so Hal had to do some serious digging. He discovered a number of bright young men who had been hidden under bushel baskets. They had the talent and the enthusiasm—they just needed to be discovered.

Fortunately, the cancer at Chrysler did not reach all the way down. Although I had to replace almost all the officers, there was plenty of dynamic young talent beneath them. As we started getting rid of the less competent people, it was a lot easier to find the good ones. To this day, I can't believe that the former management didn't notice them. I'm talking about people with fire in their eyes: you can practically tell they're good just by looking at them.

I quickly elevated Sperlich to vice-president in charge of product planning. Before long, I promoted him to head of all North American operations. As I saw it, Hal had a hand in everything that had gone right at Ford during the 1960s and 1970s. More recently, the same has been true at Chrysler.

Hal's a visionary, but a very pragmatic one. He understands how to ring the cash register and he doesn't fool around with trivia. He tolerates a fair share of facts and study, but only up to a certain point. Then he says: "Okay, what are we trying to do here?" And he does it. He's a guy who knows how to move.

Hal's also got that uncanny ability to see into the future, to know what people will want three or four years down the road. We've worked together ever since the Mustang and we test our hunches on each other. Both of us are given a lot of credit for clairvoyance. I'd say that between the two of us, we're at least as good as any *one* top auto guy in the world!

We have our disagreements, too, but that's part of our working relationship. Hal likes to kid me. He says I'm getting too old to know about the youth market. Maybe he's right. Maybe that's why I still listen to him. But hell, not always! He's only five years younger than I. He's beginning to look older, but after twenty-four years of abuse from me, that's only natural.

*   *   *

From the start, Greenwald and Sperlich were terrific, but two guys do not a management team make. I still needed more help in a hurry. And I knew where to get it. There was one pool of people who had a body of experience and proven ability that was completely going to waste: retired Ford executives. I needed to pick their brains and use their street smarts to get things organized.

Gar Laux had worked in both the marketing and the dealer side of operations at Ford. When the Mustang was introduced, he had been sales manager of the Ford Division. Later he was my general manager in the Lincoln-Mercury Division.

During the Knudsen era at Ford, Gar had left the company to head the Dallas Chamber of Commerce. Within a few years he had another job—as Arnold Palmer's partner in a Cadillac dealership in North Carolina. But it wasn't only Gar's experience that appealed to me. His personality was just as important. He's one of those guys everybody likes to go out and drink with and confide in, and I knew he'd be terrific at building better relations with our dealers. God knows we needed it.

The bad feelings between Highland Park and the dealers were astounding. I was amazed and appalled by the way the two sides were talking to each other and by the angry and insulting letters that were being exchanged between the dealers and Chrysler headquarters. At Ford I had always been on very good terms with the dealers, but it took me twenty years to win their confidence. Getting to know a whole new group of dealers was different—and I sure didn't have twenty years to do it. I couldn't build all the bridges myself. Gar Laux was the man for the job.

I brought him in to help both sides lower their voices and start listening to each other. After all, what's good for Chrysler is good for the dealers, and vice versa. Instead of allowing the two sides to harbor grudges or take potshots at each other, we needed to create an environment where somebody from top management could sit down with the dealers and go over all of their complaints and problems, one by one.

And the dealers certainly had plenty to say. They had every right to be angry with management, because they hadn't been treated well at all. For years the company had been shipping them junk and expecting them to sell it. Chrysler's quality had been so poor that the dealers got into the habit of expecting to rebuild the cars when they received them. Under those conditions, how could we ask them to be courteous and enthusiastic? How could we ask them to *trust* us?

We were flooded with letters from unhappy customers who had

visited Chrysler showrooms, letters that said: "I can't get the time of day from these guys," or: "I saw a commercial that said come in and compare. I went in to compare, but there was nobody to talk to. The salesmen all seemed to be drinking coffee or reading *The Daily Racing Form*. So what am I supposed to do?"

Every time I read one of those letters I got mad. I was furious that we were losing sales from people who really wanted to do business with us—if only to help us out.

So I sent Gar to hold seminars with the dealers and remind them of a few fundamentals: when a guy comes through your door, love him. Talk to him. Give him the information he needs to make a $10,000 purchase. He's not always too sure of what he wants. He might not know what a transaxle is or what front-wheel-drive does for him. And the hims have now given way to the hers. Over 50 percent of cars are now bought by women, and they don't always know about the technical side of things. They need some courteous help. Dealing with customers takes knowledge, time, and patience—after all, if salespeople don't have that, they should look for another line of work. (I always remembered my father's admonition to those waitresses.)

Gar informed the dealers that the new administration was going to bring a sense of discipline to all areas of our operations. He said that we recognized the quality problem and were determined to fix it. He explained that we intended to honor our commitments, operate within budgets, and keep to schedules. He told the dealers that the whole company was being turned around and that from now on they could count on us.

Originally, Gar had agreed to come up as a consultant for a few months while maintaining his dealership in North Carolina. Before long, we persuaded him to stay on for a couple of years to be in charge of sales and marketing.

When it came to a quality image, Chrysler had a really serious problem. With something so important, you can't just wave a wand and presto! Even if your product gets better right away, it takes time for the public to realize it. It's like the bad girl in town who changes her ways and goes straight. For the first couple of years, nobody believes her.

Styling and value are what sells cars, but quality is what keeps them sold. When it comes to the public's perception of quality, advertising can't do the job for you. Neither can press conferences or other public appearances. The only solution is to build good products, price them competitively, and then go out and service them. If you can do those things, the public will start beating a path to your door.

To give us a hand on quality, I brought Hans Matthias out of retirement and hired him as a consultant. Hans used to be my chief engineer at the Ford Division and later was in charge of manufacturing for the whole Ford Motor Company. His specialty was quality control; until he retired in 1972, he had done more than anyone else to improve Ford's quality. In two years at Chrysler, he did the same.

Matthias worked with Sperlich to put some discipline into the manufacturing system. Sperlich was always working on future models that were still three years away. "Don't skimp," I told him, "no matter how bad things are right now. The only way we'll ever survive is if we stay in business during alterations." Today our quality is equal to or better than any American-made cars. And we're fast closing in on the Japanese.

The public has become pretty cynical about big business and for good reason. Sometimes our cars were so bad, they felt we built them that way on purpose. Most people don't realize that it's in the company's interest to build cars right the first time. If we catch a problem at the factory, it might cost us $20 an hour to fix it. But if we let that problem go and the dealer has to fix it, it's going to cost us $30 an hour under warranty. As much as I hate paying $20 an hour, it sure as hell beats paying $30.

Good design always involves a delicate balance: what does a customer want, and how can we give it to him without compromising the other things he wants?

Cars are very complex machines, more so each year. Take air conditioning, for example. If you're paying an extra $700 to keep cool in the summer, you want your money's worth. Whoever designs the air-conditioning system has to remember: it's no good if it takes 30 minutes to cool down the car, because most trips are over by then. So you need to install high-speed blowers. But they can't be too noisy, because the guy driving the car wants to listen to his $300 stereo while the air conditioning is on. The air-conditioning guy can't say: "That's not my problem. I just want to cool him down." He's got to integrate his part into the total system of the car.

The designer has to keep several things in mind. First, the part has to be low in weight, because like anything else in the car, if it's heavy, it will affect the mileage. Second, it should be low in cost—for obvious reasons. Finally, it should be easy to manufacture. Assembling two pieces is always easier and more reliable than assembling three.

Easy to manufacture—*that's* the key to quality. "My design is super." That's a line I've heard for years. And I always think: "Yeah, it's so super that I can't build the thing."

Of course, quality doesn't stop with the engineer. It has to be part of the consciousness of the workers in the plants. Through the establishment of "quality circles," our plant workers have become far more involved than they used to be in the building process. We sit them down in a room and we say: "How about this operation? Can you do it? The engineer says you can, and the manufacturing guy says you can. But you're the ones who have to build the thing. What do you say?"

So off they go to try it for a couple of days. If it doesn't work, they come back and tell us: "That's a bad idea. Here's a better way to do it." The word gets around pretty quickly that management is listening, that we really care about quality, that we're open to new ideas, we're not just a bunch of dummies. That may be the most important consideration of all when it comes to quality—that the worker believes his ideas will be heard.

We also set up a joint UAW-Chrysler Management Quality Program that says: "Look, we'll argue about everything else, but when it comes to quality, we're not going to fight each other. Quality cannot get mixed up with other bargaining and be compromised by the usual adversarial relationship between workers and management."

At Ford, Hans Matthias had made quality really mean something. When I asked him to help us, he couldn't wait to get cracking. In a year and a half he brought discipline into the Chrysler system of manufacturing. Moreover, he did all this as a consultant, and everybody knows that consultants aren't supposed to do anything!

Matthias and I understood each other. Within ten minutes at Chrysler he was saying: "Do you know what you've got here? You've got a mess we may never unravel." But he did. He would go to the plants every morning and pull five units at random off the line. Then he'd bring in a new Toyota and ask the guys to look at the difference. Pretty soon he had the foreman saying: "Hey, our cars are really bad."

Then there's George Butts, who was there when I arrived. George has done a great job in improving the quality of Chrysler products. I've made it very clear to everybody in the company that quality is our top priority, and I think the message has filtered down. I set up a separate department for George to oversee quality. He's the watchdog for me—and my top manager on all quality issues.

During the height of the loan guarantee debate in 1979 when we were cutting costs right and left, Matthias and Butts came to me with a proposal to bring 250 new people into the plants for improved quality control. We couldn't afford it. But I approved the plan anyway because if Chrysler was going to have any future at all, we had to have a quality product.

I can't talk about quality without also mentioning Steve Sharf, who is now head of all manufacturing. He too was at Chrysler when I got there. He's a diamond in the rough, one of those guys who had been kept under a bushel basket for years. Given new responsibilities, he really made good things happen.

Then there was Dick Dauch, who came to Chrysler after working at GM and Volkswagen. Dauch proceeded to bring us fifteen top guys from his two alma maters. This is a point that's often overlooked by people trying to understand our comeback. I took all the guys from Ford that I knew in marketing, finance, and purchasing, but when it came to quality car building I went for the best GM and Volkswagen people. So I had the old and the new, the line and the staff, and the retirees—and they all got along. It was that unique melting pot that turned our quality around so quickly.

Together, Matthias, Butts, Sharf, and Dauch have brought integrity to our manufacturing system. It is this commitment to quality manufacturing—along with a brilliant group of designers and engineers led by Don DeLaRossa and Jack Withrow—that allows us to be the only car company in the world to offer a five-year, fifty-thousand-mile warranty.

That warranty is no sales gimmick. It can't be. In the fourth and fifth years, when those cars start to age, it would be too expensive to repair all those engines and transmissions if they didn't hold up. The liability would kill us.

Fortunately, quality and productivity are two sides of the same coin. Everything you do for quality improves your productivity. When you improve quality, warranty costs go down, and so do inspection and repair costs. If you're doing the job right the first time, engineering and tooling costs go down, too, and owner loyalty starts to rise.

In addition to Gar Laux and Hans Matthias, I brought another ex-Ford man out of retirement to join Chrysler. Paul Bergmoser had worked at Ford for thirty years as vice-president in charge of purchasing.

He's tough and innovative, and I knew I could count on him to figure out a dozen ways to do what everybody else said was impossible.

"Listen, Bergie," I told him on the phone, "I'm all alone over here." I tried to explain how Chrysler didn't have any of the systems and organizations we had been so used to at Ford. He too agreed to come aboard—first as a consultant, and later, for a year or so, as president of the company.

When Paul arrived in Highland Park, he was amazed at what he found. He used to come in and say to me: "You know, I'm doing the digging for you, but what is under the rocks I'm overturning you just aren't going to believe." Sometimes we would laugh, it was so wild. After a year at Chrysler, he complained to me: "Lee, I have a terrific accountant's report that tells me we lost a billion dollars this year. What I don't have is an analysis to tell me how we lost it!" All I could say was: "Paul, welcome to Chrysler."

Like all of us who had worked at Ford, Bergie was used to a highly systematic way of working. At Chrysler, he found almost no systems in place in the purchasing department, which even by the lax standards of Chrysler was known for its inefficiency. Unfortunately, Chrysler was more dependent on outside suppliers than either GM or Ford, both of whom build many of their own parts.

And as the smallest of the Big Three, Chrysler wasn't always in a position to get the best prices. To make matters worse, the company had failed to treat its suppliers well, and over the years they had reciprocated in kind. As a result, we couldn't always depend on a steady flow of parts. Bergie had his work cut out for him.

As I've already mentioned, Laux, Matthias, and Bergmoser all came out of retirement to help me. I would have been lost without these guys. Each of them had many years of experience as well as the desire to put that experience to work.

Why did they do it? Was it, as some people speculated, because of my great salesmanship? Of course not. These were my friends. I knew they were the kind of people who would respond to the challenge, who would be willing to give a hand. They thought it could be fun. When it wasn't any fun, they stuck with it anyway. They had that essential quality—inner strength.

That's true, by the way, of everybody who joined our team. Only guys of a certain temperament could hack it. It was more than a challenge—it was an adventure. And in all the travail, nobody ever got weak in the knees. There was no self-doubt. There was no wringing of hands. There was no asking: "Why did I give up a promising career with a good company to take this on?" These were spirited men, men of character and mettle. I'm grateful to every one of them and I will never forget them.

Still, I owe a special debt to the guys who came out of retirement. Let's face it: mandatory retirement is a terrible idea. I've always felt it was ridiculous that when a guy reaches sixty-five, no matter what shape he's in, we retire him instantly. We should be depending on our older executives. They have the experience. They have the wisdom.

In Japan, it's the older guys who are still running things. On my last trip over there, the youngest guy I talked to was seventy-five. I don't think this policy has done Japan much harm in recent years, either.

If you can still come to work at the age of sixty-five and do a good job, why should you have to leave? The retired executive has been there before and he's seen it all. He's learned a lot over the years. What is wrong with old age if the guy is healthy? People forget that our health standards have improved dramatically. If a man's okay physically and has the stamina to do the job, why wouldn't I want to use his expertise?

I've seen too many executives announce that they'll retire at fifty-five. Then when they turn fifty-five, they feel compelled to carry it through. They've said it so often that they're committed, even if they're not crazy about the idea. I think that's tragic.

Many of these guys fall apart when they retire. They've become used to the tough grind, with lots of excitement and high risks—big successes and big failures. Then they suddenly find themselves playing golf and going home for lunch. I've seen a lot of men die only a few months after they retire. Sure, working can kill you. But so can not working.

Well, you might say I finally had my battery and my infield in place. But I still needed an outfield. To complete the new team, I had to buy some marketing talent. Marketing is my specialty, and I wasn't impressed by what I found at Chrysler. I solved the problem in a slightly unusual way. On March 1, 1979, I called a press conference in New York to announce a very important acquisition: we were replacing Chrysler's two ad agencies, Young & Rubicam, and BBDO, with Kenyon & Eckhardt, the New York-based agency that had been so effective for the Lincoln-Mercury Division at Ford.

Even by the standards of Madison Avenue, firing our agencies was a ruthless act. It also represented the single largest account change in the history of advertising. This was a $150 million decision, and it told the business world we weren't afraid to take the bold steps that were essential if we were going to turn our company around.

At the time, K&E still had the $75 million Lincoln-Mercury account at Ford. In order to join us, they had to drop it immediately. I'm sure Henry was none too pleased to hear the news, which must have come as a shock to him. Our announcement had been planned very carefully, and the Ford people were informed only about two hours in advance. Security surrounding the deal had been terrific, and virtually nobody in Detroit knew about the switch before it was announced. After the shake-up, Young & Rubicam became the new agency for Lincoln-Mercury. A couple of years later, when we had grown too big for one agency, BBDO got back the Dodge account. So the whole thing ended up as a high-stakes game of musical chairs.

The two agencies that I replaced were perfectly okay. But I already had so much on my plate that I had to simplify things. I just didn't have the year it would take to deal with two entirely new groups. I didn't have time to teach them my philosophy—or my way of operating. Instead, I brought in familiar professionals who knew me so well that when I gave half an order, they already knew what the other half would be.

In my view, K&E are the best in the business. At Ford they had given us "Ford has a better idea," although some people at Ford actually objected to that phrase. They thought it should have read, "Ford has the *best* idea."

"Ford has a better idea" was the brainchild of John Morrissey, who until recently was chairman of the domestic board of Kenyon & Eckhardt. John started out with J. Walter Thompson and then moved over to work for Ford before joining K&E. He's a very creative guy, and we go back a long way together.

It was K&E that had come up with "the sign of the cat," which was a critical component in building up the Lincoln-Mercury Division. K&E's record in helping to double Lincoln-Mercury's market share during the 1970s speaks for itself. Lincoln-Mercury was a tough assignment, and it's during those years that I learned that Kenyon & Eckhardt could operate in a crisis mode, under pressure.

Because K&E had been involved with Ford for thirty-four years, we offered them a five-year contract, which was unprecedented in the short-term world of advertising. We also offered them the opportunity to become far more involved than any agency had in the past.

With every new car, public perception is half the battle. The deeper the agency gets involved, the better it is for both sides. K&E people were our active partners. They became members of our most important company committees, including product planning and marketing. They became an integral part of Chrysler, the closest thing to a house agency we could have. In effect, they became our marketing and communications arm.

Such a close association between the agency and the client had never been tried before in the automobile business. But I've always felt that if you're going to spend $100 million on a new car, you can't expect your advertising people to get creative overnight. They've got to be in on the whole process of developing the car. They've got to be at the meetings where the car is being thought up. They've got to give you their best advice as early as possible, such as "This won't sell because . . ." or "Don't name it that because . . ."

A big advantage of this setup is the speed with which we can now operate. One Thursday at four in the afternoon we decided to offer our retail customers a new financing rate of 10.9 percent. K&E immediately started filming a commercial. By five the next morning it was finished. By Saturday it was on the air. When something has to be done, I like to move fast. I need an agency that can keep up with the pace.

One of K&E's first decisions was to bring back the symbol of the ram, which had been used years ago by Dodge trucks and then abandoned. K&E's research showed that what people really wanted in a truck was a tough, durable, dependable, no-nonsense product. So they resurrected the ram with the theme "Dodge trucks are ram-tough" and put the word and the symbol back on the trucks and in the ads. Before long, our trucks were perceived as being in the same league as Chevrolet and Ford. We were soon getting consideration from people who until now hadn't even been thinking of a Dodge product.

At one point when sales were very low, the agency came up with a program in which we said to the public: "We want to get you to consider a Chrysler product. Come in and test-drive one of our cars. If you do, and if you then end up buying a car from one of our competitors, we'll give you fifty bucks just for considering us."

Admittedly, this idea was a little far out. Many of our dealers rebelled. They said it would be abused. But they were wrong: we got a lot of people into the showroom, and we sold a lot of cars.

Still, the dealers continued to see it as a gimmick, even though the company, and not the dealers, was putting up the fifty bucks.

After a few months we dropped the plan because of the lack of dealer support. But I still think it was a hell of an idea.

Another marketing first we put together with K&E was the money-back guarantee. "Buy one of our cars," we said. "Take it home, and within thirty days, if you don't like it *for any reason*, bring it back and we'll refund your money." The only catch was a depreciation charge of $100, since we couldn't sell the car as new.

We tried this one in 1981, and all of Detroit thought we were nuts: "What if a guy simply doesn't like the car? What if he changes his mind? What if his wife hates the color?"

If any of those things had happened more than occasionally, we'd have been swamped by customers coming in to get their money back. The paperwork alone could have killed us.

But to the surprise of the skeptics, the program worked very well. Most people play fair; very few took advantage. We had estimated that 1 percent of our customers might bring back their cars. Amazingly, the total number of returns worked out to less than two tenths of one percent.

This one, too, was a revolutionary idea, and I'm glad that we tried it. The important thing to remember is that we were trying everything possible to assure potential buyers that we stood behind what we said.

With Kenyon & Eckhardt on our team, we were now ready to play ball. Unfortunately, the season was half over, and we were deep in last place. Even so, I thought it was only a matter of time before we would be back in the race. I failed to realize that before we could ever resemble the New York Yankees of old, we had to go through a long period of looking more like the old Chicago Cubs.

XVI

THE DAY THE SHAH LEFT TOWN

Once I had my team in place, I was confident that Chrysler's recovery would only be a matter of time. But then I hadn't counted on the economy to fall apart. And I certainly hadn't counted on Iran. As it turned out, neither had Jimmy Carter.

Right after I came in, our share of the market headed due south. We started to hit numbers as low as 8 percent, which was pretty dismal even by Chrysler's modest standards. I was beginning to realize that it might take years before this company was back on its feet again.

During my career at Ford, I had taken great pride in my strong family life. No matter what was going on at work, I was always able to leave behind the concerns of the office. But that was before I came to Chrysler. Now I started waking up in the middle of the night. My mind never got settled. I was working constantly. There were times when I wondered about my sanity, about whether I could keep it all together. You can run sprints only so long before you're out of breath.

Thank God I had a wife who understood me. Yet after twenty-five years with me in the auto business, even she started worrying.

I was losing my ass out there, and it was a new experience. Ralph Nader used to claim that Iacocca was such a marketing whiz that he could make people buy cars they really didn't want. Nader complained that the monstrous Big Three, with all their power and leverage, could brainwash the public into buying whatever we told them.

But if that was true, where was this special power now that I really needed it? Where was my great marketing genius when nobody was buying our cars? I could have used some of that magic in 1979, when I was having a terrible time selling anything.

By now, Chrysler's problems were so serious that our precarious position was well known. So in addition to everything else, we had to deal with the nasty rumors of our imminent demise. When a guy puts down $8,000 or $10,000 for a new car, it's a major investment. He has to worry about whether the company is going to be around in a couple of years to provide parts and service. If he's always reading about the potential bankruptcy of Chrysler, he's not going to rush out and buy one of our cars.

It got to the point where Chrysler was fast becoming a one-word joke. The nation's cartoonists were having a field day. So was Johnny Carson:

CARSON: "Boy, is he mean."
AUDIENCE: "How mean is he?"
CARSON: "Why, he's so mean that this morning he called up Chrysler and asked, 'How's business?' "

Or: "I don't know what's going on at Chrysler, but it's the first time I ever heard anybody make a conference call to Dial-A-Prayer!"

I had been at Chrysler less than three months when all hell broke loose. On January 16, 1979, the Shah left town. Within a few weeks, the price of gas doubled. The energy crisis hit California first, and in May *Newsweek* featured it as a cover story. A month later, the crisis came East. During the last weekend in June, you had to be lucky to find a gas station open for business.

All of this had a devastating effect on sales of our larger cars as well as recreational vehicles (RVs). Chrysler was a leader in RVs and motor homes, and these huge gas-guzzlers were the first victims when the panic began. By June of 1979, the chassis and the engines we were supplying to the RV industry had virtually stopped selling. And sales of our vans, another big part of our operation, had dropped by half.

One of the public's favorite criticisms of the auto industry is that we should have anticipated the post-Iran oil shortage. But if our own government had no idea about what was going on over there, how should I have known?

No, we weren't prepared for Iran. But we sure responded to it. In 1979, we planned our 1983 models with the very rational assumption that by the time they came out, gas would be selling for $2.50 a gallon. Then somebody yelled, "April Fool's! Gas is cheap again, so give us big cars!"

If anybody had told me that gas prices would double in 1979 and that four years later they would still be at the same price regardless of inflation, I would have said he's nuts. There's no way in the world that we could have anticipated either the Iranian crisis or its aftermath.

There's a widespread myth that American car companies had all the wrong kinds of cars, whereas foreign carmakers had just what people wanted when the oil crisis hit. But that's not true. Until the Shah was overthrown, there were long waiting lists of customers who wanted big cars with big V-8s—in fact, there weren't enough gas-guzzlers to go around.

As for the Japanese, did they really anticipate the American demand for small cars? For thirty years, they've been building nothing else. Whenever the shift occurred, they would have been ready.

We all had small cars, but in 1978 we couldn't give them away. As late as January 1979, just a few weeks before the Iranian explosion, Datsun was offering rebates. Toyota and Honda weren't selling anything. We ourselves had thousands of unsold Omnis and Horizons. And our small Colt, built by Mitsubishi, was not selling even with a $1,000 rebate.

All of that changed overnight. Just two months earlier, gas had been selling for sixty-five cents a gallon. Our full-size car plants were working overtime. The Japanese had seven hundred thousand small cars sitting on the docks in San Diego and Baltimore. But by April, those seven hundred thousand little Japanese cars were gone, snapped up by Americans who wanted instant fuel economy. And many of them had been sold at black-market prices, $1,000 over the sticker price. It wasn't that Ford, GM, and Chrysler couldn't antici-pate the American market. Nobody could.

GM was lucky. They had planned to be previewing their new X-body cars in April. The Chevrolet Citation was a down-sized, front-wheel-drive, fuel-efficient car. In the first two days it was offered, GM sold every Citation in existence and took orders for twenty-two thou-sand more.

Chrysler was less fortunate. After the first oil crisis had subsided in 1974, Americans had gone back with a vengeance to big cars. As usual, Chrysler had followed the market. That meant we didn't have nearly enough subcompacts ready when the public suddenly had its mind changed again.

I vividly remember the images we saw every night on the evening news—pictures of gas lines in California, in Washington, and of actual riots at some service stations in New York. People got scared. They started topping off their tanks whenever they could. Some drivers even started carrying an extra five-gallon can in their trunk or putting a fifty-gallon tank in their garage—and to hell with safety.

Congress started talking about gas rationing. Magazines ran cover stories about how Detroit got caught with its pants down. And sure enough, whether it was panic over the availability of gas or simply the sharp rise in prices, the market for family cars, V-8 engines, vans, trucks, and recreational vehicles dried up instantly.

In a period of five months in 1979, the small-car share of the market rose from 43 percent to nearly 58 percent—a swing of 15 percent. In our business, a move of 2 percent in a single year represents a major shift. A swing of 15 percent is catastrophic. In a single month—May 1979—van sales fell by 42 percent. Never before in the history of the car business had there been such a violent change in the market as the one that occurred that spring.

As damaging as that revolution was, we at Chrysler knew that we could adapt to this new reality. We also knew we could get there before anybody else in Detroit. It wouldn't take much. All we had to do was double our investment in new plants and products over the next five years and hope we were still alive!

But just as we were starting to take those first expensive steps, the country nosedived into a recession. We were still staggering from the first punch. When the second one came, it almost knocked us out. The annual rate of car sales in this country dropped to almost half of what it had been. No industry in the world can survive in an economy that calls for double the investment with only half the revenues. For us, all bets were off. There were no rules, because we were in an unprecedented situation. These were uncharted waters.

Until then you could always say: Go look in the manual. GM originated it, Ford copied it, and Chrysler had pieces of it. I don't mean this literally. It's just that between 1946, when I came into the business, and March of 1979, there was never much doubt about how to run a successful operation.

But suddenly we had to stay loose and change our minds every week. To put it mildly, this was a very new and novel way of doing business. Everybody talks about "strategy," but all we knew was survival. Survival was simple. Close the plants that are hurting us the most. Fire the people who aren't absolutely necessary or who don't know what's going on.

I felt like an Army surgeon. The toughest assignment in the world is for the doctor who's at the front during a battle. In World War II, my cousin was a medic at a M*A*S*H-type hospital in the Philippines. He came back with some pretty ugly stories about triage. It's a question of priorities, he used to say. There'd be forty badly injured guys, and the medical staff had to think fast. "We have three hours. How many guys can we save?" They would pick the ones who had the best chance of survival—and the rest had to be left for dead.

It was the same at Chrysler. We had to do radical surgery, saving what we could. When times are good and you have a marginal plant, you can study it for two years, going over every pro and con. Ford is terrific at that. They'll study the thing to death.

But when you're in a crisis, there's no time to run a study. You've got to put down on a piece of paper the ten things that you absolutely have to do. That's what you concentrate on. Everything else—forget it. The specter of dying has a way of focusing your attention in a big hurry.

At the same time, you've got to make sure you've got something left when the immediate crisis is over. That sounds simple enough, but it's much easier said than done. It takes gritting your teeth. It takes discipline. You hope and you pray that it works, because you're doing the best you can. You're concentrating on the future, meaning you hope you'll be alive tomorrow.

We began by closing some of our plants, including a trim plant in Lyons, Michigan, and our oldest plant, Dodge Main, in Hamtramck, the Polish section of Detroit. There was a great deal of protest from the community when we closed down this inner-city factory, but we had absolutely no choice.

At the same time, we had to keep the suppliers shipping their stuff to us, even when we didn't have enough money to pay them. The first thing we needed to do was convince them that we weren't heading into bankruptcy. You can't fool suppliers. They know your business very well. We brought them in. We showed them our future products. We let them know we were here to stay. We asked them to stand by us.

To save money, we set up a system where parts would be shipped at the last possible moment. This is known as "just in time" inventory, and it's a good way to cut costs. The Japanese have been doing it for years, and they probably learned it from us. As far back as the 1920s, when the ore boats used to arrive at Ford's River Rouge plant, that ore was turned into steel and then to engine blocks within twenty-four hours. But during the boom years between 1945 and 1978, the American car industry fell into some bad habits.

One of the many changes we made was to speed up the way our parts and supplies reached the assembly plants. For example, we used to ship transaxles by train from Kokomo, Indiana, to Belvidere, Illinois. By switching to trucks, we got them there the same day, which streamlined the whole operation.

After a few months, our just-in-time system became so efficient that when our Detroit engine plant staged a wildcat strike, our assembly plant in Windsor ran out of engines four hours later!

We saved money wherever we possibly could. When we designed the K-cars, we deliberately kept them under 176 inches long so that we could fit more of them on a standard freight car. In normal times, nobody notices things like that. But in a crisis, you look for every possible way to cut costs.

When it came time to produce our 1979 annual report, we decided to forego the traditional glorious full-color magazine that most companies send to their shareholders. Instead, our two hundred thousand owners received a brief, plain-looking document printed with black ink on plain white recycled paper. It saved us quite a bit—and it gave our stockholders a message: anything so austere had to mean we were close to impoverished. And we were!

But saving money wasn't enough. We also had to raise a bundle of cash just to pay our bills. At one point we were losing money so badly that we sold all the dealership real estate we owned to a Kansas company called ABKO. Included were a couple of hundred downtown properties that ensured we'd have Chrysler dealers in strategic locations around the country. But we were scrambling for cash and we needed the money, which came to $90 million. Later, to keep our dealers where we needed them, we had to buy back about half of those properties—for twice the price.

In retrospect, selling the real estate looks like an enormous mistake. On the other hand, we needed the cash. At the time, that $90 million looked like a billion to me!

Before he retired, John Riccardo did his best to undo some of the company's more serious mistakes. He made a deal with Mitsubishi for our operations in Australia. He sold our Venezuela operations to

GM, and our Brazil and Argentina operations to Volkswagen. He negotiated a deal with Peugeot for our European operations, in return for $230 million and a 15 percent stake in Peugeot, an arrangement that made Peugeot the largest automobile company in Europe. When it was all over, Chrysler had operations in the United States, Canada, and Mexico. And nowhere else.

Sometime later, I concluded that we had no choice but to sell our tank operation to General Dynamics for $348 million. That was a very tough decision, because the Defense Division was the one part of the company that was virtually guaranteed its profit of $50 million a year by the U.S. government. But we needed the cash as a buffer to get the suppliers to give us an extension on our payments to them.

I made that decision reluctantly, in part because I was selling the only business where by law the Japanese couldn't compete. Actually, I was tempted to sell off the car business and keep the tanks! Financially, that would have made a lot more sense. But building tanks was not our main line of business. If Chrysler was going to have a future, it would have to be as a car company.

Even so, it was a painful decision. Our Tank Division was a very strong subsidiary, with plenty of great people. We had forty years of history tied up in the tank business. During World War II, we had been part of the "Arsenal of Democracy." Our people had designed and built the best battle tank in the entire world, and just a few months earlier I had personally driven the first M-1 turbine-powered tank off the line. We had some very exciting and profitable new products on the drawing boards. And some of the best talent in the whole company was running the place.

Nobody wanted to give up all that. But in the end, we had to balance our attachment to that division against our urgent need to build a substantial cash cushion with which to ride out the recession. We had no choice but to concentrate our efforts on cars and trucks.

At the time, interest rates were so high that if we hadn't needed all that cash to stay alive, we could have made $50 million a year just by putting what General Dynamics paid us into a money market fund. And $50 million was almost as much as we had been making on the Tank Division itself. It was then that I was first struck by the idea of buying a bank. You could make more money on money than you could on cars, trucks—or tanks!

There's an interesting sidelight to this story. Our contract with the UAW covered tanks as well as cars. In order to survive, we had negotiated an agreement with the union whereby we paid the workers a little over $17 an hour instead of the $20 an hour they had been getting. The tank workers didn't ratify the contract, but they were stuck with it. As a result, the Defense Department got a big break. I went to the Army and said: "Here's a refund of $62 million—my gift to you as a patriotic American." At $1 million a tank, it was like giving them sixty-two tanks free!

All of the measures we took to keep Chrysler alive were difficult. But none was more difficult than the mass firings. In 1979 and again in 1980, we had to lay off thousands of workers, blue-collar and white-collar alike. At one point, in April 1980, we cut our white-collar ranks by seven thousand people, a move that saved us over $200 million a year. A few months earlier, we had laid off eighty-five hundred salaried workers. These two moves alone cut out $500 million in annual costs! These cuts were across the board, including the chiefs as well as the Indians.

The firings were just tragic, and there's no way to pretend otherwise. Among the senior people, I handled most of the firings personally. That's not something you should delegate. You have to tell the truth. Having been fired myself, I had become an instant expert on what *not* to do. I certainly wouldn't say I just didn't like them! I always made sure to explain the reasons and to offer the guy the best possible pension he was entitled to. In some cases I even tried to bend the rules a little.

Firings are never pleasant, so you have to handle them with as much compassion as you can muster. You have to put yourself in the other guy's shoes and recognize that no matter how you dress it up, it's a pretty bad day in anyone's life. It's especially hard when the person feels it's not really his fault, that he's the victim of bad management, or that the top people never really cared about him.

I'm sure we made a lot of mistakes. Especially in the first year, there were probably guys who got laid off for the wrong reasons. Perhaps the boss didn't like them. Maybe they were too candid or outspoken. We had to move fast, and in the process it was inevitable that some good people got blamed unfairly. I'm sure we have some blood on our hands. But this was an emergency, and we tried to do the best we could.

Most of the people we fired found other jobs gradually. Some stayed in the auto business. Others found jobs with suppliers, or as teachers and consultants. It hurt me to let them go. As a group they were friendlier and nicer than the crew I had known at Ford. But in the end, that wasn't enough.

Watching people get kicked around had a big impact on me. It made me think a lot more about social responsibility, a lesson I had never learned at Ford. There, like the rest of top management, I was above it all. Also, we never had a crisis of this magnitude. In the past, I never had to do much laying off. It's not that I suddenly got religion. It's just that I reached a point where I had to say: "I wonder if I'm doing right by all these people who depend on me."

One of the luxuries we had to eliminate was a large staff. Ever since Alfred P. Sloan took over the presidency of General Motors, all management functions in our industry have been divided into staff and line positions—just like the Army. Line guys are in operations. They have hands-on involvement and specific responsibilities, whether it's in engineering, manufacturing, or purchasing.

The staff guys are the overall planners. They're the ones who integrate the work of the line guys into a workable system. Virtually the only way that a staff guy can be effective is if he's come up through the line. Yet the tendency, especially at a place like Ford, is to take a Harvard Business School graduate who may not know his ass from his elbow and make him staff. He's never run anything, but now he's telling the line guy, who's been doing his job for thirty years, that he's doing it all wrong. I've spent too much time in my career refereeing staff/line disputes that should never have come up in the first place.

You do need a staff—so long as you don't overdo it. At Ford, when Henry was trying to get rid of me, he brought in the consulting firm of McKinsey & Company. In addition to forming the office of the chairman, McKinsey also set up a superstaff of about eighty people. Its purpose was to check all the other staff and line people to make sure everybody was doing his job. Over the years, this group has become like a sovereign power at Ford—a company unto itself.

When Chrysler got hit, I had to let most of the staff go. I've been a line guy all my life, which might have made it easier. But my thinking was simple: I needed somebody to build the cars and sell the cars. I couldn't afford to have a guy who says that if we had done this or that, we could have built that car a little better. Even if he was right, we didn't have the luxury to consider it. When the bullets start to fly, the staff is always first out the door.

With all the firings, we ended up stripping out several levels of management. We cut down the number of people who needed to be involved in important decisions. Initially we did it out of the sheer necessity to survive. But over time we found that running a large company with fewer people actually made things easier. With hindsight it's clear that Chrysler had been top-heavy, far beyond what was good for us. That's a lesson our competitors have yet to learn—and I hope they never do!

XVII

DRASTIC MEASURES: GOING TO THE GOVERNMENT

$\mathbf{A}$s early as the summer of 1979, it was clear that only drastic measures could save the Chrysler Corporation. We were doing all we could—and then some—to reduce our expenses, but the economy was getting worse and our losses were continuing to mount. By now we were drifting into dangerous waters. If we were going to survive, we needed help. We no longer had the means to save ourselves from drowning.

I could see only one way out of this mess.

Believe me, the last thing in the world I wanted to do was turn to the government. But once I made the decision, I went at it with all flags flying.

Ideologically, I've always been a free-enterpriser, a believer in survival of the fittest. When I was president of Ford, I spent almost as much time in Washington as in Dearborn. Then I went to the capital for only one reason—to try to get the government off our backs. So naturally, when I was back in Washington as chairman of Chrysler to make the case for government help, everybody said: "How can you? How dare you?"

"What choice do I have?" I answered. "It's the only game in town."

We had already tried absolutely everything else. During 1979 and 1980, there had been more than a hundred meetings with potential investors. Most of these people turned out to be phonies, con men, or well-intentioned but naïve Samaritans. Still, I met with anybody who might have been able to help us, however unlikely the prospect.

Then there were the middlemen purporting to represent wealthy Arabs. I knew there were a lot of rich Arabs, but this was ridiculous. We had to follow up 156 separate Arab leads alone. I used to say to our Treasury Department, "Aren't we out of rich Arabs yet?" I must have met a dozen promising-looking guys with Arab connections, most of whom turned out to be hustlers. Each one explained that he had access to an Arab prince who was going to come up with the big bucks. But they were all dead ends.

A noteworthy exception was Adnan Khashoggi. He's a zillionaire from Saudi Arabia who made a huge bundle from the inflow of oil money. Khashoggi is a savvy guy who got an American education. He's a broker who gets involved in all kinds of deals for war matériel and capital investment goods in return for a handsome commission.

I tried to sell him on the fact that the Arab world was in disrepute because of OPEC. I told him that in terms of public relations, whether he was representing Yasir Arafat or King Faisal, an investment in Chrysler could only help the Arab image. But nothing ever came out of my talks with Khashoggi or anyone else from the Arab world.

My discussions with Toni Schmuecker, head of Volkswagen, were far more serious. Toni and I have known each other as good friends for over twenty years, ever since he worked for me as a purchasing agent in Ford of Germany. We had a few hush-hush discussions about a partnership between Volkswagen and Chrysler, which we called the Grand Design. The plan was that we'd both manufacture the same car. Chrysler would sell it on the American side, and Volkswagen would sell it in Europe. Earlier we had arranged to buy three hundred thousand Volkswagen four-cylinder engines a year for our Omnis and Horizons, which had a lot in common with the Rabbit. So in a way, we had already taken the first step.

There were some obvious advantages to the plan. Our dealer network would increase dramatically. Our purchasing power would be much greater. We could spread our fixed costs over a much larger volume of cars. It really was a marriage made in heaven. And it was so simple a baby could have figured it out.

When I joined Chrysler, I hadn't stopped thinking about the idea of Global Motors. From time to time, Hal Sperlich and I continued to talk about it. A merger between Chrysler and Volkswagen would have represented a real beginning, and both Hal and I were tremendously excited about the possibility. If we succeeded in merging with Volkswagen, we could have added on a Japanese partner without too much difficulty.

Our talks with Volkswagen got pretty specific. It was a very interesting episode at a time when we were dying. But that was the problem—we really *were* dying. Once Volkswagen studied our balance sheet, they pulled back. We were deeply in debt, and we weren't making any money. At the time the plan was much too risky. Instead of their lifting us up, we might have pulled them down.

As our talks were ending, word of the meetings leaked out. The rumor of an imminent merger between Volkswagen and Chrysler was leaked by *Automotive News*, the weekly trade journal of the car industry. That was proof enough for Wall Street, where our stock jumped from $11 to $14. According to the rumors, Volkswagen had decided to buy out Chrysler for $15 a share.

When the "news" broke, Riccardo was in Washington, meeting with Stuart Eizenstat of the Carter staff and Michael Blumenthal, secretary of the treasury. Both Eizenstat and Blumenthal urged him to accept the offer. Unfortunately, there was no offer to accept.

Schmuecker had certainly been interested, but Werner Schmidt, their vice-president for marketing, had opposed it strongly. Schmidt, who had once been a trainee in my office at Ford, was a big German fellow who proceeded to tell me in no uncertain terms why Volkswagen could never join up with Chrysler: our image was bad, our cars were lousy, and our dealer organization wasn't strong enough. I must have trained him well, because Schmidt summed up the case against the merger in a few brash words.

Four years later, in 1983, we had further talks with Volkswagen. Ironically, our positions were reversed. Now it was *their* dealer organization that was having trouble: nobody was buying Rabbits anymore.

Because our government still doesn't have an energy policy, any company that makes only small cars is at the mercy of fluctuating gas prices. And because Volkswagen produces *only* small cars, the Japanese were walking all over them. For one thing, the German mark, like the dollar, can't compete against the controlled yen. For another, whether Rabbits are made in Germany or in Pennsylvania, the labor costs are very high. On top of that, Volkswagen had to absorb the cost of shipping their cars from Germany, which is another big expense. That's why they finally started to build some of them in the United States.

Volkswagen was our most serious suitor, but there were others, including John Z. DeLorean. DeLorean, who had started his own automobile company after leaving General Motors, came to see me about the possibility of merging his company into Chrysler.

At the time of John's visit, both our companies were in deep trouble. "My father told me never put two losers together," I told him. "So either you make it or I will, and then we'll come back and talk."

DeLorean is a first-rate auto man. I knew him when he was a super engineer for Pontiac and later when he was the top guy at the Chevrolet Division. We were great competitors, going at it head-to-head. When I was on the cover of *Time* in 1964 for the Mustang, he used to kid me: "Why did you make the cover of *Time*, and not me with the GTO?" In 1982, when he made the cover of *Time* for his alleged part in the drug bust, I thought: "Well, John, you finally made it." I felt bad for him, because he had more than enough talent to get there the right way.

After the merger idea didn't pan out, John came to see me again. This time he wanted me to consider an R&D tax shelter, which became known as a "DeLorean Shelter." This project, which he had masterminded with a couple of his associates, got a lot of publicity in *Fortune*. It involved selling off limited partnerships, which are then written off against the government.

He thought Chrysler should go that route, and he had prepared a huge study for me that cost him something like fifty or sixty thousand dollars. I said: "John, I appreciate it. But even if it worked"—and it might have worked in a modest way—"the IRS would flip if I took them for a couple of billion dollars." That's one shelter that would be thrown out—because of sheer size.

Finally, after many more meetings with possible saviors, we ran out of alternatives. And that's when we finally went to the government. But our approach to Washington did not begin with a request for loan guarantees.

Like me, John Riccardo was getting more frantic by the day. Technically he was still the chairman, although he was on his way out and I was running the company. Riccardo could see that we were going down the tubes in a hurry unless something happened soon. That's when *he* started traveling to Washington.

First he tried to line up congressional support for a two-year freeze on government regulations. That way we could spend our money on new fuel-efficient cars instead of squeezing the very last gram of hydrocarbons out of the tailpipe. But nobody in Washington would listen.

Riccardo had the right approach. Although many of Chrysler's problems were the direct result of bad management, the government had to share at least part of the blame for our situation. After setting some tough, ill-considered regulations for automotive safety and emission controls, it then said to the American automakers: "You guys aren't allowed to get together for joint research and development on these problems. You each have to do it on your own." Mind you, Japan was pursuing the opposite strategy. Since they didn't have to conform to U.S. antitrust laws, they could pool all their genius.

Now, we can do some pretty dumb things in Washington when we work at it. Regulated items should not be competitive. If one of the companies develops a more effective, more efficient, less costly way of controlling emissions, it should be shared. I don't mean the company has to give it away. Let them sell the thing.

But until recently, we couldn't talk about it in the same room without going to jail. We couldn't even hear General Motors describe its system. We literally had to get up and leave, or we'd be guilty under the consent decree by which all of us were operating.

As I write these words, Washington is finally starting to change its tune. It's getting the message that our antitrust laws have been too severe and that we can't be competitive with the Japanese until those laws are reconstituted. Unfortunately, the government's new attitude seems to be starting with a marriage between Toyota and General Motors, the two giants of the industry. We need that like a hole in the head.

At any rate, because of the antitrust laws, General Motors, Ford, American Motors, and Chrysler each had to set up, staff, and finance separate facilities to work on the same problems—problems whose solutions would be of no economic benefit to any of us.

Ever since the Motor Vehicle Safety Act of 1966, all the various gadgets and devices designed to protect motorists from hurting each other came to a cost of around $19 *billion*. General Motors can spread that cost over five million cars a year. Ford spreads it over two and a half million, and Chrysler over about a million.

You don't need a calculator to see that if GM's expenses on a particular item were $1 million and they sold a hundred thousand cars, each buyer paid an additional $10. And if Chrysler's costs were the same but we had only twenty thousand buyers, each one would pay an additional $50.

But that's only for research and development. Then we have to *manufacture* the stuff. Here the same disproportion applies, except with larger numbers. GM, with its huge sales volume, can build them cheaper and sell them cheaper than we can. And so the gap widens.

Another factor that slowed us down was the sheer volume of staff time and paperwork necessary to report on our EPA regulatory confirmations. In 1978 alone we had to file 228,000 pages to the EPA!

There are any number of studies by widely respected economic institutions that prove beyond a shadow of a doubt that the application of the government's safety, emission, and environmental controls on automobiles and trucks is discriminatory and retrogressive. That's why both Riccardo and I came to the same conclusion. The government helped get us into this mess, so the government should be willing to help get us out.

But Riccardo's proposal for a freeze on regulations fell on deaf ears. At that point he began to lobby for a refundable tax credit. According to this plan, the money we spent on meeting government safety and pollution standards would be refunded to us, dollar for dollar. The total amount came to $1 billion—$500 million in 1979, and another $500 million in 1980. We would repay the debt from higher taxes on our future earnings.

We would not have been the first to ask. In 1967, American Motors had received a special tax credit of $22 million. Volkswagen had received a tax break of $40 million from the state of Pennsylvania in order to set up a plant there. Oklahoma had recently provided tax relief for General Motors. Renault, which is wholly owned by the government of France, had just been given a loan of $135 million for the assembly of new cars in an American Motors plant in Wisconsin. Michigan and Illinois have been known to engage in bidding wars to compete for new business. The city of Detroit has itself given tax relief to Chrysler. And in a number of European countries, American car companies routinely receive outright grants and subsidies from the host government.

Riccardo proposed that companies should get some tax benefits while they're in a loss position. When you're losing money, you can't write anything off. Everything costs you more, from air bags to robots. With all the government regulations to contend with, as well as the energy crisis, the guy in a loss position was really getting a raw deal.

Riccardo went down to Washington to try to get some congressional action, but once more they threw him out. He was a good fellow, but he wasn't an effective communicator. He had a short fuse and a hot temper, and those qualities don't get you very far in the halls of Congress.

John knew there was no viable alternative to government help. We were losing money, and we weren't cutting our overhead fast enough. Volume was going to hell due to the international oil crisis. And because gas prices had just doubled, we had to switch over to front-wheel-drive and high-fuel-efficiency cars in a big hurry. Chrysler had to commit $100 million a month—$1.2 billion a year—just to provide for the future.

Moreover, every Friday we had to come up with $250 million to meet the payroll and pay for the parts we had bought the previous week. It didn't take much foresight to realize where we were headed.

On August 6, 1979, G. William Miller left his position as chairman of the Federal Reserve Board to become secretary of the treasury. It was an important move. As head of the Fed, Miller had told Riccardo that Chrysler should go into bankruptcy rather than approach the government for help. But in his new position, Miller apparently changed his mind. His first official act was to announce that he favored government support for Chrysler as being in the public interest. Miller rejected the idea of tax credits. But he said that the Carter administration would be willing to consider loan guarantees if we submitted an overall plan for our survival.

Only then did we decide to ask for a loan guarantee. Even so, we went through some pretty tough soul-searching in Highland Park.

Sperlich in particular was dead set against it. He was convinced that government involvement would ruin the company, and I wasn't sure he was wrong. But I didn't see any other option. "Fine," I said. "You don't want to go to the government? Neither do I. Show me a better way out."

But there wasn't any. Someone else brought up the case of British Leyland, the English car company. When they went to the government, it destroyed people's confidence in the company. Their market share was cut in half, and they never recovered. It wasn't an encouraging precedent, but there was no other choice except bankruptcy. And bankruptcy was no choice at all.

With great reluctance, we decided to proceed with an application for government loan guarantees.

I knew that this proposal would be highly controversial, so I made sure I did my homework. I found that there were a number of precedents for what we were asking. In 1971, Lockheed Aircraft had received $250 million in federally guaranteed loans after Congress decided to save its workers and suppliers. Congress established a loan-guarantee board to oversee the operation, and Lockheed repaid its loans, including an additional $31 million in fees, to the federal treasury. The city of New York had also received guaranteed loans, and it, too, was still in business. But these were merely the best-known examples.

Loan guarantees, I soon learned, were as American as apple pie. Among those who had received them were electric companies, farmers, railroads, chemical companies, shipbuilders, small-businessmen of every description, college students, and airlines.

In fact, a total of $409 billion in loans and loan guarantees was outstanding when we made our $1 billion request. But nobody knew this. They all said that loan guarantees to Chrysler would set a dangerous precedent.

Over and over, I told editors and reporters about the $409 billion in previous loan guarantees—it's now grown to more than $500 billion. Setting a precedent? On the contrary. We were only following the crowd.

Who had received all those guaranteed loans? Five steel companies under the Import Relief Act of 1974, including $111 million to Jones & Laughlin alone. More recently, the Wheeling-Pittsburgh Steel Corporation had been granted $150 million in loan guarantees for plant modernization and the installation of antipollution equipment.

Then there's the housing industry. And subsidies for tobacco farmers. And loans for keeping up our marine freight capability—the maritime industry literally floats on government subsidies. Loans for airlines, such as People Express. Loans from the Farmers Home Administration, the Export-Import Bank, and the Commodity Credit Corporation. Loans guaranteed by the Farmers Home Administration, the Small Business Administration, and the Department of Health and Human Services.

There were even loan guarantees for the Washington subway. The Metro had received $1 billion so that senators, congressmen, and their aides could get around town better.

Up on Capitol Hill, they didn't like it when I talked about that one. But I don't think they'll ever see that money again.

"Let's face it," I said. "The subway is just a showpiece for the capital."

"Showpiece?" they said. "This is a transportation system!"

"Fine," I replied. "What the hell do you think Chrysler is?"

But nobody seemed to remember these other loan guarantees. At least the media should have reported that side of the story. Even today, most people are surprised to learn that our case wasn't totally without precedent.

To be honest, when I was president of Ford, I don't think I would have listened to these arguments either. I probably would have said to Chrysler: "Leave the government out of this. I believe in survival of the fittest. Let the marginal guy go broke."

Back then I had a very different view of the world. But if I had known about some of the guaranteed loans that never got much publicity and if I had followed the arguments in the great national debate that accompanied our approach to Congress, I might have come to see things another way. At any rate, I'd like to think so.

To anyone who would listen, I continually stressed that Chrysler wasn't an isolated case. Instead, we were a microcosm of what was going wrong in America and a kind of test lab for everybody else. No industry in the world got hit harder than autos. Government regulation, the energy crisis, and the recession were almost enough to put us away.

As the weakest link in the chain, Chrysler got hit first. But what happened to us, as I explained again and again, represented only the tip of the iceberg when it came to the problems facing American industry. I predicted flatly that GM and Ford would soon join us in the loss column. (I didn't know they'd join us to the tune of $5 billion. But they did. Within six months they were in the ditch to keep us company.)

What I had to say wasn't what people wanted to hear. It was so much easier to find a scapegoat. And who was a better candidate than the tenth-largest industrial corporation in America—a corporation that had the nerve to approach its own government for help?

XVIII

SHOULD CHRYSLER
BE SAVED?

F rom the very start, the prospect of government-backed loans for Chrysler was opposed by just about everybody. Predictably, the greatest outcry came from the business community. Most business leaders came out strongly against the plan, and many of them went public with their views, including Tom Murphy of General Motors and Walter Wriston of Citicorp.

For most of them, federal help for Chrysler constituted a sacrilege, a heresy, a repudiation of the religion of corporate America. The aphorisms started flowing like water as all the old clichés got dusted off. Ours is a profit-and-loss system. Liquidations and closedowns are the healthy catharsis of an efficient market. A loan guarantee violates the spirit of free enterprise. It rewards failure. It weakens the discipline of the marketplace. Water seeks its own level. Survival of the fittest. Don't change the rules in the middle of the game. A society without risk is a society without reward. Failure is to capitalism what hell is to Christianity. Laissez-faire forever. And other assorted bullshit!

The National Association of Manufacturers came out strongly against federal loan guarantees. And at its meeting on November 13, 1979, the policy committee of the Business Roundtable approved the following statement on the Chrysler situation:

A fundamental premise of the market system is that it allows for both failure and success, for loss as well as profit. Whatever the hardships of failure may be for particular companies and individuals, the broad social and economic interests of the nation are best served by allowing this system to operate as freely and fully as possible.

The consequences of failure and reorganization under the revised statutes [bankruptcy, in other words], while serious, are not unthinkable. The loss of jobs and production would be far from total. Under reorganization, the many viable components of the business could be expected to operate more effectively while other elements might be sold off to other producers. It is at this stage that a better case can be made for targeted Federal assistance to deal with any resulting social problems.

At a time when government, business, and the public are becoming more and more aware of the costs and inefficiencies of government intervention in the economy, it would be highly inappropriate to recommend a course of even deeper involvement. Now is the time to reaffirm the principle of "no federal bailouts."

This statement made me furious. I tried to find out exactly who in the group had voted for it, but everybody I checked with seemed to have been out of town at the time. Nobody wanted to take responsibility for zapping us.

In reply, I sent the following letter:

Gentlemen:

I was deeply disturbed to learn that on the same day I testified in Washington on behalf of Chrysler Corporation's request for loan guarantees, the Business Roundtable, of which Chrysler is a member, issued a press release against "federal bailouts."

I have several observations to make.

First—the basic charter of the Roundtable is to contain inflation. Its goals have since been extended to a discussion of other economic issues of national importance. These discussions have traditionally taken place in an open and free atmosphere in which all points of view are considered. The fact that we did not have an opportunity to present the facts of the Chrysler case to the members of the Policy Committee runs directly counter to that tradition.

Second—it is ironic that the Roundtable took no similar position on federal loan guarantees to steel companies, to shipbuilders, to airlines, to farmers, and to the housing industry. Nor did it protest the establishment of "trigger prices" on foreign steel, or the provisions for federal assistance to American Motors.

Third—the Roundtable statement invokes the principles of the free market system which "allows for both failure and success." It totally ignores the fact that government regulatory intrusion into the system has contributed greatly to Chrysler's problem. It is in fact entirely consistent with the workings of a free market system for the government to offset some of the adverse effects of federal regulation. Federal loan guarantees to steel companies were made precisely for that reason.

Fourth—the Roundtable statement is wrong in its declaration that reorganization under the new bankruptcy statute is practical. Our need is not to scale down debt, but to raise huge amounts of new capital. It would be impossible for us to raise the necessary amounts of capital during a bankruptcy proceeding. We have consulted with one of the nation's leading experts on bankruptcy, Mr. J. Ronald Trost, of Shutan and Trost, whose analysis of the new law led him to testify that bankruptcy is not practical for Chrysler and would lead quickly to liquidation.

Your own Roundtable staff has indicated that no bankruptcy experts were consulted during the preparation of your statement. If they had been, I feel sure the statements would have been considerably less confident on the subject of the virtues of bankruptcy.

Fifth—it is most unfortunate that the Roundtable has chosen to engage in sloganeering in this campaign. To proclaim a policy of "no federal bailouts" in a press release is to reduce the discussion to its lowest level. The hundreds of thousands of workers across the country who depend on Chrysler for employment deserve far better in the debate over their future.

Finally, I believe my acceptance of your current invitation to become a member of the Roundtable would be a source of embarrassment to the other members. I had looked forward to joining a business forum that openly discusses vital economic and social issues in an atmosphere of mutual trust and respect. The Roundtable's press release indicates that such an opportunity does not exist in the Policy Committee. Therefore, please accept my sincere regrets and the resignation of Chrysler Corporation from Business Roundtable membership.

That was what I told the Business Roundtable. This is what I would have *liked* to tell them: "You guys are supposed to be the business elite of this country. But you're a bunch of hypocrites. Your group was founded by some steel guys who've spent their whole lives trying to screw the government. Remember President Kennedy blowing his cool with Big Steel and calling them a bunch of SOBs? You're against federal help for Chrysler? Where were you when loan guarantees were made available for steel companies, shipbuilders, and airlines? Why didn't you speak up about trigger prices on foreign steel? I guess it depends on whose ox is being gored!"

In all these prior cases, the Business Roundtable had been silent. But when I came in asking for federal loan guarantees, they put out a manifesto! As long as it benefits them, they really don't object to a little government interference. But when it comes to saving Chrysler, they suddenly stand on principle.

Even some of our major suppliers joined in the chorus of gloom. We were isolated, captives of an outmoded ideology.

Let me be clear where I stand. Free-enterprise capitalism is the best economic system the world has ever seen. I'm 100 percent in favor of it. All things being equal, it's the only way to go.

But what happens when all things are *not* equal? What happens when the real-life causes of a company's problems are not determined by free enterprise but by its opposite? What happens when one company—because of the industry it's in and because of its size—is driven into the ground by the unequal effects of government regulation?

That's what happened to Chrysler. Certainly, past management errors were a big part of the problem. Chrysler never should have built all its products on speculation. It shouldn't have tried to expand overseas. It never should have been in the used-car business. It should have paid more attention to quality.

But what ultimately brought the company to its knees was the relentless lash of more and more government regulation.

I had a week of hell in Congress trying to explain that.

They kept saying: "Why do you keep coming down here and crying, 'Regulation!'?"

I said: "Because you guys made the regulations, but you're pointing the finger at us."

Then they would turn around and say: "It was stupid management."

Finally I'd had enough. "Okay," I told them, "let's stop this
crap. It's fifty percent your fault—regulation—and fifty percent our
fault, because I know all the management sins. What do you want me
to do? Crucify the guys who aren't here? They made mistakes. Now
let's get back to the matter at hand: you guys helped us get into this
mess!"

Why is our free-enterprise system so strong? Not because it stands
still, frozen in the past, but because it has always adapted to changing
realities. I'm a great advocate of free enterprise, but that doesn't mean
I live in the nineteenth century. The fact is that free enterprise no
longer means exactly what it used to.

First, the free-enterprise system adapted to the industrial revolution.
In 1890, it adapted to Samuel Gompers and the labor movement.
The corporate executives all fought against the new movement, but
they were the ones who were really responsible for it. They had set up
the sweatshops, kept small children working all day at the sewing
tables, and created a hundred other injustices that needed to be
corrected.

If you go back and read the history books, you'll see that the
businessmen of that era were convinced that the new labor unions
spelled the end of free enterprise. They thought capitalism was finished and that the specter of socialism in America lurked just around
the corner.

But they were completely wrong. They failed to understand that
free enterprise is flexible and organic. Free enterprise adapted to the
labor movement. And the labor movement adapted to free enterprise—so
well, in fact, that in some industries labor has become almost as
successful and as powerful as management.

Free enterprise also survived the Great Depression. Here, too,
our business leaders thought it was the end of the road for capitalism.
They were furious when Franklin Roosevelt decided to create work for
people who had lost their jobs. But while the business leaders were
only theorizing, F.D.R. was playing with live ammunition. He did
what had to be done. And when he was finished, the system was
stronger and more successful than ever.

Whenever I praise F.D.R., I hear the business leaders mumbling:
"Iacocca's a turncoat. He's lost his mind. He *loves* F.D.R." But they

forget where they'd be without his amazing vision. F.D.R. was fifty years ahead of his time. The SEC and the FDIC are just two of the agencies he set up to prevent the terrible things that happen when business cycles go haywire.

These days, free enterprise has to make further adjustments. This time, it has to adapt to a new world—a world which now includes a formidable rival, Japan, and a world where nobody else is playing by the rules of pure laissez-faire.

While all these ideological arguments were raging, the nation's tenth-largest corporation was falling apart. Obviously, that's not the time to talk ideology. When the wolf is at the door, you get pragmatic in a big hurry.

You certainly don't have the luxury of saying: "Now, wait a minute. I wonder how they would argue this one down at the Union League Club in Philadelphia? What would they say: Free enterprise forever!"

But what is free enterprise really about? Competition. And competition was something the loan guarantees stood to provide a lot more of. Why? Because they would guarantee that Chrysler would still be around to compete with GM and Ford.

Competition is something that the auto industry both needs and understands. During the great debate over the future of Chrysler, a Ford dealer wrote a letter to *The New York Times*: "For the past twenty-five years, I have been a competitor of Chrysler. Yet I take basic issue with the editorials you have written against Chrysler's request for Federal assistance. . . . The proper role of the federal government in a democratic free-enterprise system is not to aid the survival of the fattest [sic], but to preserve competition. If Chrysler fails, as the industry strains to reinvent the automobile more quickly than anyone expected, can Ford be far behind?"

Another dealer, in Oregon—this time for Chevrolet—ran a full-page ad in his hometown paper with the headline, "If we can't sell you a Chevrolet or a Honda, buy a Chrysler!" The ad went on to say: "Competition is good for us, good for the industry, good for the country, and good for you, the consumer."

In addition to preserving competition, saving Chrysler would also preserve jobs—lots of them. Altogether, counting our workers, dealers, and suppliers, six hundred thousand jobs were at stake.

Some people believed that if we went under, our workers could have found positions with Ford and General Motors. But that wasn't the case. At the time, both Ford and GM were selling just about all the small cars they could manufacture. It wasn't as if they had empty factories and were looking for additional workers to fill them. If Chrysler folded, almost all our workers would have been unemployed.

Only the imports could have met America's sudden and insatiable demand for small cars. And so if Chrysler went under, America wouldn't only be importing more small cars. We would also be exporting jobs.

We were asking: "Would this country really be better off if Chrysler folded and the nation's unemployment rate went up another half of one percent overnight? Would free enterprise really be served if Chrysler failed and tens of thousands of American jobs were lost to the Japanese? Would our free-market system really be more competitive without the million-plus cars and trucks that Chrysler builds and sells each year?"

We went to the government and we said: "If it makes sense to have a safety net for individuals, it makes sense to have a safety net for their companies. Work, after all, is what keeps individuals alive."

So we argued about competition and we argued about jobs. But most important of all were our arguments about economics. Quite simply, we bottom-lined them. The Treasury Department had estimated that if Chrysler collapsed, it would cost the country $2.7 billion during the first year alone in unemployment insurance and welfare payments due to all the layoffs.

I said to the Congress: "You guys have a choice. Do you want to pay the $2.7 billion now, or do you want to guarantee loans of half that amount with a good chance of getting it all back? You can pay now or you can pay later."

That's the kind of argument that causes people to sit up and take notice. And it brings up an important lesson for young people who may be reading this book—*always* think in terms of the other person's interests. I guess that's my Dale Carnegie training, and it's served me well.

In this case, I had to talk in terms of the representative sitting in Congress. On ideological grounds, he might be against helping us. But he sure changed his mind fast after we did our homework and provided a district-by-district breakdown of all the Chrysler-related jobs and businesses in his state. When he realized how many people in his constituency depended upon Chrysler for their living, it was farewell, ideology.

While the battle was being fought in and out of Congress, I was busy doing everything I could to raise money, including selling debentures to other companies. I felt like a rug merchant who needed to raise some cash in a hurry. And my spirits were low because wherever I turned, there was nobody saying: "Give it a go, you can make it."

During the debate, the bankruptcy "solution" for Chrysler was very popular. Under Chapter 11 of the Federal Bankruptcy Act, we'd be protected against our creditors until we got our house in order. A few years later, we would supposedly emerge as a smaller but healthier company.

But when we called in all kinds of experts, they told us, as we already knew, that in our case bankruptcy would be catastrophic. Our situation was unique. It wasn't like Penn Central. It wasn't like Lockheed. It wasn't like dealing with the government on defense contracts they've already given you. And it wasn't like the cereal business. If Kellogg's were known to be going out of business, nobody would say: "Well, I won't buy their corn flakes today. What if I get stuck with a box of cereal and there's nobody around to service it?"

But cars are different. Just the whisper of bankruptcy would shut off the cash flow to the company. We'd see a domino effect. Customers would cancel their orders. They'd worry about future warranty coverage and the availability of parts and service—not to mention the resale value of the car.

Here there was an instructive precedent. When the White Truck Company declared bankruptcy, they thought they could strong-arm their lenders by hiding under the rules of Chapter 11. Technically it might have worked. Except for one problem. Every one of their customers said: "Oh, no, they've gone bankrupt! I think I'll buy somebody else's truck."

Some of the banks wanted us to go that route. "What are you messing around with the government for? Go declare bankruptcy, and run your company out of bankruptcy." They'd give us examples of other companies that had done that. But we kept saying: "Look, we're a major consumer company in a consumer industry. We wouldn't survive for two weeks trying that."

In a bankruptcy, our dealers would lose their ability to finance purchases from the factory. Nearly all dealer vehicle financing would be shut off within a day or two by the banks and the finance companies. We estimated that about half our dealers would themselves be forced into bankruptcy. Many others would be recruited by GM and Ford, leaving us without outlets in major markets.

Suppliers would demand payment in advance—or on a COD

basis. Most of our suppliers are small businesses with fewer than five hundred employees. The strain of a Chrysler bankruptcy would be impossible for thousands of small companies who depended on us for their very existence. Many of them, too, would have to declare bankruptcy, which in turn would deprive us of essential parts.

And forget about Chrysler. What would the largest bankruptcy in American history have done to the nation? A study by Data Resources estimated that the demise of Chrysler would ultimately cost the taxpayers $16 billion in unemployment, welfare, and other expenses.

So much for the bankruptcy option.

During the national debate over Chrysler's future, everybody was taking potshots at us. Writing in *The New York Times*, columnist Tom Wicker said that Chrysler should suddenly devote its energies to building mass transit instead of automobiles. Editorial cartoonists had a marvelous time with the story that Chrysler was asking the government for help.

But *The Wall Street Journal* was particularly relentless. They went crazy on the subject of loan guarantees, which they called, in a memorable editorial headline, "Laetrile for Chrysler."

Their objections to government help for Chrysler went far beyond the editorial pages. They just wouldn't leave us alone. They duly reported every single item of bad news but neglected to report any of the more hopeful signs. Even after we had received the loan guarantees, they pointed out that although we had enough money, although we had a restructured company, although we had new management, the right product, and great quality, lightning *could* strike. The economy *could* get worse. Car sales *could* be even lousier.

It seemed that almost every day the *Journal* would run a negative article about the Chrysler situation. And whenever that happened, we'd have to spend some of our limited energy trying to control the damage to public opinion.

For example, in the first quarter of 1981, Ford lost $439 million. Chrysler was improving but we still lost close to $300 million. What was the *Journal*'s headline? "Ford Has Narrower-Than-Expected Loss While Chrysler's Is Wider Than Forecast." That was the only way you could possibly write a headline that made us look worse than Ford. The numbers just didn't support it.

A couple of months later, our monthly sales showed a 51 percent gain over the previous year. But the *Journal* felt compelled to point out that "the comparison is distorted, however, because Chrysler's year-earlier sales had plunged to rock-bottom levels." Fine. But the previous year, do you think the *Journal* had excused our low sales by statements to the effect that business had been great the year before?

It reminds me of an old Jewish joke. Goldberg gets a call from the bank that his account is overdrawn by $400.

"Look up last month's statement," he says.

"You had a balance of nine hundred dollars," says the bank official.

"And the month before that?" says Goldberg.

"Twelve hundred dollars."

"And the month before that?"

"Fifteen hundred."

"Tell me," says Goldberg. "All those other months, when I had plenty of money in my account—did I call *you?*"

That's how I felt about *The Wall Street Journal.*

In college, as one of the editors of the school paper, I had learned firsthand how much power the headline writer has. Since most people don't read the whole story unless they're especially interested in the subject, for the majority, the headline *is* the story.

In the middle of the loan guarantee crisis, after we had borrowed only part of what we were entitled to under law, the *Journal* ran an editorial suggesting that Chrysler be "put out of its misery." It was their now-famous "Let Them Die With Dignity" editorial, which should go down in history as a classic—if only as an example of how abusive freedom of the press can get in this country. I know, I know, the First Amendment guarantees them that right.

I was furious. I fired off a letter to the editor in which I said: "In effect, you have announced that because the patient has not yet been restored to full health by the ingestion of half the prescribed medicine, he should be put to death. I'm grateful you are not my family physician."

I think *The Wall Street Journal* is living in the last century. Unfortunately, it's the only game in town. The *Journal* is a monopoly and it's become arrogant, like General Motors.

Incidentally, the *Journal's* snipings didn't stop when Chrysler recovered. On July 13, 1983, I announced at the National Press Club that we would repay all of our government-backed loans by the end of the year. Two days later, *The New York Times*—which had opposed the loan guarantees—ran a story called "Chrysler's Sharp Turnaround." According to the article, "It is hard to overstate the magnitude of the turnaround. . . . How was it possible to turn such a desperately sick company around so quickly?"

That same day, *The Wall Street Journal* also ran a big story about Chrysler. Its headline? "Chrysler, Having Cut Muscle as Well as Fat, Is Still in a Weak State." Could there be any doubt that the *Journal* carries a bias? They have a right to their opinions, but opinions belong on the editorial page. They could at least have said something like: "It's too bad they had to do it *this* way, but what a great job Chrysler's done!"

With that kind of coverage in the nation's business press, it's not surprising that so much of the public had trouble understanding what was really going on.

A big part of the problem was the language being used to describe our situation. "Bailout" is a colorful metaphor. It conjures up images of a leaky boat foundering in rough seas. It implies that the crew was inadequate. At least "bailout" is a better phrase than "handout," which was also being tossed around. We didn't ask for any free gifts, and we sure didn't get any.

One popular view was that we were a big, monolithic company that didn't deserve help. To counter this myth, we explained that we're really an amalgam of little guys. We're an assembly company. We have eleven thousand suppliers and four thousand dealers. Almost all of these people are small-businessmen, not fat cats. We needed a helping hand—not a handout.

Many people didn't even know *that*. They thought we were asking for a gift. They seemed to think that Jimmy Carter sent me a get-well card with $1 billion in laundered tens and twenties tucked inside. Many well-intentioned Americans were apparently under the impression that Chrysler had received $1 billion in cash in a brown paper bag and that we never had to pay it back.

If only it were true!

XIX

CHRYSLER GOES
TO CONGRESS

To say the least, testifying before congressional and Senate committees has never been my idea of fun and games. Believe me, it was the last thing in the world I ever wanted to do. But if we had even the slightest chance of getting Congress to approve the loan guarantees, I knew I would have to appear in person to state our case. No delegating this time!

The Senate and House hearing rooms are designed to intimidate the witness. The committee members sit at a semicircular table a couple of feet above the floor, looking down. The witness is at a real psychological disadvantage, because he's always looking up at the questioner. And to make matters worse, there are those television lights in your eyes.

I was referred to as the witness, but that's a misnomer. In reality, I was the defendant. Hour after hour I had to sit in the box and go on trial before Congress and the press for all of Chrysler's so-called sins of management—both real and imagined.

At times it was like a kangaroo court. The ideologues lined up and said: "We don't care what you're saying. We want to break you." I was on my own in those hearings. I had to ad-lib everything. The questions came fast and furious, and they were always loaded. Staff members were constantly passing notes to the senators and congressmen, and I had to respond to everything off the cuff. It was murder.

We were scolded for not having the foresight of the clever Japanese to build cars that get thirty miles per gallon, even though the

American consumer had continually demanded bigger cars. We were lectured for not being prepared for the overthrow of the Shah of Iran. I had to point out that neither Carter, Kissinger, David Rockefeller, nor the State Department had anticipated that event, although they were all far better informed than I on these matters.

We were excoriated for not having prepared for the screwed-up fuel allocation system devised by the Department of Energy and for the subsequent riots at the gas pumps. Never mind that gas had been sixty-five cents a gallon one month earlier. Never mind that its price had been artificially depressed because of government price controls, which sent precisely the wrong signals to the American consumer. Never mind that we were investing the bulk of our capital in meeting government regulations. In the minds of Congress and the media, we had sinned. We had missed the market, and we deserved to be punished.

And punished we were. During the congressional hearings, we were held up before the entire world as living examples of everything that was wrong with American industry. We were humiliated on the editorial pages for not having the decency to give up and die gracefully. We were the object of scorn by the nation's cartoonists, who couldn't wait to paint us into the grave. Our wives and kids were the butt of jokes in shopping malls and schools. It was a far higher price to pay than just closing the doors and walking away. It was personal. It was pointed. And it was painful.

On October 18, I made my first appearance before the House Subcommittee on Economic Stabilization of the Committee of Banking, Finance, and Urban Affairs. All of the members showed up, which in itself was unusual. Normally, hearings are held without most of the members, who always have a dozen other commitments at the same time. The real work is usually done by the congressional staff.

I began my testimony by stating our case very simply: "I am sure you know that I do not speak alone here today. I speak for the hundreds of thousands of people whose livelihood depends on Chrysler remaining in business. It is that simple. Our one hundred forty thousand employees and their dependents, our forty-seven hundred dealers and their one hundred fifty thousand employees who sell and service our products, our nineteen thousand suppliers, and the two hundred fifty thousand people on their payrolls, and, of course, the families and dependents of all those constituents."

Because there was so much confusion about what kind of help

we were asking for, I made it clear that we were not requesting a handout. We were not asking for any.gifts. I reminded the committee that we were petitioning for the guarantee of a loan, every last dollar of which would be repaid—with interest.

In my opening statement, I outlined seven essential points to the committee. First, our problems were due to a combination of bad management, excessive regulation, the energy crisis, and the recession. We had completely changed our management, but the other three factors were beyond our control.

Second, we had already taken prompt and decisive steps to solve our problems. We had sold off our marginal assets. We had raised a significant amount of new money. We had reduced our fixed costs by almost $600 million a year. We had lowered the salaries of our top seventeen hundred executives. We'd suspended all merit pay increases. We had cut out our employee stock purchase plan. We had eliminated the dividend on our common stock. We had gained new and important commitments from our suppliers, our bankers, our dealers, and our workers, as well as state and local governments.

Third, in order to remain profitable, we had to remain a full-line producer of cars and light trucks. We could not survive as a one-product company. We could not stay in business and manufacture only small cars. The profit margins on subcompact cars are about $700 each, which was not enough to keep us in business—not with the Japanese enjoying low labor rates and favorable tax advantages.

Fourth, we would not be able to survive a bankruptcy.

Fifth, we had no offers to merge with other companies, either American or foreign. And unless we received the loan guarantees, it wasn't likely that anyone was going to ask us to dance.

Sixth, despite our reputation for building gas-guzzlers, Chrysler already had the best average fuel economy of the Big Three. We offered more models with at least twenty-five miles per gallon than GM, Ford, Toyota, Datsun, or Honda.

Finally, I asserted that our operating plan for the next five years was sound and that it was based on conservative assumptions. We knew that we could improve our market share and soon become profitable once again.

Later in the hearing I elaborated on each of these points in much greater detail.

The questions and the accusations were endless. Some of the committee members just could not get it through their heads that Chrysler was now under new management. Not surprisingly, most of them didn't want to consider the real costs of federal regulation. So they continually pointed a finger at the mistakes made by the previous management team and asked me to defend them.

CONGRESSMAN SHUMWAY OF CALIFORNIA: "My concern is what assurances can you give this subcommittee and give the government that you are not going to repeat the mistakes of yesteryear? You assert that some of the fallacies that have pervaded management in the company now have been resolved and you are on your way toward profitability. I frankly do not see the kind of answers that would really convince me that that is the case."

MR. IACOCCA: "Congressman, I couldn't convince you. You will have to take my word for it. I put together a new team at Chrysler. They are the best automobile men in the United States, in my opinion. We have got a track record. We have been through all that. We know how to build small cars. We have been at it for thirty years and we're saying we can do it. That is all we can say to you. You go on track records, you go on experience. We offer ours up to you. That is all I can say."

MR. SHUMWAY: "The track record of Chrysler is not what you're relying on today to persuade us."

MR. IACOCCA: "People make companies. I think we are doing enough to help ourselves. You just watch us. You will see a lot of action at Chrysler. You will see better cars and you will see better service and better quality. And that, in the end, is all that is going to matter."

Everybody was looking for a scapegoat, but I refused to blame the previous Chrysler administration for all our problems. After all, during the third quarter of 1979, the Ford Motor Company had lost $678 million. Even GM had a third-quarter loss of $300 million. What about those numbers? We couldn't have *all* gotten stupid at the same time! Obviously there had to be other, more compelling reasons for these unprecedented losses. And so I talked a great deal about regulation.

And I talked about the common misconception that Chrysler built gas-guzzlers rather than fuel-efficient small cars. I pointed out that Chrysler was the first American producer of small, front-wheel-drive cars, ahead of both GM and Ford. At the time of my testimony, there were more than half a million Omnis and Horizons on the road—more small, front-wheel-drive cars than any other American manufacturer could offer. Moreover, the new K-car was due out within the year.

No, I explained, the problem wasn't that we had too many gas-guzzlers. In reality, we didn't have *enough*. Big cars are where the profits are, for the same reason that in a butcher shop there's a bigger markup on steak than on hamburger.

I said that General Motors makes 70 percent of all the big cars, including Cadillac Sevilles, which sell at a profit of $5,500 a pop. We had nothing to compare. To make as much money as GM did on one Seville, we had to sell eight Omnis or Horizons. Moreover, GM is the price leader. They're not going to raise their prices on small cars by $1,000 just so Chrysler can break even.

I talked about all these things and more. But when I look back on the hearings, it's other voices I hear. I vividly remember Congressman Richard Kelly from Florida, our most outspoken opponent. He began by saying: "I think that you are trying to put a con on us. I think that you have made your presentation in the open market, and the people out there, acting on a voluntary basis—not the people of the quality you see sitting up here, but the kings of industry that really know how to make the thing hum—they have told you to get lost.

"And they told you to get lost because, in the same conditions in which they survived, you could not make it. So now you are coming here, and you are expecting this bunch of dummies here on this subcommittee to fall for this baloney about human suffering."

Kelly was smart. He manipulated the media by using the right words to titillate people on the evening news. He lashed out at us again and again. "The Chrysler bailout will be the beginning of a new era of irresponsibility in government. The Chrysler bailout is a rip-off of the American worker, American industry, and the taxpayer and consumer. The Chrysler charity is the most blatant con job in our time."

Kelly lectured us about how Chrysler had failed to compete. He repeatedly urged us to declare bankruptcy and opposed federal loan guarantees in every way, shape, and form.

A couple of years later, by the way, Congressman Kelly, the great defender of the American way of life, was convicted twice in the Abscam affair and sentenced to a term in jail. He lost the election, and went out in disrepute. Poetic justice!

*   *   *

Kelly wasn't our only opponent. In the midst of the debate, Congressman David Stockman, from our own Michigan delegation, wrote a major article for the *Washington Post Magazine* entitled "Let Chrysler Go Broke." A few weeks earlier, he had written a piece for *The Wall Street Journal* called "Chrysler Bailout: Rewarding Failure?" Stockman, who later became the budget director, was the only member of the Michigan delegation to vote against us. He was a former divinity student, but I guess he was playing hooky the day they learned about compassion.

Fortunately, not everybody was hostile. Stewart McKinney, the ranking minority member on the committee, was very supportive. Here I got a break, as McKinney was a friend whom I knew from my days at Ford. As a Republican from a silk stocking district in Connecticut, he took a lot of flak from his more doctrinaire colleagues.

McKinney favored us from the beginning, mostly because the alternative to federal help was so bad. His position was: "I know autos, and I know what this guy did at Ford. He'll make it work." At one point in the hearings, he said: "If you do for Chrysler what you did for Ford, we're going to have to put up a statue."

To which I thought: "And you know what happens to statues— the pigeons shit all over them!"

McKinney had done his homework, which is more than I can say for some of his colleagues. Henry Reuss, chairman of the House Banking Committee, proposed at one point that Chrysler ought to be building railroad cars! We couldn't afford to maintain the facilities we had, but this guy thought we should be getting into a whole new line of vehicles. This little project would have entailed an investment of a couple of billion dollars—at a time when we were already broke.

Our other big supporter on the subcommittee was Michigan Congressman Jim Blanchard, author of the loan guarantee bill, who later went on to become governor of Michigan. Blanchard was the number two Democrat on the committee, and he and McKinney were a great team.

Tip O'Neill was our real point man in the Congress. Early on, I had a meeting with him to explain our position. He listened carefully, and he understood what he heard. As soon as he turned on his lights to help us, the tide started to turn.

Tip set up a Speaker's task force, a group of about thirty who lobbied their colleagues. There was also a small ad hoc support group on the Republican side—their job was much more difficult.

There were similar hearings in the Senate. There my chief nemesis was William Proxmire, chairman of the Banking Committee. Proxmire was tough, but he was always straightforward and fair. He told us from the beginning that he was totally opposed to loan guarantees. But he was scrupulous in letting us make our case. He promised only to vote against us—not to do any lobbying.

I had a good sparring session with Proxmire, because for all his talk about free trade, he had previously agreed to some special help for American Motors.

In 1967, American Motors had received a federal tax credit that resulted in a cash rebate of $22 million.

In 1970, American Motors was granted special permission to purchase emissions control technology from GM as an exception to a federal court consent decree.

In 1974, American Motors was designated a small business by the federal government in order to give it preferential treatment on its requests for government contracts.

In 1977, American Motors was given the right to request a two-year waiver from the final emissions standards for oxides of nitrogen.

In 1979, American Motors' request for a waiver was granted by the EPA. A similar waiver for Chrysler, by the way, could have saved us over $300 million.

Proxmire has made himself quite a reputation out of ridiculing government expenditures he disagrees with. But he made a blatant exception for American Motors. Why? Because Proxmire happens to be a senator from Wisconsin, where American Motors has a major assembly plant.

I went head to head with him. I said: "I remember you were the prime mover for loan guarantees for American Motors, and they're owned by the French. So you were aiding and abetting the French government." We were fighting for our lives, and by that time I really didn't care whether I was polite.

Proxmire struck back. He raked me over the coals for being inconsistent in my own ideology. "More than any other executive in Detroit," he said, "you have led the anti-Washington campaign, and what you said has made a lot of sense. I would support it and other members might support it more vigorously." He then went on to say that if the guarantees were passed, the government would be deeply involved with Chrysler. "Doesn't this fly in the face of what you have been preaching so eloquently for so long?"

"It sure does," I replied. "I have been a free-enterpriser all my life. I come here with great reluctance. I am between a rock and a hard place. I cannot save the company without some kind of guarantee from the federal government.

"I am not going to preach to you," I continued. "You gentlemen know this better than I do, that we are setting no precedent. There are already four hundred nine billion dollars of loan guarantees on the books, so don't stop now, men. Go to four hundred ten billion dollars for Chrysler because it is the tenth biggest company in the U.S. and there are six hundred thousand jobs involved here."

When I talked about precedents, even the adversarial guys had a hell of a time. The best they could come up with was to say: "Well, just because we've done some stupid things in the past doesn't make this one right."

At the end of my long testimony and the subsequent interrogation, Senator Proxmire paid me a high compliment. "As you know," he said, "I am opposed to your request. But I have rarely heard a more eloquent, intelligent, well-informed witness than you have been today. You did a brilliant job and we thank you. We are in your debt." I thought: "No, no, you've got it backwards. We're trying to get in *your* debt!"

After Proxmire's great compliment, I smiled for a moment. But then he made clear that he was going to fight me down to the last shot—and he made good on his word.

Another opponent on the Senate committee was Senator John Heinz, Republican of Pennsylvania, who went out of his way to be hostile. He had it in for our stockholders, and he wanted them to suffer. We had to point out that Chrysler stock was not held by institutions. Thirty percent of our shareholders were employees. The rest were private individuals. They had already seen the value of their stock erode considerably.

But Heinz wanted us to issue another fifty million shares immediately, which would reduce the value of our stock from $7.50 to $3.50—a price it later reached quite nicely on its own. He couldn't get it through his head that with the shape we were in, nobody out there had any interest in buying Chrysler shares at *any* price.

The House and Senate hearings were only part of the story. I spent most of my time in small, private meetings. I had a good talk with Kansas Senator Nancy Kassebaum, the only woman in the Senate. I made a strong case, and I thought she was coming around. But in the end, she voted against us.

I had better luck with the Italian caucus in the House. Congressman Pete Rodino of New Jersey brought me in and said: "I want you to talk to my pals here." There were thirty-one guys (well, actually, thirty guys and Geraldine Ferraro, a representative from Queens), and all but one voted for us. Some were Republicans, some were Democrats, but in this case they voted the straight Italian ticket. We were desperate, and we had to play every angle. It was democracy in action.

There wasn't time for a meeting with the black caucus, but I did meet with its leader, Congressman Parren Mitchell of Maryland. In 1979, 1 percent of the black payroll in the entire United States was paid by the Chrysler Corporation. Blacks comprised an important part of the coalition that made the loan guarantees possible.

Coleman Young, the black mayor of Detroit, came to Washington several times to testify on our behalf. He minced no words in outlining what a Chrysler bankruptcy would do to Detroit. Young had been an early supporter of Jimmy Carter, and he spoke forcefully to the President about the Chrysler situation.

During the last three months of 1979, the pressure on me was tremendous. I was going to Washington a couple of times a week and trying to run Chrysler at the same time. Meanwhile, Mary was sick with periodic diabetic attacks. On two or three occasions I had to drop everything and run back to Detroit to be with her.

Every time I went to Washington, I was on a crazy schedule of eight or ten meetings a day. Each time I went, I had to make the same speech, outline the same points, present the same arguments. Repeated, repeated, one at a time.

Once I was walking down one of the marble corridors in Congress and I just didn't feel right. It was as if I were walking on eggs. I was dizzy and close to fainting. I was also seeing double.

They took me to the surgeon general's office and then to the House infirmary, where they checked me out. It was vertigo, something I had experienced only once before, twenty years earlier. Back then, I had been walking down the corridor at Ford with McNamara, and I started bumping into the wall. McNamara said: "What's going on, Lee? Are you drunk or something?"

"Why?" I asked, not even realizing anything was wrong.

"Because you keep hitting the wall, that's why."

Vertigo is a problem with equilibrium in the inner ear, and I was suffering a recurrence. They discharged me from the infirmary, but then it happened again. All the tension and pressure made me feel like I had rocks in my head. But somehow I muddled through.

*   *   *

Our highest priority during this period was to maintain the confidence of the consumer. While the hearings were going on, our sales dropped off dramatically. Nobody wanted to buy a car from a company that was about to go belly up. The percentage of consumers who were willing merely to *consider* a Chrysler product plunged overnight from 30 percent to 13 percent.

There were two schools of thought as to how we should respond to this crisis. By and large, our PR people maintained that silence was the best policy. "Just sit tight," they advised. "It will all work out. The last thing we want to do is call attention to our miserable situation."

But Kenyon & Eckhardt, our ad agency, strongly disagreed. "The situation is critical," they said, "and you've got a choice. You can die quietly, or you can die screaming. We recommend that you die screaming. That way, there's always the chance somebody will hear you."

We took their advice. We asked K&E to put together an ad campaign that would reassure the public about our future. We had to let people know two things—first, that we had absolutely no intention of going out of business, and second, that we were making the kind of cars America really needed.

Instead of our regular advertising, which featured pictures and text describing our new models, we ran a series of editorials expressing our point of view about the loan guarantees as well as Chrysler's long-range plans. Instead of promoting our products, we were promoting the company and its future. We weren't getting our message across through the normal channels—it was time to advertise our cause instead of our cars.

Ron DeLuca of K&E's New York office drew up a series of full-page print ads explaining our position. Before writing each one, he used to come into my office for an hour or so to talk things over. Then I'd edit his copy, and we'd go back and forth until we were both satisfied.

In these ads, which K&E began to refer to as "paid PR," we set the record straight. We exposed some of the more prevalent myths about Chrysler: We were not building gas-guzzlers. We were not asking Washington for a handout. Loan guarantees for Chrysler did not constitute a dangerous precedent.

The ads were unusually straightforward and frank. Ron took an aggressive approach, which I liked very much. We knew all too well what the man on the street was thinking about Chrysler, so we tried to put ourselves in his place and anticipate his questions and doubts. There was no point in ignoring the bad press. Instead we had to meet it head on and replace rumors with the facts.

One of these ads carried a bold headline that spelled out what many consumers were starting to wonder: "Would America be better off without Chrysler?" In the other ads, we asked—and answered— some pretty tough questions:

- Doesn't everyone know Chrysler cars get lousy gas mileage?
- Aren't Chrysler's big cars too big?
- Did Chrysler wait too long to downsize?
- Isn't Chrysler building the wrong kind of cars?
- Doesn't Chrysler have more problems than anyone can solve?
- Is Chrysler management strong enough to turn the company around?
- Has Chrysler done everything it can to help itself?
- Does Chrysler have a future?

These ads were unusual in another way, too. We decided that they should all carry my signature. We wanted to show the public that a new era had begun. After all, a chief executive of a company that's going broke has to reassure people. He's got to say: "I'm here, I'm real, and I'm responsible for this company. And to show that I mean it, I'm signing on the dotted line."

At long last, we would be able to convey that there was some genuine accountability at Chrysler. By putting my signature on these ads, we were inviting the public to write to me with their complaints and their questions. We were announcing that this large, complex company was now being run by a human being who was putting his name and his reputation on the line.

The ad campaign was a major success. I'm pretty sure it played a role in the massive effort to convince Congress to approve the loan guarantees. The great frustration of advertising, of course, is that you never really know what finally makes a difference in the battle for people's minds. But we heard reports of people in the Carter administration and the Congress running from one office to another with these ads in their hands—either furious or delighted, depending on their views.

And there's no question that the ads had a real impact on the public. People would see the front page of the newspaper, which said that we were going broke. Then they'd look inside and find our side of the story.

Meanwhile, on another front, our Washington office had organized a massive dealer lobby. Groups of Chrysler and Dodge dealers were coming to Washington every day. Wendell Larsen, our vice-president of public affairs, would brief them, telling them which congressmen to talk to and what to say.

Car dealers tend to be wealthy (or at least they used to be), and they also tend to be active in their communities, so they have a lot of clout with their representatives. Since most of them are conservative and Republican, their presence had a big impact on the congressmen who were against us on ideological grounds. And many of the dealers had made campaign contributions, which is something a congressman can't always ignore.

When you send a bunch of car dealers into Washington, it's amazing what they can accomplish. We even had a few dealers from other companies, who argued that competition was good for the entire industry and that Chrysler deserved a chance.

In order to make our case, we had to force the congressmen to think of the loan guarantees in real human terms instead of ideology. We delivered to each representative a computer printout of all the suppliers and dealers in his district who did business with us. We outlined exactly what the consequences for that district would be if Chrysler went under. As I recall, there were only 2 districts out of the entire 535 that had no suppliers or Chrysler dealers. This list, which made our problems hit home, had a tremendous effect.

Then there was Doug Fraser, who constituted a lobby effort of his own. Doug didn't fall for any crap about a bankruptcy. He knew what would happen to his people if Chrysler failed. And he knew we weren't crying wolf.

Fraser testified brilliantly. He talked vividly about the cost in human lives and suffering if the loan guarantees were not passed. "I don't come here to plead for the Chrysler Corporation," he told the committee. "My concern is the terrible impact that a bankruptcy would have upon the workers and on their communities."

Fraser was a tireless and effective lobbyist who met individually with a number of congressmen and senators. He was also a good friend of Vice President Mondale, and he paid a couple of important visits to the White House.

At one point I went to the White House myself to see the

President. Carter didn't get very involved in the Chrysler debate, but he did support our cause. During my visit, he told me how much he and Rosalynn liked my TV commercials. He joked that I was becoming as well known as he was.

Carter delegated the Chrysler problem to the Treasury Department, but he made it clear that he stood behind us. Without the support of the executive branch, the bill would never have passed.

Since leaving office, Carter has come to see me twice. He's proud that Chrysler is thriving. I think he feels as if he fathered the baby. "Of all the things we accomplished in my administration," he told me, "I look back on this as something we really did right." Jimmy Carter had his drawbacks, but his accomplishments have been underrated.

By the time the vote came, we had a lot of backers in Congress. Still, Tip O'Neill's support was crucial. Just before the vote, he stepped down as Speaker and spoke as the representative from Massachusetts. In an impassioned plea for the loan guarantees, he recalled the effect of the Great Depression in Boston, when workers who had lost their jobs had to beg for work shoveling snow. "I have always fought hard to save a hundred jobs," he told his colleagues. "Isn't it a little crazy for us to sit here and argue about this when more than half a million families are out there tonight waiting to hear our verdict?"

Tip used raw emotion to sell his guys in the House. He was one of our leaders in this whole episode. Once you've got the Speaker of the House, you have a lot of clout. When the vote came in, the House had agreed by a two-to-one margin (271 to 136) to help Chrysler get back on its feet.

The Senate vote was a lot closer, 53 to 44, but that's routine in these situations. The bill was passed just before Christmas, and a lot of American families had reason to celebrate. I was exhausted and relieved, but I wasn't wildly optimistic. All too often since coming to Chrysler I had seen a light at the end of the tunnel. And all too often it had turned out to be another train coming at me. I knew that a great many parts of the puzzle had to fall into place before we would ever see a penny of those guaranteed loans.

The legislation called for a restructuring of Chrysler that, according to Treasury Secretary G. William Miller, was to be the most complicated financial transaction in the history of American business. I got tired just thinking about it.

The act created a Loan Guarantee Board with authority to issue

up to $1.5 billion in loan guarantees over the next two years, which
were to be repaid by the end of 1990. But there were a number of
strings attached:

- Our current lenders were required to extend $400 million in
  new credit and $100 million in concessions on existing loans.
- Foreign lenders were required to extend an additional $150
  million in credit.
- We had to raise an additional $300 million through the sale of
  assets.
- Suppliers had to provide the company with at least $180 million,
  of which $100 million was in the form of stock purchases.
- State and local governments with Chrysler plants had to provide $250 million.
- We had to issue $50 million in new stock.
- Union members had to come up with $462.2 million in
  concessions.
- Nonunion employees had to contribute $125 million in pay
  cuts or freezes.

In addition—and very few people realize this—the government
took all of Chrysler's assets as collateral. Everything we owned—cars,
real estate, plants, tools, and all the rest—was carried on the books for
$6 billion. The government appraisers estimated that the liquidation
value of our assets came to $2.5 billion. In a worst-case scenario,
the government had first lien. If we went under, they would recover
all $1.2 billion of the loans before any other creditors could make
claims.

Even if the $2.5 billion estimate was generous, and even if the
true value of our assets came to only half of that, the government was
still protected. If we had defaulted on our loans, the Loan Guarantee
Board could have liquidated our assets and still come out whole. In
other words, the government was taking no financial risk at all!

A couple of weeks after the Loan Guarantee Act was passed, the
Republicans came into power. Their attitude was: "This is a Carter
program. We'll honor the letter of the law, but not one iota beyond
that. It's against our ideology. If Chrysler makes it, we'd be embarrassed.
And we wouldn't want other companies to get any fancy ideas."

We were lucky that when push came to shove, we had appealed
to a Democratic administration that put people ahead of ideology.
Democrats usually do. They deal with labor, they deal with people,

they deal with jobs. Republicans deal with trickle-down theories of investment.

I realize that I'm stereotyping. I'm the first to admit that when things are going well, when I've made a lot of money, I've always favored the Republicans. But ever since coming to Chrysler, I've leaned toward the Democrats. Overall, I'm for the commonsense party, and when the chips are down, that's usually the Democrats.

There's no question in my mind that if there had been a Republican administration in 1979, Chrysler wouldn't be around. The Republicans wouldn't even have said hello to us. Chrysler would have gone bankrupt, and today they'd be writing books about having protected free enterprise. It's not just Reagan; most Republicans would have said: "Federally guaranteed loans? You must be nuts." Republicans just aren't used to thinking like that.

If our crisis had occurred three years later, when Ford and GM were also in big trouble and International Harvester was going broke, not even the Democrats would have responded. They would have seen that there were fifty other guys lined up right behind us, with no system to handle it all.

So maybe it's a good thing that Chrysler got into trouble a little earlier than it might have with stronger management. If our crisis had come at the same time as Braniff and Pan Am, Washington would have said: "Sorry, boys. The line's already too long."

I'm sure those other companies considered asking for government help. After all, they're not crazy. But they got the message early. What would happen if they came down to ask for a deal like Chrysler? Answer: "Forget it."

As I write these words, it's been four years since the loan guarantees were passed. During that time, we've kept hundreds of thousands of people off the dole. We paid hundreds of millions of dollars in taxes. We preserved competition in the auto industry. We paid back the loans seven years early. We paid large fees to the Loan Guarantee Board. And the government enjoyed a windfall from selling our warrants.

In view of all this, you have to ask a philosophical question. By going to Congress, did we really violate the spirit of free enterprise? Or has our subsequent success actually helped free enterprise in this country? I don't think there's any doubt about the answer. Even some of our opponents from 1979 now concede that the Chrysler loan guarantees were a good idea.

Oh, there are still some diehards such as *The Wall Street Journal* and Gary Hart—but what the hell! You can't convert them all.

XX

EQUALITY OF SACRIFICE

With the passage of the Loan Guarantee Act, we now had a fighting chance to survive. And I do mean "fighting"!

Our mission was the economic equivalent of war. Although no one was getting killed for Chrysler, the economic survival of hundreds of thousands of people depended on whether we could arrange the various concessions that the Loan Guarantee Act required.

I was the general in the war to save Chrysler. But I sure didn't do it alone. What I'm most proud of is the coalition I was able to put together. It shows what cooperation can do for you in hard times.

I began by reducing my own salary to $1.00 a year. Leadership means setting an example. When you find yourself in a position of leadership, people follow your every move. I don't mean they invade your privacy, although there's some of that, too. But when the leader talks, people listen. And when the leader acts, people watch. So you have to be careful about everything you say and everything you do.

I didn't take $1.00 a year to be a martyr. I took it because I had to go into the pits. I took it so that when I went to Doug Fraser, the union president, I could look him in the eye and say: "Here's what I want from you guys as your share," and he couldn't come back to me and ask: "You SOB, what sacrifice have *you* made?" That's why I did it, for good, cold, pragmatic reasons. I wanted our employees and our suppliers to be thinking: "I can follow a guy who sets that kind of example."

Unfortunately, austerity was a new idea at Chrysler. When I came in, I heard all kinds of horror stories about the extravagance of the previous administration. But I wasn't impressed. After all, I had lived for years with Henry Ford, who thought he owned the company and who was powerful enough to act as if he did. Henry spent enough money to make Lynn Townsend look like a beggar. He made the head of General Motors look like he was on welfare.

Although my reduced salary didn't mean I had to skip any meals, it still made a big statement in Detroit. It showed that we were all in this together. It showed that we could survive only if each of us tightened his belt. It was a dramatic gesture, and word of it got around very quickly.

I learned more about people in three years at Chrysler than in thirty-two years at Ford. I discovered that people accept a lot of pain if everybody's going through the chute together. If everybody is suffering equally, you can move a mountain. But the first time you find someone goofing off or not carrying his share of the load, the whole thing can come unraveled.

I call this equality of sacrifice. When I started to sacrifice, I saw other people do whatever was necessary. And that's how Chrysler pulled through. It wasn't the loans that saved us, although we needed them badly. It was the hundreds of millions of dollars that were given up by everybody involved. It was like a family getting together and saying: "We got a loan from our rich uncle and now we're going to prove that we can pay him back!"

This was cooperation and democracy at their best. I'm not talking about a Bible lesson here. I'm talking about real life. We went through it. It works. It's like magic and it awes you.

But our struggle also had its dark side. To cut expenses, we had to fire a lot of people. It's like a war: we won, but my son didn't come back. There was a lot of agony. People were getting destroyed, taking their kids out of college, drinking, getting divorced. Overall we preserved the company, but only at enormous personal expense for a great many human beings.

Our task was made a little easier by the knowledge that much of America was rooting for us. We were no longer seen as the fat cats asking for welfare. With the congressional hearings behind us, that part of the saga was over. By now, our advertising campaign was beginning to get results. We were the underdog engaged in a heroic struggle, and the public responded accordingly.

Many unknown people wrote to us, saying in a hundred different ways that they were with us, that Henry Ford's loss was Chrysler's gain. The little people said a lot, and they said it well. They understood what we were doing.

Some pretty big people helped us, too. Bob Hope came to see me. He told me that while having a massage he'd seen one of my commercials on television. Now he wanted to do something for us.

I ran into Bill Cosby at dinner one night in Las Vegas. That same night, he called me in my hotel at 1:00 A.M.

I said, "Hey man, you woke me up."

He said: "Hell, we're just getting going. We're up all night. Anyway, I admire what you're doing, and I appreciate how much you're helping the black people. I'd like to do something for you. I make a lot of money and other people are starving." He came to Detroit to do a show for our workers—20,000 of them. Then he got on a plane and left. He never asked for a dime. He never asked for a car. He just wanted to help us out and show his support.

One night Pearl Bailey came up to me at a diabetes function in downtown Detroit. She said she just had to talk to me. She thanked me for trying to preserve jobs and for giving people hope. Instead of doing a concert, she wanted to give a lecture to our workers at the Jefferson Avenue plant.

She made a rousing speech about patriotism and the need to sacrifice. But while she was talking, a couple of hecklers started in: "Easy for you to say, Pearl, you're rich!"

Before we knew it, we almost had a riot on our hands. I had to jump up and bring the meeting to a close. But it was a great gesture, and I really appreciated it.

Frank Sinatra wanted to help, too. He said: "Lee, if you're working for a dollar, I will, too." He did some commercials for us, and during the second year we gave him some stock options. I hope Frank held on to them, because if he did, he made a bundle.

There were a number of these cases. During that period, I got to see the positive side of human beings. I had never really known how people would act when the chips were down. I learned that the majority will rally around. They won't think about greed, even though the media seem to believe that greed is the only motivating force in business. Most people, when called upon, will serve—so long as they're not being singled out to get the short end of the stick.

I also learned that people can act very serenely in a crisis. They accept their fate. They know it's going to be a tough grind, but they grit their teeth and go with it. Watching that happen was the pleasant part—maybe the only pleasant part—of this whole episode.

After I cut my own salary, I started in on the executives. We threw out the stock incentive plan, where we paid half and they paid half. We cut their salaries by up to 10 percent, which had never been done in the auto industry. We cut salaries in all but the lowest levels—we left the secretaries alone. They deserved every cent they made.

The executives were pretty docile about it. They read the papers. They knew very well that the whole ball game could be over at any moment. At such a time, there's no periphery anymore. You see only one thing: the track that leads to survival. Nothing stops you, so you go on adrenaline.

It started with me, but it permeated down through the ranks. For the good of the cause, I could have asked them to jump through the window—and all because of the shared perception that everybody was bleeding equally.

Once I had dealt with the executives, I started in on the unions. Here I had the help of a real pro, Tom Miner, who handles our industrial relations. Today the business world takes union concessions for granted. But back then, we were pioneers.

The union has always had the attitude that the executives are fat cats and the workers get screwed. I said: "Well, now you're looking at some pretty skinny fat cats, okay? So what do you have to say?"

From that day on, I was their pal. The union loved me. They embraced me. They said: "This guy is going to lead us to the promised land."

I don't mean it was easy. I had to lay it on the line. I talked tough to them. "Hey, boys," I said, "I've got a shotgun at your head. I've got thousands of jobs available at seventeen bucks an hour. I've got none at twenty. So you better come to your senses."

A year later, when things got even worse, I had to go back to them a second time. One bitter winter night at ten o'clock I spoke to the union negotiating committee. It was one of the shortest speeches I've ever given: "You've got until morning to make a decision. If you don't help me out, I'm going to blow your brains out. I'll declare bankruptcy in the morning and you'll all be out of work. You've got eight hours to make up your minds. It's up to you."

That's a hell of a way to negotiate, but sometimes it's what you've got to do. Fraser said it was the worst economic settlement he had ever agreed to. The only thing worse, he added, was the alternative—having no jobs at all.

Our workers made some pretty big concessions. Right away, $1.15 an hour came out of their paychecks. Over the year-and-a-half period of concessions, that amount grew to $2.00 an hour. Over a nineteen-month period, the average working guy at Chrysler gave up close to $10,000.

The union had grown used to my new salary of $1.00 a year, and they ragged me when I didn't do it again the second year. They actually got mad about it. But I didn't see the top guys at Ford or GM taking any salary cuts after the union had agreed to concessions.

As a matter of fact, after GM and the UAW negotiated a contract in which the workers gave up wage increases and benefits that came to $2.5 billion, what did the company do? Roger Smith, the chairman of GM, cut his own salary by all of $1,620 a year! To add insult to injury, on the very day that the union signed the new contract, which included major wage concessions, GM announced a new and bigger bonus plan for its top executives. There's a company that doesn't quite understand equality of sacrifice.

For the first time in many years, the attitude of Chrysler workers began to improve. When the Canadian union went out on strike in 1982, they didn't sabotage the cars or wreck the machinery, which used to be routine. They wanted more money, but they didn't want to do anything to damage the company.

One of the provisions of the loan guarantees was an employee stock ownership plan for our workers. It cost us $40 million a year for four years. But it made good economic sense. If you let workers share in the profits, they're much more motivated to do a good job. (Each worker now has credited to his account about $5,600—a nice nest egg.)

Here, too, the free-enterprise crowd went nuts. And once more I was ready for them. I pointed out that the big pension plans in this country own plenty of stock. They own a large chunk of General Motors and many other major publicly traded companies. So what's wrong with cutting the workers in *while they're working*?

The laissez-faire crowd thinks that this represents the first step to socialism. But I don't see anything wrong with the workers owning a piece of the action. It certainly doesn't interfere with good management. What do I care if the company's stock is owned by a broker's account on Wall Street or by Joe Blow who works on the assembly line? Which one can do more for me? Today, by the way, our workers own about 17 percent of the company.

We also got the union to side with us on absenteeism. There are always a few guys who never come to work but who still want to get paid. Together with the union, we put some teeth into the rules to penalize the chronic offenders.

During this same period, we had to close a number of plants. A lot of people were thrown out of work. It's a very emotional thing for people who have been working in the same plant for twenty or thirty years. In some cases their parents had worked there, too. All of a sudden they find out you're going to lock the doors.

There was plenty of screaming over some of the plant closings. But the union understood very well that we had to take drastic measures. They were able to accept these actions because they knew we were asking for equivalent concessions from our suppliers, our executives, and our banks.

During 1980, I went to every single Chrysler plant in order to speak directly to the workers. At a series of mass meetings, I thanked them for sticking with us during these bad times. I told them that when things got better, we'd try to get them back to parity with Ford and GM workers but that it wouldn't happen overnight. I gave them my pitch, and they hooted and hollered, and some of them applauded and some of them booed.

I also conducted sessions with the plant supervisors. I'd ask if anybody had questions for me. We didn't always agree on the answers, but just having the chance to talk together was a big step forward.

That's communication at the highest level: the chairman talking to the guy on the floor. Everybody hears it and everybody feels part of it. I'd like to do that more often. I did a lot of it at Ford, but then I could afford to—things were running pretty smoothly back at the office.

At Chrysler, however, it's been one crisis after another. You get worn out from it all. And it's an awfully long day shaking hands with hundreds of guys. Inevitably some of the assembly line workers want to come up and hug you, or give you a present, or let you know that they pray for you in church because you saved their job.

During this period a woman named Lillian Zirwas, a maintenance clerk at the Lynch Road plant in Detroit, wrote a piece in the plant newspaper. In effect she told her fellow workers to shape up. She said: "Maybe now you'll have plenty of time to think as you're being laid off of the times you goofed off, or the times you turned an eye on shoddy stuff."

I wrote her a letter telling her how much I liked the piece and invited her to my office. She came in with a cake she had baked. I remember that it had chocolate icing and one of the ingredients was beer. However she made it, it was the best cake I ever ate. My wife wrote to Lillian Zirwas to ask for the recipe.

Of course, not all our workers shared her attitude. It's hard to be happy about a $2.00-an-hour cut. Still, it's not quite accurate to say, as the news media always do, that this put Chrysler workers $2.00 an hour below Ford and GM workers.

That's because, unlike Ford and GM, Chrysler had an unusually large number of retirees. To begin with, we had a work force that was older than average. Then we had to lay off thousands of people. For all the workers who were now at home, the corporation had to pay pensions, health care costs, and life insurance premiums. And it's the active workers who have to produce the money that pays for those expenses.

In normal times, that's not a problem. At least two guys were working for every retiree, and they produced enough to cover his pension and other costs. But by 1980 we were down to the ridiculous and unprecedented ratio of ninety-three workers for every hundred retirees. In other words, we now had more guys sitting at home than coming to work! As a result, every Chrysler worker had on his shoulders the economic burden of supporting himself—*and* somebody else.

This is one more area where Chrysler's problems reflect what's going on in our society. It's this same phenomenon that's breaking Social Security. People are retiring early, living longer, and there's not a large enough base of workers to support them.

Although our workers took a $2.00-an-hour pay cut, the large number of retirees meant that our labor costs did not go down accordingly. Some of our workers didn't see it this way. Their attitude was: "That's not my problem. I'm not my brother's keeper."

My response was: "Wait a minute. Your union is based on solidarity forever. You put in these pension plans, and now there are a lot of people sitting home, and that's too bad. The industry went to hell. Chrysler was too big, so we cut it down to size. Somebody has to pay those costs. We can't renege on the pension plan."

Even before the union had made any concessions, I invited Doug Fraser to sit on our board of directors. Despite what the press has reported, Fraser's appointment was not part of a package deal with the union.

Now, it's true that the union had been asking for labor representation on the board for many years. But it had become a kind of ritual. I don't think they ever expected to get it. I put Doug Fraser on our board because I knew he could make a special contribution. He's smart, he's politically savvy, and he says what he thinks.

As a board member, Doug found out firsthand what was going on at Chrysler from the perspective of management. He learned how our suppliers contributed and that our turnaround wasn't only due to the workers. He learned that our profit-and-loss statements were real and that profit wasn't a dirty word. He learned and understood so much that some of the workers began to see him as a turncoat, because he told them the truth when we were too weak to take a strike.

He's had an enormous effect. When there's a plant closing, he advises us on how to minimize the dislocation and the suffering that go with it. He's chairman of our public policy committee. He's also on the health care committee, along with me; Joe Califano, former secretary of HEW under Carter; and Bill Milliken, former governor of Michigan. As a foursome we probably know as much about health care as any four guys in the world. The four of us represent labor, management, and federal and state government. Over the years, we were the ones who made the decisions that landed us in the health care mess the country's in today. It took all four groups to screw up the health care system, so it will take the same combination to straighten it out.

Naturally, when I brought Doug Fraser onto our board, the business community went wild. They said: "You can't do that! You're putting the fox into the henhouse. You've lost your mind!"

I said: "Wait a minute. Why is it all right to have bankers on the board when you owe them $100 million, but not a worker? Why is it all right to have suppliers on the board? Isn't that a conflict of interest?"

Until then, no representative of labor had ever sat on the board of a major American corporation. But it's pretty standard in Europe. And in Japan they do it all the time. So what's the problem? It's that the average American CEO is a prisoner of ideology. He wants to be pure. He still believes that labor has to be the natural, mortal enemy of the manager.

That's obsolete thinking. I want labor to understand the inner workings of the company. The old days are gone for good. Some people don't believe it, but they'll find out soon enough. America's economic future depends upon increased cooperation among government, union, and management. Only by working together can we take on the world market.

It wasn't only management types who opposed the Fraser move. Plenty of union guys were against it, too. They were afraid that Fraser's being on the board might compromise their leadership's ability to extract the last drop of blood out of the turnip. All their lives they've had an attitude of get all you can because management will never do anything for the good of the worker unless it's extracted with violence or bloodshed.

For this kind of thinking to change, you need to have reasonable men who can discuss the concept of sharing profits only when we have some to share and wage increases only when we have improved productivity. Maybe that's a concept whose time has not yet come. But it will *have* to come, because if we continue to slug it out and fight each other for a bigger piece of the pie when all the while that pie is getting smaller, the Japanese will continue to have us for lunch.

When I was at Ford, labor and management saw each other only every three years when it came time to negotiate a new contract. And every three years you'd walk into the room with a chip on your shoulder. You wouldn't know the guy and you'd immediately think: "I don't like him, he's the enemy." It's like meeting at a bridge and trading spies. You hate the other side, even though the exchange is a good thing.

I'm very glad I put Doug Fraser on the board, because he's first-class. I'd put him on any board I was on. He's just that good. He knows how to negotiate. He knows how to compromise. He knows the difference between a good deal and a bad deal. He's so good that I once recommended him to President Reagan as a government negotiator.

If Doug Fraser had served on Lynn Townsend's board, maybe Chrysler wouldn't have bought up the lousiest companies in Europe.

Some of those terrible moves could have been stopped by just one bold man asking: "Why are we doing this? Does it really make sense?"

Besides, what have we got to hide from the union? What are we trying to keep from the workers? We need to build better cars for less money. And who else can help us reach that goal if not the head of the union?

Whenever I was taken to task for having Fraser on the board, I gave my standard argument: "Why are you so upset? Either way, you can only gain. If it turns out to be a mistake, you'll know not to try it. You'll be able to talk about it at the country club. You can say: 'Wasn't Iacocca a jerk?'

"But if it does work, then I'll have been the guinea pig, and you'll thank me for leading the way. Some day you may even prosper from it!"

XXI

THE BANKS:
TRIAL BY FIRE

Nne of our constituencies found it easy to make concessions. But once they understood how bad the situation was and once they were convinced that other groups were also doing their part, they all went along pretty quickly.

Except the bankers. It took longer to get $655 million in concessions from our four hundred lending institutions than it did to get the loan guarantees of $1.5 billion passed by the entire United States Congress. Compared to dealing with the banks, the congressional hearings were as easy as changing a flat tire on a spring day.

I was disappointed by the attitude of the banks, but I wasn't surprised. During the House and Senate hearings, the bankers had been very negative. Walt Wriston, the head of Citibank, Tom Clausen, president of the Bank of America, and Pete Peterson, head of Lehman Brothers, had all testified against the loan guarantees. Peterson had gone so far as to compare our situation to Vietnam, suggesting that Chrysler might represent an endless quagmire.

I had a couple of very tough meetings with Peter Fitts, who represented Citibank, and Ron Drake from Irving Trust. Fitts and Drake were workout men—specialists in financial restructurings. Their general attitude was that we at Chrysler were dummies who didn't know what we were doing. These guys didn't care about jobs or investments. The only thing that mattered was the return on their money.

Like almost everyone else in the banking world, they wanted us to declare bankruptcy. But I resisted. I did my best to convince them that with equality of sacrifice and with our new management team, Chrysler would be able to make it.

Ron Drake and I had some especially bitter arguments, but then a funny thing happened: today, he's my personal financial adviser at Merrill Lynch. We hated each other in 1980, but we also went through hell together and ended up great friends.

When the Loan Guarantee Act was passed at the end of 1979, Chrysler Corporation and Chrysler Financial, our credit wing, were in debt to over four hundred banks and insurance companies to the tune of $4.75 billion. These loans had accumulated over a period of years, during which our bankers must have been asleep at the wheel. None of them ever seemed to wonder about the health of the company, even though the ominous signs were there for anybody to see.

Chrysler had been a bonanza for the bankers, and nobody had wanted to look a gift horse in the mouth. For over fifty years, Chrysler had borrowed steadily from the banks without missing a single payment.

Chrysler has traditionally been a highly leveraged company, paying generous dividends and borrowing heavily from the banks. That may be good for the banks, but it hasn't always been good for Chrysler. When you're highly leveraged, everything is exaggerated. Good times are better—but bad times are much worse.

It also meant that our credit rating has never been as good as GM's or Ford's. As a result, we've always had to pay a premium on the money we've borrowed. Unlike General Motors, which is big enough and profitable enough to function as its own bank, Chrysler has had to borrow money at the prevailing interest rates. And the banks have been only too happy to oblige.

Through the fat years, the bankers were always right there by our side. But in bad times they backed off in a hurry. As good conservative Republicans, most of the bankers were skeptical of the Loan Guarantee Act. Because most of the bank loans were to Chrysler Financial rather than to Chrysler Corporation itself, the bankers figured that if we declared Chapter 11, they'd still make out pretty well.

But they were in for a big shock. Late in 1979, Jerry Greenwald asked Steve Miller and Ron Trost, a Los Angeles expert on bankruptcy, to prepare a "memo of liquidation." This document made it clear that essentially it didn't matter whether the loans had been made to Chrysler Corporation or Chrysler Financial. In the event of a bankruptcy, *all* the loans would be tied up for between five and ten years in the courts, and the banks would lose a significant percentage of their investment. And under a quirk in the Michigan law, the interest rates on the outstanding loans would drop to 6 percent a year until the matter was resolved. It didn't take long for the banks to realize that it was in their best interest to grant the concessions that would keep us in business.

Even so, they were far less inclined to compromise than our suppliers and our workers. For one thing, their survival didn't depend on our recovery. For another, the sheer number of banks was overwhelming. When Lockheed received federal loan guarantees in 1971, only twenty-four banks were involved, and all of them were American. Our banks, however, were spread out over most of the fifty states—and all over the world. They ranged from Manufacturers Hanover Trust in New York, where we owed over $200 million, to the Twin City Bank of Little Rock, Arkansas, where we owed a mere $78,000. We owed money to banks in London, Toronto, Ottawa, Frankfurt, Paris, Tokyo—and even Tehran.

Each bank had its own agenda. Manufacturers Hanover, known in the business world as Manny Hanny, had been connected with Chrysler for years. Lynn Townsend had been on their board for nine years, while two of Manny Hanny's chairmen had served on ours. More than once they had helped us through hard times. John McGillicuddy, the current chairman, had established a $455 million revolving credit agreement for Chrysler. In addition, he testified in Congress in favor of the loan guarantees. "I believe that Chrysler Corporation ought to survive," he told the committee. "I am not categorically opposed to government assistance in every case and do not see its sparing use as a threat to the free-enterprise system."

John McGillicuddy was one of our white knights. Manny Hanny was our lead bank, and McGillicuddy pushed his colleagues to accept our package of concessions.

Our other white knight was G. William Miller, secretary of the treasury. He testified before the House committee that Chrysler represented an exceptional case and that the loan guarantees were a good idea. Miller was tough on the banks. He felt they should take their losses and lick their wounds.

But over at Citibank, Walter Wriston was deeply opposed to the guarantees. As the most influential banker in the country, Wriston was our albatross. Citibank was sure we were going bankrupt, and they couldn't wait to get their fifteen cents on the dollar—which is what we had proposed as a settlement. (We were also offering another fifteen cents in preferred stock.) Citibank seems to enjoy its reputation as a hard-nosed outfit. Anytime they could set up a roadblock in our way, they did.

But the conflict between Manny Hanny and Citibank was just the tip of the iceberg. Our lenders included both big-money banks and small-town banks, domestic banks and foreign banks, and even a couple of insurance companies. There were loans to Chrysler Corporation itself, loans to Chrysler Canada, and loans to Chrysler Financial. There were also loans to various foreign subsidiaries and letters of credit against future invoices.

To make matters worse, we had loans outstanding at many different interest rates. There were low-interest, fixed-rate loans at 9 percent. Then there were high-interest, floating-rate loans, which floated with the prime, ranging from 12 percent in January, when we began dealing with the banks, to 20 percent in April, when we formulated an agreement, back to around 11 percent by the time the deal was completed.

There were banks whose lines of credit were fully extended, and others that were only partly drawn down. There were loans that were already six months overdue, such as the one for $5 million from a bank in Spain that was issued in July 1979 and was supposed to have been repaid ninety days later. And there were longer loans, too, including some from insurance companies that didn't come due until 1995.

Naturally, there was a lot of tension and disagreement among the banks about what constituted a fair resolution. Generally speaking, the bankers were in no mood to compromise. Their major conflicts were not with Chrysler but with each other. Everybody had a reason why someone else should bear the brunt of the concessions.

The American banks said: "To hell with the foreign banks." Little did I know that what the big American banks were really worried about were *their* loans to Mexico, Poland, and Brazil. With all the postponements and defaults on their international loans, the big American banks are now going through the same problems as Chrysler. But unlike us, they have a rich uncle to bail them out—without a lot of the hoopla and publicity.

Not too long ago, when Mexico needed $1 billion to avoid defaulting on loans to New York banks, Paul Volcker of the Fed just wrote them a check over the weekend. That's what I call curb service for the banking fraternity. There were no hearings and no attempt to impose controls. There were no penalties for the banks. And of course the $1 billion came directly from the taxpayers.

The bankers sure didn't like the idea of loan guarantees for Chrysler. But guarantees for them were another matter. They plainly made a lot of mistakes in granting loans to foreign countries, but the International Monetary Fund bailed them out. The banks wanted us to cut executive pay, skip dividends, and all the rest. But I don't see anybody getting tough with them for making bad loans. I'd sure like to be the workout guy who asks Citicorp to start skipping dividends and its officers to take pay cuts!

There's a funny orientation at the Federal Reserve Board—they're all bankers, no businessmen. If a bank goes under for making bad decisions, it gets immediate attention. Two little banks go under in Oklahoma, and you have Paul Volcker yelling about a liquidity crisis and loosening the strings on money. But when Chrysler and International Harvester, two companies with almost a million jobs at stake, are going under, that's good old free enterprise at work.

Not really. That's nothing but a double standard and totally unfair.

Meanwhile, the foreign banks had their own complaints. The Japanese banks said: "Look, when there's a problem in Japan, the home banks cover it and the foreign banks get paid off. This is an American problem—let the American banks deal with it."

The Canadian banks said: "We're not going to let the Americans tell us what to do. We've been pushed around long enough." The Canadian government supported this position. In return for guaranteed government loans, Canada wanted us to provide assurances of a fixed employment level.

The Canadians felt like the youngest kid in the family who gets all the hand-me-downs. We were building our rear-wheel-drive vehicles in Canada—our big van and the New Yorker. At the time it seemed as if these cars were a dying breed.

We ended up with a compromise. Rather than any absolute numbers, we guaranteed the Canadians a percentage of our North American employment, and we agreed on 11 percent. As things turned out, that was an easy promise to keep. Because the United States never did come up with an energy policy, as gas prices dropped these bigger cars took off like rockets. At one point Canadian workers constituted 18 percent of Chrysler's North American employment.

The European banks said: "We're not going along with you. What about Telefunken?" A couple of years earlier, the German government had designed a bailout program for Telefunken, but the American banks had pulled out, leaving the German banks holding the bag. Like the Japanese, the German attitude was: "This is an American problem. Your banks should bear the brunt of it."

When they realized what they were up against, the American banks suddenly got religion. Their position became the same as ours: "No, everybody's in this together. In a bankruptcy, the court is going to treat us all the same." It was beginning to dawn on them that the only way we were going to solve this thing was to ask for fair and equitable contributions from *all* the banks involved.

Still, there were problems. The smaller banks said: "To hell with New York. Our loans to Chrysler make up a bigger percentage of our assets than the loans from those big New York banks. So let's have everybody's concessions based on the size of the bank."

To induce the banks to make the concessions we needed, we were forced to offer a sweetener: 12 million stock warrants, good until 1990, which could be exercised if the stock ever reached $13 a share. When the Loan Guarantee Board heard about that, they demanded a similar arrangement, on the theory that they too were a lender, with 50 percent more money at risk than the banks. So the government ended up with 14.4 million warrants.

In the end we gave up 26.4 million warrants, representing a major potential dilution of our equity. At the time, we didn't think very much about those warrants. We needed everybody's cooperation, and with our stock as low as $3.50, $13 a share seemed like a distant dream.

It took months to come up with an acceptable plan for the banks. I kicked the whole thing off and went to a few of the early meetings, but the great bulk of the work was handled by Jerry Greenwald and Steve Miller.

The negotiations with the banks were so complicated that Jerry did little else but coordinate the master plan from Highland Park. He set up twenty-two task forces that met every Friday with himself and Steve Miller. Miller, meanwhile, was running all over the place, flying to New York or Washington, with side trips to Ottawa, Paris, London, and dozens of other cities.

Miller's schedule was unbelievable. He spent much of his time in New York, where a typical day would began at six-thirty with a breakfast meeting with one of our lawyers. This would be followed by a series of meetings throughout the day with bankers and their lawyers.

At six in the evening he would meet with yet another group of bankers for drinks. At eight, there would be dinner with still others. At ten, he would be back at the hotel trying to prepare for the next day's meetings. Around midnight he would be on the phone to Japan to work out our arrangements with Mitsubishi and the Japanese banks.

Steve worked his tail off, and he also brought a little camaraderie to the task. His attitude to the bankers was: "Hey, this is hard, and I know you've never done anything like it. But neither have we, so let's see if we can't go through these uncharted waters together."

Steve Miller had the perfect personality for the job. He was tough and well-organized, but he also knew when to loosen up. In one meeting where the various banks were all fighting among themselves, he pointed a toy pistol at his head. "If you guys can't agree on this stuff," he said, "I'm going to have to kill myself."

At another of those meetings, the group sent out for sandwiches from a local delicatessen. The response came back immediately: "You guys are from Chrysler? Sorry. We won't deliver unless you pay us in advance!" That's the kind of atmosphere we were living in. Here we were trying to get hundreds of millions of dollars in concessions from the banks, and the local deli wouldn't even carry our corned beef and pastrami sandwiches for half an hour!

At first, Steve had been meeting with the bankers in separate groups. But this method only encouraged their divisiveness. Soon he decided to get everybody together in the same room. That way, each would have to talk to the other and see for themselves how pissed off grown men can really get.

This was a watershed event. It was also the first time that some of the bankers had ever met. Steve made a little speech. "I realize there's no way that my plan is going to strike you as fair," he told the bankers. "I just hope it's equally unfair to everybody. I want you to take the plan home and study it over the weekend. We'll meet again next Tuesday, April 1, and you'll tell me yes or no. But we can't discuss this thing much further. If you don't like the plan, we'd better just forget the whole thing."

Some of the bankers threatened that they wouldn't be back on Tuesday, but they all showed up. As it turned out, the meeting took place at a terrible time in the banking world. The silver market had just gone crazy with the Hunt Brothers. Bache was in big trouble. Interest rates had gone to 20 percent and they looked as if they might soar to 25 percent.

If we couldn't get the bankers to agree at this meeting, it would be all over. And with the nation's economy already shot to hell, it's quite possible that a Chrysler bankruptcy could have started a landslide of economic disasters.

When the whole group had convened for the April 1 meeting, Steve opened with a real shocker: "Gentlemen," he began, "last night Chrysler's board of directors held an emergency meeting. In view of the terrible economy, the declining fortunes of the company, and skyrocketing interest rates—not to mention the lack of support that we've had from our lenders—at nine-thirty this morning we decided to file for bankruptcy."

The room was silent. Greenwald was flabbergasted. He was on the board, of course, but this was the first he had heard of any such meeting. Then Miller added: "I should probably remind you all that today is the first of April."

There was a great sigh of relief. Unfortunately, the Europeans had never heard of April Fool's. They kept staring at the wall, wondering what on earth the date had to do with all of this.

Miller had thought up his little joke about five minutes before the meeting. It was risky, but it worked—it got everybody in the room to focus on the larger picture and to consider the consequences of no agreement. Steve's compromise plan was accepted by all the banks who attended: a total of $660 million in interest deferrals and reductions plus a four-year extension of $4 billion in loans at 5.5 percent.

But the plan could work only if every single bank to whom we owed money agreed to cooperate. Some of these banks, such as Bank Tejarat in Iran, made us pretty nervous. We owed them only $3.6 million, but this was right after the hostage crisis, and the U.S. government had frozen about $8 billion in Iranian deposits. To our great relief, the Iranians agreed to the plan without any problem.

By June, almost every bank had accepted the plan. When we had them all, we could finally get our hands on the first $500 million in guaranteed loans. But we were quickly running out of cash to pay our bills. On June 10, 1980, we had to stop paying our suppliers. Once again, bankruptcy was a real possibility.

The first $500 million in guaranteed loans was only a few days away, but how long would our suppliers stay patient? Even if they didn't force us into immediate bankruptcy, they could always decide to stop shipping, which would have been almost as bad. Because of our very tight inventories, any disruption of parts would be a disaster.

Fortunately, as we stood on the edge of the precipice, the suppliers came through.

By this time more than 90 percent of the banks had agreed to go along with our plan. They represented more than 95 percent of the outstanding loans. But we still needed a participation rate of 100 percent. Otherwise, the whole deal was off. Meanwhile, time was quickly running out. Even if every bank agreed to accept the plan, there was still the problem of all the paperwork and the proper signatures.

For example, there was a bank in Alaska that had signed the agreements but had put them in the mail instead of returning them by express courier. The papers were going to arrive too late, so we had to express them another set.

In Minnesota a bank officer had put the agreements in a box next to his desk, planning to sign them the next morning. That night, the cleaning lady picked them up and put them through the shredder.

A bank in Lebanon had signed the documents but couldn't get them out of the Beirut airport during the civil war. We finally got them delivered to the U.S. embassy. Eventually the Loan Guarantee Board accepted the embassy's testimony that the papers were all signed and in order.

In a financial reorganization, the usual practice is that the big banks agree to buy out the little guys at an appropriate discount to make the whole process go more smoothly. But we stood firm that there would be equal treatment for everybody. We knew that if we made any exceptions, it would open the floodgates.

A few of the small bankers honestly believed that extending the loans was just throwing good money after bad. To them it was a matter of taking their losses now rather than down the road.

In May, Steve Miller went on a whirlwind trip to Europe to visit the most stubborn banks over there. His job wasn't made any easier by an article in the *Financial Times* that said Chrysler had developed a secret plan to pay off the holdouts. As he arrived at each bank, they were all eager to learn the details. They were highly disappointed to find that their only options were to go along with the existing compromise or to send us into bankruptcy.

Back home, the recalcitrants were mostly small rural banks. One of them was threatening to screw up the entire Chrysler deal for a loan of $75,000. Here, too, there were rumors that we were quietly paying off the banks that weren't going along. These rumors encouraged the holdouts, but one by one we got them. As the number of holdouts became smaller, the pressure on each of them became overwhelming. Still, as May stretched into June, I was beginning to wonder just when this agony was finally going to stop.

The most dramatic conflict of all came in Rockford, Illinois, with the American National Bank and Trust Company. David Knapp, the bank president, was convinced that even with federal loan guarantees, Chrysler was about to go broke. He didn't want any part of it. His bank had sued to recover its loan of $650,000, and he was determined to hold out to the bitter end.

Fortunately for us, however, Rockford was also the site of one of our major assembly plants, and many of its residents worked for Chrysler or our suppliers. As soon as they heard about the problem, they started putting pressure on the bank to go along with the general agreement.

When that didn't help, Steve Miller flew down to meet with Knapp. Miller wasn't even sure that Knapp would see him, but if he refused, Steve intended to go to the local newspaper and tell them that Mr. Knapp was going to put five thousand people in Rockford out of work.

The mayor of Rockford set up a meeting with Knapp and Miller at City Hall. Miller gave Knapp a pep talk. He tried to explain that the deal wasn't to everybody's complete satisfaction but that the other banks were going along with it. He said that he just couldn't cut a special deal with any of the banks. Knapp heard him out, but he wouldn't change his mind. His position was: "I'm sorry, but if you take a loan you've got to pay it back."

A few days later the Rockford bank agreed to the plan. David Knapp had received a number of phone calls from companies that depended on Chrysler's survival. He had heard from politicians at every level. Thousands of UAW members had threatened to withdraw their money from his bank. There had even been a bomb threat from somebody in town, which he was sure had come from us.

After the trip to Rockford, Miller went to visit one or two other holdouts. By the end of June we had them all. And that was the end of it.

Or so we thought. Once we had the indicated agreement of all the banks, the only remaining task was to collect all the signed documents and have a closing. Normally, a closing consists of a bunch of lawyers who get together, look over some documents, and declare that the deal is complete.

But Chrysler's case was a bit more complicated. To start with, there were ten thousand individual documents. The printing bill alone for the final agreements came to close to $2 million! Stacked in a pile, the documents would have reached as high as a seven-story building.

Moreover, the documents were scattered in law firms all over New York, and in several other cities, too. Most of them, though, were in the Westvaco Building at 299 Park Avenue in Manhattan, in the law offices of our counsel, Debevoise, Plimpton, Lyons, & Gates.

On Monday evening, June 23, there was a meeting in these offices to get all the papers in order for the next day's closing. We had a large group of lawyers on hand, because if even a single document was missing, the whole deal was off.

At around 7:30 P.M., Steve Miller was in the cafeteria on the thirty-third floor of the Westvaco Building when he noticed black clouds of smoke out the window. He assumed that there was a grease fire in the kitchen, but he soon learned that the twentieth floor of the building was burning.

Steve says that he was sorely tempted to ignore the fire, because he didn't want to jeopardize the closing. But a few minutes later the building was evacuated, and everybody who could walked down thirty-three flights to the street.

By the time the group made its way downstairs, Park Avenue was completely blocked off by fire engines. Flames were leaping out of the windows. Steve's first thought was: "This is definitely a message from God. He's casting His vote against the deal. I guess we shouldn't have fooled around with the free-enterprise system."

Our people and the lawyers watched with growing horror as one after another the offices in the building burst into flames, while glass from the big windows went crashing into the street. Fortunately, the fire was being contained on the twentieth floor. All our documents were above the thirtieth floor.

Eventually the fire was under control, and the Chrysler people walked over to a local restaurant to have dinner. While Miller was walking down the street, he ran into Jerry Greenwald, who had just flown into the city to sign the documents. Jerry was on his way to the Westvaco Building when he spotted Steve.

"Boy," said Greenwald. "The traffic here is impossible. There's some kind of fire going on. Could you imagine what would happen if it was our building?"

Steve replied: "It *is* our building!"

Greenwald was familiar with Miller's sense of humor, so he

naturally assumed that Steve was joking. Jerry kept walking until he couldn't go any farther, at which point he realized it wasn't funny.

Finally, at two in the morning, Jerry, Steve, and the lawyers met in the Citicorp Center. They decided that it was essential to retrieve the papers from the smoldering building or the entire deal would be at risk. At two-thirty they were arguing their way through the police lines. A lot of firemen had already been injured in the fire, but our people were allowed in because they insisted that Chrysler's survival depended on removing those documents.

And so twenty guys went up in the elevator. They threw all the documents into cartons and mail carts. An hour later, in the middle of the night, a convoy of lawyers started pushing their mail carts down the middle of Park Avenue, over to the Citicorp Building to the offices of Shearman & Sterling, one of the law firms that represented the banks. They spent the rest of the night putting all the papers together so that the closing could proceed as planned.

The papers were reassembled between nine and noon the next day. Miraculously, nothing had been lost or damaged. At noon a large group of lawyers and bankers marched into a big conference room at Shearman & Sterling for the closing. There were speakerphones with connections to Paris, Detroit, Wall Street, Toronto, and Washington—where the Loan Guarantee Board was standing by.

Bill Matteson, our principal lawyer, called the roll. He went through the long list of banks represented in the room as well as those hooked up on the speakerphones. Are you ready to close, Toronto? Are you ready, Paris? Each group said yes.

At 12:26 P.M. on June 24, the deal was concluded to resounding cheers. We were finally entitled to receive the first installment of our federally backed loans. Later that day, after Salomon Brothers, our financial advisers, took their fee of $13,250,000 off the top, Steve Miller endorsed a check for $486,750,000. He walked over to Manny Hanny and filled out a deposit slip, just like any other depositor.

At long last, the New Chrysler Corporation was in business to stay.

XXII

THE K-CAR—
AND A CLOSE CALL

During our darkest days, the promise of the K-car was always the light at the end of the tunnel. For a couple of years, the prospect of an American-made, fuel-efficient, front-wheel-drive car was just about all we had to offer. Throughout the congressional hearings, and during the endless negotiations with the banks, our expectations for the K-car were what got us through.

The K-car is a sensational product. It's perfectly okay for me to brag about it, because I arrived at Chrysler too late to play much of a role in its creation.

This is the car that Hal Sperlich had been working on ever since he'd come to Chrysler in 1977. In many ways, it's what Hal and I had always wanted to build at Ford. It's the one we *would* have done if Henry hadn't been so stubborn about small cars.

The K-car was and is a comfortable, front-wheel-drive vehicle that ran well on only four cylinders. It offered twenty-five miles per gallon in city driving and forty-one on the highway. These figures were impressive in their own right. But even more important, they were slightly better than GM's X-car, which had been launched a year and a half earlier. Detroit had come out with small cars before, but the K-car was the first one roomy enough to accommodate a family of six while still light enough to deliver super fuel economy.

Sperlich's great triumph was that the car was strong and well stanced. It was solid. It wasn't flimsy-looking, like some of the other compacts on the market. Like the Mustang, the K-car was small and stylish. The difference was that the K-car could run on a very small engine.

In our ad campaign we announced that the K-car was an American alternative. To drive that point home, many of the ads were done in red, white, and blue. We also pointed out that the K-car was roomy enough to hold "six Americans" —a little shot at our Japanese competitors. We even had to install six seat belts in each car, which added slightly to our cost.

But our master stroke of marketing was to use the term "K-car" instead of the real names, Aries (for the Dodge line) and Reliant (for Chrysler). I'd love to take credit for that decision, but this was just one of those happy accidents that happens on its own. With all that we had been through, we were certainly overdue for a lucky break.

When a new car is in the early stages of development, the stylists usually assign it a code name for internal use. At Ford, we always used the names of animals. Chrysler and GM use letters of the alphabet. Later the marketing team goes through a list of possible names and researches them in detail.

At Chrysler, the K-car was the last train in the station. If we failed here, it was all over. With that awareness, we began talking about the car at a very early stage in its development, long before we had settled on the actual names. Without our planning it, the letter K seemed to stick in the public mind.

Naturally, once the public picked up on the "K-car" theme, we stuck with it in our advertising by announcing that "the K-cars are coming." We even decided upon a special promotion with a major retailer, which we called "K-car comes to K-Mart." Before long, the "K" designation had grown so popular that the real names, Reliant and Aries, had become more like subtitles. In 1983, when we finally removed the letter K from the back of the cars, our advertising agency was convinced it was a big mistake.

The Aries and Reliant are definitely the right cars for the times. They provide great fuel economy and a comfortable ride, and they look pretty good, too. That isn't just my judgment, by the way. *Motor Trend Magazine* named the Aries and Reliant as cars of the year for 1981, an award we had won three years earlier for the Omni and Horizon.

"These are the cars we need," wrote the magazine. "Surely these must be indicators of quality, signs of times that have come. But more than this, they reveal that maybe for the first time an American automaker has calculated the demeanor of the general car-buying public. With the Aries and Reliant, Chrysler will be able to serve up a substantially better car that will last longer in the face of heavy rock salt *and* traditional buyer neglect."

And Jim Dunne, automotive editor of *Popular Science*, observed: "If Chrysler could have designed a car that was right for today's market just three weeks ago instead of three and a half years ago, they still would have designed this car."

Today the K-car serves as the foundation for almost everything we do. Virtually all our other cars have been derived from its platform, including the LeBaron, Chrysler E Class, Dodge 600, the New Yorker, and to a lesser degree our sports cars, Dodge Daytona and Chrysler Laser.

Because we've done so much off the K platform, we've taken a lot of heat from the press—especially *The Wall Street Journal*. The way they describe it, you'd think we had invented some new way to cheat the customer!

Now, it's true that once upon a time, the ideal in Detroit was to create a completely new car for every price range. But these days, a totally new model requires an investment of about $1 billion. These days, "new" cars are an illusion. Each "new" car is invariably a mixture of new and previous parts. The new parts may include the sheet metal, the transmission, or the chassis. But nobody, not even GM, can afford to make a new car from scratch anymore.

Building a new car off the platform of another model has been going on in Detroit for fifty years. The Japanese have done it from the start. GM has been masterful at doing it, and many parts of the Chevrolet have found their way into Buicks and Cadillacs. And at Ford, as we've already seen, the Mustang was a restyled Falcon.

The smart guys use interchangeable parts to get their costs down. That's not only permissible, it's also essential. These days, to do a new car from scratch when you're unsure of the volume is a sure formula for bankruptcy.

At the same time, there *is* such a thing as going too far in that direction. GM learned this the hard way on two different occasions. In 1977, GM found themselves short of Oldsmobile V-8 engines, so they began to install comparable Chevrolet V-8's in some of their Oldsmobiles, Pontiacs, and Buicks.

Unfortunately, they forgot to tell their customers about the switch. Some of them got so angry that they filed lawsuits. When it was all over, the engine switch had cost GM more than $30 million.

GM had a similar problem with the Cadillac Cimarron. The

Cimarron was rushed into production when some of the marketing guys at Cadillac noticed that the median age of Cadillac buyers was somewhere between seventy and "deceased."

But the new model was little more than a fancied-up Chevrolet Cavalier. Even Pete Estes, a former GM president, complained that the Cimarron looked too much like a Chevrolet. Leather seats and automatic headlight dimmers were not enough to distinguish it from the basic J-car. The consumers sensed that something was wrong, and the Cimarron bombed in the marketplace.

Even with the perfect product, you can make mistakes. Eventually the K-car saved us. But its first year on the market coincided with some of the worst problems we ever had.

To our great distress, the K-car got off to a poor start. In October 1980, when we introduced the Aries and Reliant, they fizzled. We had some unexpected problems with our new robotic welders in the factories, which led to production snags. For a proper launch, we needed thirty-five thousand cars in the showrooms on Introduction Day. Instead, there were only ten thousand.

Worse, we had sticker-shocked the consumers right off their feet. At the time, we were involved in a tough price war with GM's X-car, our primary domestic competitor. Their basic Citation Hatchback went for $6,270, so we'd priced the basic K-car at $5,880.

The only way we could underprice GM and still survive was to make it up on options. And so we built a lot of cars with air conditioning, automatic transmissions, velour upholstery, and electric windows, which added a couple of thousand dollars to the price.

We should have paid more attention to our research. We had advance information that customers would be more interested in the basic models, which sold for around $6,000. But we were in a crisis mentality. As a result, we sent out too many cars whose total price was between $8,000 and $9,000.

It was a costly mistake. We should have waited until the K-car had gained some initial acceptance and *then* introduced the options. We had no business reaching for the wealthier customers. These weren't the people who were going to buy the K-car in the first place.

The good news is that we identified the problem very early and were able to correct it. We knew that the customers were coming into the showrooms, so the interest was certainly there. But we also knew that most of them were leaving without placing an order. When we interviewed these people on their way out the door, they all told us the same thing: "I thought this car was supposed to be a good buy. Then I looked at the sticker price." As soon as possible, we started producing more basic models. Before long, sales picked up.

But by December we had run into another problem. The prime rate had now zoomed up to 18.5 percent. Two months earlier, when the K-cars were first introduced, interest rates had been 5 percent lower. If they had *stayed* at 13.5 percent, we could have sold a lot of cars. But in those days, interest rates were changing almost daily. And cars as well as houses were going unsold.

I was furious with the Fed's mercurial behavior on interest rates, but there was nothing I could do to change it. I could, however, respond to the situation. And I did.

To fight the specter of high interest rates, we came up with a floating rebate plan. We would grant a refund to any customer who bought a car on credit—based on the difference between 13 percent and the prevailing interest rate when the car was purchased.

When I announced the new plan, I said: "The Lord helps those who help themselves." He must have been listening, even though Paul Volcker wasn't, because our gamble paid off. Before long, Ford and GM were offering rebates of their own.

By early 1981, sales had picked up considerably. Despite the awkward beginning, the K-cars finished the year with more than 20 percent of the compact-car market. And they've been selling well ever since. While some people were still writing us off, we sold a million Aries and Reliants, which gave us the cash to start developing other new models.

But that came later. Because our K-cars got off to such a slow start, we began 1981 in very bad shape. Although we had fought so hard all year to keep Chrysler's bad news off the front pages, we soon had to go back to Washington to draw down another $400 million in guarantees.

When it came to actually borrowing that money, the Loan Guarantee Board had put a number of roadblocks in our way. For example, we couldn't get the loans all at once, but only in installments. The first two installments were pretty close together in 1980.

But the third drawdown, a year later, was a complete disaster from the perspective of public relations. Most people just didn't understand what was going on. They saw the story on television and they thought: "Here we go again. Those guys just got a billion and a half dollars. Why are they going back for more?"

I should never have agreed to borrow the money in three installments. For each drawdown, we had to face up to the bad headlines. It was terrible. I don't think the Loan Guarantee Board would have let us borrow the entire sum all at once, but instead of three installments, we could probably have arranged for two installments of $600 million each.

Each time we went back for more money, our sales dropped off. The public was under the impression that Chrysler was a bottomless pit. Plenty of people who were considering our products changed their minds and bought cars from our competitors. It's impossible to know for sure, but my guess is that about one third of the $1.2 billion that we actually received in guaranteed loans was wasted through lost sales as a result of all the bad publicity. Even so, I don't know any other way we could have survived.

To qualify for the final $400 million of our loan, we had to arrange for yet another round of concessions. We asked the banks for an additional $600 million through the conversion of debt into preferred stock. We asked labor for a freeze on cost-of-living adjustments. We asked our suppliers for more time to pay and a 5 percent price reduction during the first quarter of 1981. And G. William Miller, secretary of the treasury, asked the banks to forgive half of our remaining debt. Once again, the alternative was bankruptcy.

This time, the banks forgave a total of $1.1 billion worth of debt in exchange for preferred stock in the company. Preferred stock normally pays a dividend, but in our case there wouldn't be any until we had paid off the guaranteed loans. The bankers didn't take our stock offer too seriously. But the optimists among them knew that if Chrysler ever came back from the grave, they'd eventually recover a good part of their money.

Throughout 1981, our survival was never more than a week-by-week proposition. Even with the K-car, our losses were still staggering—$478.5 million for the year. To make matters worse, the Loan Guarantee Board was putting some additional strictures on us that did little to lift our morale.

One of their rules was that we had to pay them an administrative fee of $1 million every month. That really ticked me off, because our January payment alone covered their annual expenses, so the next $11 million was pure profit for the Treasury. Hell, if I could have had a deal like that for Chrysler, I wouldn't have needed the loan guarantees in the first place!

Under the terms of the act, the government was required to

charge us an annual fee of .5 percent of the total amount to administer the loans. But William Miller had the authority to raise the fee to 1 percent if he believed the loans were at risk. He did—and 1 percent of $1.2 billion comes to $12 million a year. We had no negotiating leverage on that one, no opportunity to say: "That's too much, we don't like it." That extra $6 million could have gone for something more productive to help ensure our long-term future.

My second quarrel with the board was the ridiculous amount of paperwork with which they burdened us. One good comprehensive report a month would have given them all the information they needed. Instead, they asked us for a continuing mountain of documents, and it was a pain to keep up with it all.

To make matters worse, they didn't even *read* the stuff. If they had any questions, they'd just pick up the phone and call. I can understand that early on in the whole process the Loan Guarantee Board must have been nervous and that it was important to them to make sure that everybody knew what was going on. But as we gradually became healthier, there was no mechanism to change the rules.

Then we ran into a problem that could only have come from the fertile mind of a real bureaucrat. The board ordered us to sell our Gulfstream jet. To the little minds in Washington, the Chrysler jet was a symbol of the profligate spending of a big corporation. Never mind that the government had a hundred private jets—all at taxpayers' expense—to help them conduct *their* business. Nobody blinks when you spend $100 million for new robots, but when you send one of your top guys around to the factories to teach the workers how to use those new robots, that's OK—but only if he flies commercial.

So what if he has to get from Highland Park, Michigan, to Rockford, Illinois, or Kokomo, Indiana. Some of our plants can't be reached very easily by commercial aircraft. And if I'm paying a guy two hundred grand a year, I don't want him spending his time in airports.

Private planes save a lot of wear and tear on our employees. People outside the business world often have the impression that most executives goof off. Not the ones I know. They work twelve and fourteen hours a day, and their time is valuable.

The corporate jet is not a perk. It's a necessity. Believe me, it would be a lot nicer to fly first class in a commercial airplane with a friendly stewardess serving us drinks. But the company jet is a great time-saver—and a stress-saver as well.

✻　　✻　　✻

To be fair, not everything that the Loan Guarantee Board asked us to do was trivial or unduly meddlesome. Among their more reasonable demands was that we look actively for a merger partner. When I first came to Chrysler with Global Motors on my mind, I assumed that any conceivable merger would involve a foreign company such as Mitsubishi or Volkswagen. But after one look at our balance sheet, nobody would even talk to me.

In 1981, as the roof was caving in, it seemed a merger might be the only way out. They say that necessity is the mother of invention. Well, when the tide turned against us once more, we got as inventive as we could. We came up with a last-ditch plan, an idea that sounded preposterous on the surface but that actually made a lot of sense. Because we had the K-car and they had no real equivalent, we proposed a merger between Chrysler and Ford.

There were a thousand obstacles to such a plan, but the first thing that came to everyone's mind was the personality question. "Let's say it all works," said our bankers. "But Henry's still around and so are you—how could you two make a go of it?"

"Listen," I replied, "here's what I'll do. Henry has already announced that he's stepping aside. I'm willing to do the same. I'd like to stick around for twelve months to help put this deal together. After it's done, I'll walk away. This thing is obviously bigger than both of us."

The other major problem was that this kind of merger would normally be a violation of the antitrust laws. So I checked with Pete Rodino of Watergate fame and with some of the other guys on the Judiciary Committee. They thought that because we were failing, the rules could be waived. I also called Bob Strauss, a great lawyer and major figure in the Democratic party. He too thought that we might be able to pull it off.

Once the antitrust problem was out of the way—at least in theory—we could focus on the positive. The previous year, 1980, had been a disaster for us: we ended up losing $1.7 billion. But 1980 had been no picnic at Ford, either. Their losses were almost as bad as ours—over $1.5 billion. Far more important was that their market share was plunging. Back in 1978, it had been as high as 28 percent. Three years later, it had dropped as low as 15 percent.

I asked Tom Denomme of our staff to draw up some plans. Within a few weeks Tom put together a proposal that made beautiful sense.

Under its terms, Ford would physically take over Chrysler. Because they were so much larger as well as healthier, Ford had to be the surviving company. Chrysler and Dodge would continue to operate, but as a third and fourth division at Ford, alongside the Ford and Lincoln-Mercury Divisions.

Tom and I saw great benefits for both companies in a merger. Their strengths were our weaknesses—and vice versa. Both of us had spent many years at Ford before coming over to Chrysler, so we understood the problems and the needs of each side.

If the merger went through, the benefits to Chrysler would be obvious—so obvious, in fact, that they could be summed up in a single world. Survival.

But what was in it for Ford? A great deal. At the time, Ford was very strong in Europe, where they were spending a disproportionate amount of money. But in America they were dying in the marketplace. After the second oil crisis, they were being badly hit by the imports. Aside from the Escort/Lynx subcompact—Ford's "world car" and their equivalent of our Omni/Horizon—they didn't have any small front-wheel-drive cars.

Moreover, Ford was about to embark on a massive investment of billions of dollars in order to produce the Tempo and Topaz, only to duplicate the kind of roomy, front-wheel-drive product that already existed at Chrysler in the K-car. If we merged, we could begin selling a version of their Escort to replace our own Omni/Horizon, and they could begin selling a version of our new Aries and Reliant. Under the terms of our plan, Ford would provide a larger, front-wheel-drive car, originally planned for 1987, and most of the larger models as well as the trucks. We would supply the 1984 minivan.

For Ford, a merger with Chrysler represented the fastest, easiest way to get back to their original position of being a strong number two. With a stroke of the pen, they would surpass GM in truck sales and also be number one in the Canadian and Mexican car markets. Domestically, a merger would mean that Ford's market share would jump straight up from 17 percent to 27 percent.

If a merger with Chrysler went through, Ford would have been at 75 percent of GM's strength in U.S. car sales. Then we would have seen a real horse race. Alfred Sloan would have turned over in his grave, because the new company would have four divisions against GM's five. It would have been a fantastic thing to have these two great companies going at it head to head. It would have been great for America. And the bankers and the lawyers would have loved it, because it would have been the biggest deal in the history of American industry.

On the other hand, if Chrysler simply folded, our research showed that Ford's share would rise only minimally. In that scenario, the great bulk of our business would be picked up by GM and especially by the imports.

We showed the plan to some of the top bankers in New York, and they flipped. "Made in heaven," they said. "The products fit. The dealer organizations fit. Everything works."

We had drawn up hypothetical balance sheets, and they looked terrific. We had an operating plan. We were in a position to add $1 billion in profit to the combination. There was strength in those numbers.

Salomon Brothers, our investment bankers, thought the plan was pretty good. Jim Wolfensohn, who handled the Chrysler account, agreed to approach Goldman Sachs, who represented Ford. Using financial data from Chrysler plus whatever they could dig up on Ford, Salomon Brothers fleshed out the idea and put together a point-by-point guide as to why the merger made sense for both parties and how it could best be brought about.

Goldman Sachs showed some interest in the proposal, and they passed it along to the top people at Ford. At this stage the plan was absolutely secret. Because this was a once-in-a-lifetime opportunity, I went to see Bill Ford and I pitched it to him. But aside from that meeting, we had taken great pains to conceal it from the world. Everything had been done behind the scenes, hush-hush, without any leaks to the media.

Suddenly the whole thing came tumbling down. Philip Caldwell, chairman of Ford, blew the whistle. He preempted the whole discussion by making a statement to the press. In effect, what he said was: Chrysler has proposed a merger with us, but we'd never be that stupid.

Ford put out that statement to rag us a little. But at no point did they give the proposal a thorough analysis. Caldwell simply announced that the board had voted unanimously not to open any negotiations with Chrysler. Later one of the Ford board members told me that they got about a two-minute look at the plan. They had responded in twenty-four hours; it would have taken them twenty-four *days* to study that proposal properly. In a single day all they could do was declare it was a bad idea and go along with management.

The way I see it, Ford's management was opposed because they knew that we had already taken most of their good guys, and they figured that if the deal went through, they might be left out in the cold. I imagine that Henry, who was supposedly retired, also retched at the idea. So they outlined only the worst-case scenario. I think they missed a great opportunity.

I responded with a statement of my own that such a merger would have been good for the country and that America needed a real competitor to General Motors. It was a shame, because I had already gotten the right people in Washington to start nodding. They'd said that if we could get Ford to agree, they'd do their best to make sure it could fly. But the plan got blown out of the water by Ford without a fair test.

If we could somehow have put this deal together, the only ones going crazy trying to stop it would have been General Motors. Their attitude would have been: "We already did that in the 1920s. Nobody should be allowed to do it again. A Chrysler-Ford cartel? No way! That would make things too hot for us."

If the merger had gone through, the American automobile industry would have been permanently changed. The morning after the merger, there would have been no duplication between Chrysler and Ford. We'd be saving three or four billion dollars in investments. Purchasing would be easier in a larger company. And fixed costs would be cut drastically because, like GM, we'd have a lot of interchangeable parts.

The timing was right. Perhaps it still is. But I don't think the Justice Department would allow it now. They'd yell and scream because it's a perfect horizontal integration of two giants in an oligopoly that has only three players. It would get knocked down in the Justice Department on antitrust grounds. But with the GM-Toyota deal and Washington's new philosophy on mergers, who knows?

A merger would still make sense, even though Chrysler is now healthy. GM has five divisions, but Ford and Chrysler have only two each. That's a recipe for losing your shirt on fixed costs.

The way things are going, by the year 2000 there will be only two fighters in the ring anyway: GM and Japan, Inc. A merger between Ford and Chrysler is probably the single most dramatic action that could be taken to strengthen the American automotive industry vis-à-vis the Japanese.

Of course, it all depends on your perspective. Over at Ford they still believe the industry will bounce back to what it was in the good old days and that Ford will become a contender once more. But they'll always be caught in the middle, with the Japanese underpricing them on the low end and GM owning most of the high-price and luxury business. Ford is the meat in the sandwich, gradually being eaten up.

Even without a merger with Ford, I had hoped that we would be on solid footing by the end of 1981. What I hadn't counted on were continuing high interest rates and a terrible economy. On November 1, we reached yet another crisis point: we were down to our *last one million dollars*!

At Chrysler we generally spend about $50 million *a day*. To be down to our last $1 million was absurd. It was like having a buck and a half in your checking account. In the car business, $1 million is like the spare change you keep in your top drawer.

At this point any one of the big suppliers could have knocked us off. You've got to realize that our accounts payable to suppliers was running about $800 million a month. The only way out was to ask all of our suppliers for more time. But that's harder than it sounds. If we went to them and said, "Hey, we're going to be a little slow in paying you," it could have started a chain reaction. Confidence is what keeps the company and its suppliers glued together. If that starts to come undone, the suppliers begin to act in their own interest. They get nervous, and their fear can easily lead to disaster.

A couple of small suppliers actually did stop shipping. We were forced to shut down our Jefferson Avenue plant for a couple of days. But we managed to work out deals with them to extend credit terms from twenty to twenty-two or twenty-three days, and in some cases as much as thirty. Goodyear Tire and National Steel made deals with us on the side. Chuck Pilliod and Pete Love, I will remember you forever— you kept the faith!

I also worried a lot about meeting our payrolls, but we never missed a single one. We always paid our people on time. Amazingly, we never missed paying a supplier, although we did stretch things out and pay slowly at times—but only by prior agreement. There were times when I said: "God, we need to ship a thousand more cars to get this much cash or we can't meet a twenty-eight-million-dollar payment on Thursday, or a fifty-million-dollar payroll on Friday." Day by day, it was that close, and oh, the numbers were so big.

We had to be magicians. We had to know which ones we could

delay payment on, whose calls we had to take. When you scramble, you scramble like a son of a bitch.

These days, of course, they see our cash in the bank and they give us sixty days. Now we can get credit without even asking for it!

It's the old Catch-22. Want a loan? Show us that you don't need it, and then we'll give it to you. If you're rich, if there's money in the bank, there's always plenty of credit. But if you don't have the cash, then you can't get any.

My father had taught me this fact of life thirty years earlier, but I guess I wasn't listening. I sure saw the light in November of 1981!

It Only Hurts When I Laugh

Of all the forms of reporting, there is nothing more concise and cutting than the newspaper cartoon. During the Chrysler crisis, hundreds appeared. A caricature and a caption captured the news in a hurry. The chronology over the four years shows our changing fortunes. Here are some of the best—or worst—depending on your point of view.

Summer 1979

PAUL CONRAD/© 1979, LOS ANGELES TIMES. REPRINTED WITH PERMISSION.

"This is not a stickup! . . . I'm from Chrysler!"

Winter 1979

Winter 1981

Winter 1981

REPRINTED BY PERMISSION OF UNITED FEATURE SYNDICATE.

Spring 1982

DICK WRIGHT/SCRIPPS–HOWARD NEWSPAPERS.

Summer 1982

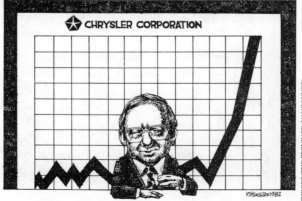

BOB KRIEGER/THE PROVINCE (VANCOUVER).

Winter 1983

ED ASHLEY/THE TOLEDO BLADE.

Spring 1983

REPRINTED BY PERMISSION. © 1983 NEA, INC.

Spring 1983

JON MCINTOSH/THE BOSTON GLOBE.

XXIII

PUBLIC MAN, PUBLIC OFFICE

By the middle of 1983, when the company was solidly on its feet again, there were stories floating around that I was running for President. I guess the rumors started because of all the TV commercials I did for Chrysler. Many people now think I'm an actor. But that's ridiculous. Everybody knows that being an actor doesn't qualify you to be President!

During the congressional debate, the ads we ran to explain our position were all signed by me. The campaign was highly effective, and when it was over, our ad agency decided to take the idea of my accountability one step further by featuring my face in television commercials.

This wasn't the first time that idea had come up. Prior to K&E's arrival on the scene, Young & Rubicam had also urged me to appear on TV. I was against it, and I turned for advice to my old friend Leo-Arthur Kelmenson, the president of Kenyon & Eckhardt.

Leo shared my skepticism. "Lee," he said, "if I were you, I wouldn't do it. The timing's wrong." Kelmenson stressed that the only valid reason for my appearing in our ads was to strengthen Chrysler's credibility. But at that point, he said, I was still too new on the job, and the company was too weak. Credibility is something you can earn only over time. And if you haven't earned it, you can't use it.

When Kenyon & Eckhardt asked me to go on television, they made a better case. A year had passed and a lot had happened.

During the congressional hearings, I had become a nationally known figure. The Chrysler story was constantly in the news, and the advertising people were eager to turn this liability into an asset.

At our strategy meetings in Highland Park, the agency made a strong presentation: "Everybody thinks Chrysler's going bankrupt. Somebody has to tell them you're not. The most believable guy to do that would be you. First, you're well known. And second, the viewers know very well that after you make the commercial, you have to go back to the business of making the cars you just touted. By appearing in these ads, you're putting your money where your mouth is."

In retrospect, I have to admit they were right. It's clear that my appearing in the television ads was an essential part of Chrysler's recovery.

But when the idea was first suggested, I was totally negative. Signing the print ads was one thing. That was like writing a series of open letters to the American public. But television ads were a completely different kettle of fish. Among other problems, I didn't see how I had the time to do them. There's a very good reason why commercials are the best thing on television—they're made with far more care and creativity than almost anything else on the tube.

But all that care and creativity are enormously time-consuming to produce. Making a commercial is the most tedious thing in the world. It's like watching the grass grow. I like to move fast, but shooting a single sixty-second spot can easily take up eight or ten hours. Every day I spent in front of the television cameras would mean that much less time to work at the car business. You just can't be an actor and a CEO on the same day.

I was also convinced that any corporate chairman who appears in his company's ads has got to be on an ego trip. Whenever I've seen a CEO pushing his own company, it's left a bad taste in my mouth. I had spent thirty years in marketing, and there were certain broad standards you just didn't violate. One of them goes something like this:

When a client proves refractory
Show a picture of his factory.
If the boss still moans and sighs,
Make his logo twice the size.
But only in the direst cases
Ever show the clients' faces.

Naturally, I was concerned that my appearing in television commercials would be seen by the public as a final act of desperation that would cause the entire enterprise to backfire.

For years, celebrities had been pitching products on TV. At Chrysler, we had used Joe Garagiola and Ricardo Montalban. Then we added John Houseman and Frank Sinatra. But until recently, only a handful of national business leaders have starred in their companies' advertising—and the three most notable are all named Frank: Frank Borman of Eastern Airlines, Frank Sellinger of Schlitz—and of course Frank Perdue, the chicken king.

Besides credibility, there's another reason to feature the boss in the ad, although it's not a very good one. If the ad fails, it's *his* ass on the line. You can always blame it on the chairman's enormous ego. After all, the public routinely assumes that it was his idea—even when it wasn't.

Some months earlier, the people at K&E had asked me to allow one of their people to come to our meetings with a hand-held movie camera to prepare a film record of our recovery. They shot some footage of me addressing a group of dealers, and as an experiment, they used a few seconds of it at the end of one of our commercials.

They liked what they saw, and they asked me to make a couple of commercials on my own. While I understood their reasoning, I still didn't like the idea. But one day I was on a plane with John Morrissey, the agency head in Detroit, and he put it to me flatly: "We have to tell the public that we're a new company, different from the old Chrysler bunch. The best way to get that message across is to feature the new boss. I don't think there's any other answer except for you to do it." So I agreed to give it a shot.

There was only one aspect of all of this that appealed to me. Unlike some of the spokesmen we had used in the past, I work cheap. Once I did 108 takes in about ten hours, and all I got for it was a corned beef sandwich and a cup of coffee!

At first I delivered only tag lines—brief announcements at the end of commercials, such as: "I'm not asking you to buy one of our cars on faith. I'm asking you to compare." Or: "If you buy a car without considering Chrysler, that'll be too bad—for both of us."

Later we got bolder and developed a more aggressive approach, including: "You can go with Chrysler, or you can go with someone else—and take your chances," and the now-famous line in which I pointed my finger at the camera and said: "If you can find a better car—buy it." That one was my own, by the way, which may explain why I could deliver it with such conviction.

"If you can find a better car—buy it" has already been parodied in a hundred different ways. It must have been effective, since I'm always getting letters telling me: "I did what you said. I shopped around and I couldn't find a better car."

But of course, others said: "I followed your advice. I *found* a better car, and it sure as hell wasn't yours!" But that's part of the risk—and part of the fun. My phrase became part of the jargon. I tried to ignore the hundreds of innovative suggestions that played on this same theme, like a big billboard in Dallas that announced: "If you can find a better Bourbon, drink it," or a letter that said: "If you can find a better lemon, suck it!"

The more commercials I made, the more active I became in deciding exactly what I would say. Of course, whenever the chairman comes up with a good line, it makes things a little awkward for the agency. They start to wonder: "Gee, if that line is so good, why didn't *we* think of it?"

In a later commercial, which has also become famous, I started out by saying: "There was a time when 'Made in America' meant something. It meant you made the best. Unfortunately, a lot of Americans don't believe that anymore." At that point I wanted to add the following line: "And for good reason. We probably deserved that reputation, because we shipped a lot of crap out of Detroit in our day."

When they heard that, even in the cleaned-up version, the agency went bananas. They said: "This isn't the place to make confessions. If you say that, the guy sitting in front of the tube whose 1975 Volaré has rusted through is going to write in for a thousand-dollar adjustment." So we compromised. I added the words "And maybe with good reason" —and we left it at that.

At the time, these ads were pretty unusual. But given our situation, we needed something dramatic. Due to circumstances beyond our control, Chrysler already had an identity all its own. We were already perceived as being very different from the rest of the American auto industry.

In marketing terms, the choice we faced was simple—either we could try to join the crowd and become one of the boys, or we could accept our separate identity and try to make it work to our advantage. By featuring the chairman in our ads, we chose the second course.

In the television ads, as in the print ads that preceded them, we decided to deal directly with the public's reservations and doubts. It was no secret that American consumers had a low opinion of American cars. Most people believed that German and Japanese cars were inherently better than anything Detroit was turning out.

We let them know right off the bat that this was no longer the case. And we backed up our claim with an offer of $50 to any customer who compared one of our cars with anyone else's—even if they ended up buying from the competition.

At the same time, we were careful not to be *too* bold. We wanted to project a spirit of confidence but not arrogance. Given the perception of Chrysler products, we didn't want to claim directly that Chrysler made the best cars—although that's what we believed.

Instead, we wanted the customer to come to that decision on his own. And so we maintained that anyone who was looking for a new car ought to at least *consider* one of ours. We believed that the quality of our cars would be apparent to anyone who checked them out. If we could only get enough customers into the showrooms, our sales would increase accordingly. And that's what happened.

But I can't stay on as a pitchman forever. I get tired of it, and so does the public. In a disposable society like ours, there are no real heroes. Nobody lasts very long. Every week *People* magazine serves us up a new bunch of celebrities. Within a few months most of them have disappeared.

So I don't want to wear out my welcome. I'm in people's living rooms fairly often, and I want to stop before they say: "Oh, no, here comes that man again."

Ever since I started making commercials, I've been trying to stop. But K&E has always found ways to keep me in the picture. I found out only recently that they had even worked up a secret plan for a Lee Iacocca Muppet to join Miss Piggy, Kermit, and the rest of them. Without telling me, they tested the idea before some audiences around the country. The audiences thought the commercials were fun but too cute. Thank God for that.

The crisis at Chrysler has been over for a couple of years now, and I want to convey that in the commercials. When I disappear from television, I hope people will say: "We're not hearing from that guy anymore because he's on his feet again. He came to us when he was sick, and now he's healthy." Otherwise there's the danger of crying wolf.

There's another problem with the commercials: they've wrecked my privacy. In a one-industry town like Detroit, I've been a celebrity for years. But now, because of the commercials, I can't even walk down the street in New York. I walk a block, and there are five double-takes, six people stopping me, and seven drivers yelling out my name. It was fun for about a week. After that, it's a pain in the ass.

A couple of years ago I was watching a TV show in Detroit. The host was interviewing a local columnist, and he said: "I want to throw out some names, and I'd like you to tell me what they mean in this town."

The first name was "Iacocca."

Right away, the guy answered: "Fame."

"Fame?" asked the host. "What do you mean? Is he powerful?"

"Oh, no," said the columnist. "He doesn't have any power. He's just famous—famous for his TV commercials."

I nodded and thought: "I agree." It's like somebody said a few years back: in our society, a celebrity is a person who's famous for being well known.

Fame is fleeting. To me, what it means most of all is that loss of privacy. Don't get me wrong—there are times when it can be very pleasant. I remember being on an elevator at the Waldorf in New York when a woman got on and pointed to me: "Iacocca," she said, "we're so proud of you. Keep doing what you're doing. You're a real American." Then she shook my hand and got off.

One of our board members turned to me and said: "Doesn't that make you feel good inside?" You're damn right it does.

A few minutes later, I was out on the street and a little old lady came up to me. "I know who you are," she said. "I come from Puerto Rico. I've only been here a few years, but I think you're doing a very good thing for this country. You're so strong and so American." There's an element of pent-up patriotism to many of these encounters, probably because of the "made in America" commercial, or just because America roots for the underdog.

But fame has other sides, too. Whenever I'm trying to have dinner in a restaurant, every five minutes some guy comes over to talk about his '65 Mustang or his Dodge Dart that's still running—or not running!

Believe this or not, I'm really a very private person. That was pretty hard for even me to remember when a couple of years ago I was asked to be grand marshal of the Columbus Day parade in New York. It was a great honor, but it also made me pretty nervous, being exposed like that in front of a million people and waving like I was Douglas MacArthur or someone coming home from the wars.

I certainly like being recognized for what I've done, but I'm always being reminded that my fame has little to do with my accomplishments. Am I famous for the Mustang? For guiding Ford through the most profitable years in its history? For having turned around Chrysler? It's a hell of a note, but I have a feeling I'm going to be remembered only for my TV commercials. Oh, that cursed tube!

Twenty-five years ago, I ran across an astounding number. I learned that in American homes, television sets were on an average of 42.7 hours per week! From that day forward, I have been awed by the power of television. I started committing millions of dollars to the purchase of TV commercials. At one point at Ford, I got carried away and bought 100 percent of all NFL games. At a half a million dollars a minute, that would be impossible today.

I knew then how powerful TV was, but I hadn't yet experienced it personally. As a result of my Chrysler commercials, I've now heard from just about everybody. A dozen optometrists zeroed in on my eyeglasses and concluded the frames were made in France. They didn't think this appropriate for a guy who was delivering a made-in-America commercial. Then there were three oral surgeons who wrote me about my loose dentures. I was offended and wrote back that my teeth were all mine—and in great shape. They were disturbed that my teeth never showed, even when I smiled, but they said the cure was simple. They had what they called "an aesthetic procedure" to buck my teeth out or cut my lips back! Now I'll do anything to sell cars, but that is going a little too far.

If my mail is any indication, I also seem to have popularized blue shirts with white collars. By the way, even though I've never smoked a cigar during a TV commerical, I've been seen a number of times on television with a cigar in hand. And that is a no-no, believe me! The press insists I smoke somewhere between 12 and 100 cigars a day. Pure fiction. Three cigars is a big day for me.

It's those damn commercials that started all the stories that I was running for President. I got patriotic and said, "Let's make America mean something again," and people identified with it. I really had no idea that the commercials would be seen in this light.

The presidential rumors got a major boost in June of 1982 with a front-page story in *The Wall Street Journal* that began: "Lee Iacocca, it is whispered around Detroit, has a hankering for public office. Not just any public office, but one grand enough to satisfy a man with an ego as big as all outdoors. Lee Iacocca, the chairman of Chrysler Corp., it is said, yearns to be the president of all the people. If a Hollywood star can, why not a Detroit car salesman?"

The logic was somewhat less than compelling. Iacocca gives a lot of speeches. He does those TV commercials. He's involved with the Statue of Liberty. He's a colorful figure in an industry of faceless men. He obviously has a big ego. Therefore, he's running for President.

Nevertheless, the story resulted in a tremendous amount of attention. Lots of articles, lots of mail. How did it start? My best hunch is that a few of the Detroit journalists got together over drinks one day and cooked it up as a gag. When they first asked me if I'd like to be President, I didn't know how to answer, so I kidded with them and said: "Yeah, I'd like to be President, but only if I were appointed and only for one year." I didn't even say one term, because it makes you too old. I got old enough during my first term at Chrysler.

Amanda Bennett's article appeared in the *Journal*'s semihumorous column in the middle of the front page. Amanda had just done a piece on the last whorehouse in Michigan, and this one ran in the same spot. That pretty well describes what I thought of the article.

A few months later, there was a story in *Time* about possible presidential candidates in 1984, and again my name was mentioned. The magazine said I could run for President because I have "an expressive face." Another example of persuasive political logic.

It's a funny thing about that phrase. Back in 1962, *Time* threw a big reception in Detroit, and Henry Luce, the founder, was there. I was invited because I was an up-and-coming young Ford vice-president, although this was a couple of years before the Mustang came out.

At one point in the evening I was introduced to Mr. Luce. He looked at me and said: "An expressive face." A few minutes later one of his guys said to me: "Someday he'll put you on the cover. He likes expressive faces." And I'll be damned if the ghost of Henry Luce didn't use that same phrase to describe me twenty years later. It hit me like a ton of bricks. Is that really how we choose our leaders?

People end up in the White House for all kinds of reasons. I once asked Jimmy Carter why he ran for President, and he said: "As governor of Georgia I had visits from some of the other people running for President, and they didn't seem very smart." I know the feeling.

But while I might enjoy being President, it's strictly a fantasy because I couldn't imagine running for office. These guys are programmed like robots sixteen hours a day—lunches, dinners, the banquet circuit, shaking hands, going to the gates of the factories—it's endless. If you run for President, you've got to be enthusiastic. To endure all that drudgery, you've got to want it really badly.

I've already shaken millions of hands. Over the past forty years I've gone to more meetings and conventions than I can possibly remember. I've held so many cocktail glasses that my right hand is permanently bent. I feel like I've seen every factory in the world.

I've now made something like a hundred speeches just in the ballroom of the Waldorf-Astoria. By now, the staff there knows the Chrysler story as well as I do. During one of my recent speeches, I noticed some of the waiters lip-synching my text as I spoke. Later one of them came up and asked me for a loan guarantee of $200 until payday!

But in all seriousness, I'm exhausted. I've grown old during my years at Chrysler. If I were ten years younger—then maybe I could see myself going into politics. Back then, I was full of piss and vinegar. But the firing at Ford and the long crisis at Chrysler and especially the loss of my dear wife have taken a lot out of me.

I also don't have the temperament for politics. I watched McNamara, and if he couldn't cut it and really help this country, I couldn't possibly do it, because he's more disciplined than I am. Besides, I'm far too impatient. I'm candid to a fault, not a diplomat. I can't exactly imagine myself waiting eight years to see if we could get an energy bill passed.

I'm too outspoken to be a good politician. If a guy's giving me a lot of baloney, I tell him to buzz off because he's wrong. Somehow I don't think the presidency works that way.

But I do think that our national leadership consists of too many lawyers and not enough people from business. I'd like to see a system where we brought in twenty top managers to run the business side of the country and maybe even paid them $1 million a year, tax-free. That would be a real incentive, and then we'd see a lot more talented people interested in public life.

A couple of years ago, a high-powered group of political types from Michigan tried to get me to run for governor. Why? Because being a governor is the best springboard to the presidency. They said: "You've saved Chrysler, and now it's doing very nicely. What about Michigan? It's got all the same problems and it's your home state now."

I had a good answer for them. "Look," I said, "if I'm ever going to run for governor, find me a nice cash-rich state like Arizona. Maybe then I'll consider it. But no more going with anybody without a little money in the bank. Once is enough!"

Ever since that *Wall Street Journal* story appeared in 1982, I've had to spend a lot of time denying that I'm running for President. But it's a no-win situation, because even the *real* candidates tell you that they're not running until they finally decide to go public with their ambitions. So a lot of people don't believe me. "If he's not running," they ask, "then why is he writing a book? Why is he involved with the Statue of Liberty unless he's planning to wrap himself in the flag?"

When nobody bought my denials, I decided to have some fun. Whenever I was asked if I intended to run for President, I would say: "Let me get those rumors out of the way. I find them unjustified and unsettling. Besides, they stir up a lot of unrest in my campaign staff."

For the most part, there was nothing I could do to put an end to the speculation. If you talk only about cars, people say you're parochial. If you talk about national and world issues, they say you're running for office.

Finally, at the end of 1983, I signed a three-year contract with Chrysler. And that, more than anything else, put an end to the talk of my alleged political ambitions.

Although I was never a candidate, I learned a lot from all the presidential talk. Shortly after the whole business began, I was having a conversation with a guy in advertising. He said something interesting: "I've decided why everybody talks about you as a presidential candidate. It's very simple. They don't believe anybody anymore. You talk to them and you make them believe that you stand for something and then you pursue it. You don't bullshit them, and the American public has been bullshitted too often."

Another thing that I apparently represent to people is that I'm a good manager. I can cut costs and make money and manage a large institution, and if there's anything I'm sure of, it's that. I know how to control a budget, and I've had experience in turning around a failing company. Americans must be looking for a leader who can balance the budget as well as restore a sense of purpose to the country.

I get a lot of mail about running for President. It's made me aware that there's a real vacuum out there. People are hungry for somebody to tell them the truth—that America isn't bad, it's great—or at least that it can be made great again if we just get back on track. They write to me because I'm on TV, because I make speeches, and because Chrysler is back on its feet. A guy will write in longhand: "Why don't you turn this country around? Why are you wasting your time selling cars?"

People are hungry to be led. I don't believe for a moment that we live in an antihero society. It's just that since Eisenhower, we haven't found ourselves a leader we can depend on. Kennedy got killed. Johnson dragged us into a war. Nixon disgraced us. Ford was an appointed, interim leader. Carter, for all his virtues, turned out wrong for his time. Reagan lives in the past.

Eventually we'll find somebody who can be a real leader. I'm deeply honored that a lot of people think it could have been me. That, in itself, gives me all the satisfaction I'll ever need.

XXIV

A BITTERSWEET VICTORY

In 1982, when the smoke of battle finally cleared, good things began to happen.

Only three years earlier, the Chrysler Corporation had to sell 2.3 million cars and trucks just to break even. Unfortunately, we were only selling around 1 million. With a little quick math, you can understand how that doesn't add up.

But now, through the combined effort of a lot of different people, we had reduced our break-even point all the way down to 1.1 million units. Before long we were actually adding people to our payroll and signing up new dealers.

In other words, we were poised for a major upswing. Unfortunately, the economy wasn't.

But late in 1982, as the economy began to heat up, so did car sales. Finally! When the year was over, we actually showed a modest profit.

My first instinct was to call a press conference to bury all the adjectives that had been used to describe us during our long crisis. Attention, reporters. Effective immediately, Chrysler is no longer "cash-starved," or "struggling," or "financially troubled." If you insist, you may continue to call us "the nation's number three automaker." But those other phrases are now banished forever!

The following year, 1983, we made an honest operating profit of $925 million—the best by far in Chrysler's history.

We had come a long way since the loan guarantee hearings,

when we had made so many promises. We promised to modernize our plants and convert them to the latest technology. We promised to convert our entire fleet of cars to front-wheel-drive technology. We promised to be the leaders in fuel economy. We promised to maintain employment for half a million workers. And we promised to offer exciting products.

Within three years we had made good on every one of those vows.

By the spring of 1983, we were actually in a position to make a new stock offering. Originally we had planned to sell 12.5 million shares, but there was so much demand for our stock that we ended up issuing more than twice that number.

The buyers were lined up and waiting. Our entire offering of 26 million shares was sold out within the first hour. With a combined market value of $432 million, this was the third-largest equity offering in American history.

Now, whenever you issue more equity, you naturally dilute the value of each outstanding share. But a funny thing happened on this one. At the time of the offering, our stock was selling at $16⅝. Within a few weeks, there was so much demand for Chrysler stock that the price zoomed all the way up to $25—and then shortly thereafter to $35. If that's the effect of dilution, I'm all for it.

Not long after the stock sale, we paid off $400 million—or one third—of our guaranteed loans. This represented the most expensive of the three drawdowns, as the interest on those loans was a whopping 15.9 percent.

A few weeks later we made a momentous decision—to pay back the *entire* loan right away, seven full years before it came due. Not everybody at Chrysler thought this was a wise move. After all, you have to be pretty sure of the next couple of years if you're going to give up that much cash.

But by now I was confident of our future. Besides, I was determined to get the government off our backs as soon as possible.

I announced the loan payback at the National Press Club. The date was July 13, 1983—and, by an eerie coincidence, exactly five years to the day since Henry Ford had fired me.

"This is the day that makes the last three miserable years all seem worthwhile," I said. "We at Chrysler borrow money the old-fashioned way. We pay it back."

I was having a good time. "The people in Washington have a lot of experience in handing out money," I said in my speech, "but not much in getting it back. So maybe the surgeon general should be standing by in case anyone faints when we hand over the check."

Actually, the government couldn't even accept the check that day. Because of red tape it took them over a month to figure out how to do it. It seems no one had ever paid them back that way before.

At a ceremony in New York I presented our bankers with the largest check I had ever seen: for $813,487,500. I also collected a bushel of apples for my trouble. During the congressional hearings, Mayor Koch of New York had bet me a bushel of apples that the city would repay its federally guaranteed loans before we would. But when we cleaned up our balance sheet, New York City still had an outstanding balance of more than $1 billion.

Now that we were out of danger, it was time to think about having fun again.

Ever since Detroit stopped making convertibles almost ten years ago, I really missed them. The very last domestic convertible was the Cadillac Eldorado, which was produced until 1976. The last Chrysler convertible was the Barracuda in 1971.

A lot of people are under the impression that convertibles were suddenly outlawed by the government. That's not really true, although things were certainly moving in that direction. In Washington, the regulators did make a push to ban the convertible—or at least to make serious changes in its structure. By that time, we already had more than enough regulatory headaches. Nobody was looking for still more problems, so convertibles were phased out.

What really killed the convertible was air conditioning and stereo. Neither one makes much sense if you're driving around without a roof.

In 1982, as we began to get healthy again, I decided to bring back the convertible. As an experiment, I had one built by hand from a Chrysler LeBaron. I drove it over the summer, and I felt like the Pied Piper. People in Mercedes and Cadillacs started running me off the road and pulling me over like a cop. "What are you driving?" they all wanted to know. "Who built it? Where can I get one?"

When they recognized my now-familiar face behind the wheel, they would sign up for one right on the spot. I drove to my local shopping center one day, and a big crowd gathered around me and my convertible. You would have thought I was giving away $10 bills!

It didn't take a genius to see that this car was creating a great deal of excitement.

Back at the office, we decided to skip the research. Our attitude was: "Let's just build it. We won't make any money, but it'll be great publicity. If we're lucky, we'll break even."

But as soon as word got out that we were bringing out a LeBaron convertible, people all over the country started putting down deposits. One of them was Brooke Shields, and we delivered the very first convertible to her as a special promotion. By then it was clear that we'd be selling quite a few of these babies. Turned out, we sold 23,000 the first year instead of the three thousand we had planned.

Before long, GM and Ford were bringing out convertibles of their own. In other words, little old Chrysler was now leading the way instead of bringing up the rear.

The convertible was done mostly for fun—and for publicity. But in 1984 we brought out a new product that was both fun *and* very profitable—the T115 minivan.

The minivan is an entirely new vehicle for people who want something bigger than a conventional station wagon but smaller than a van. The minivan holds seven passengers. It has front-wheel drive. It gets thirty miles a gallon. And best of all, it fits into a conventional garage.

Whenever I speak to students in our nation's business schools, somebody always asks me how we managed to bring out the minivan so quickly after our prolonged crisis. "How could you as a business-man put seven hundred million dollars on the line three years in advance while you were going broke?"

It's a good question. But really, I had no choice. I knew we couldn't eat the seed corn. There would be no point to our struggle if there was nothing to sell when we were back on our feet again.

And only half-kiddingly I used to say: "Look, I'm already in hock up to my eyeballs. So what's another seven hundred million among friends?

The minivan was actually born over at Ford. Shortly after the first OPEC crisis, while Hal Sperlich and I were working on the Fiesta, we designed a project we called the Mini-Max. We had in mind a small front-wheel-drive van that was compact on the outside and roomy on the inside. We built a prototype and we fell in love with it.

Then we spent $500,000 to research it. And in the process we learned three things. First, the step-up height had to be low enough to appeal to women, who mostly wore skirts in those days. Second, we had to make the car low enough to fit into a garage. Third, there had to be a "nose" with an engine up front to provide a couple of feet of crush space in case of an accident.

If we took care of these things, the research shouted, we were looking at a market of eight hundred thousand a year—and that was in 1974! Naturally, I went to see the king right away.

"Forget it," said Henry. "I don't want to experiment."

"Experiment?" I said. "The Mustang was an experiment. The Mark III was an experiment. This car is another winner."

But Henry wouldn't buy it.

In my book, if you're not number one, then you've *got* to innovate. If you're Ford, you've got to beat GM to the punch. You've got to find market niches that they haven't even thought of. You can't go head to head with them—they're just too big. You've got to outflank them.

So instead of doing the minivan in 1978 at Ford, Hal and I did it in 1984 at Chrysler. And now it's *Ford's* customers we're stealing.

This time, by the way, the research is even more convincing. As I write these words in the middle of 1984, the new minivan is completely sold out.

Moreover, Ford and GM are falling over each other to bring out their own versions. I guess imitation really is the sincerest form of flattery.

Even before the minivan came out, *Connoisseur* magazine selected it as one of the most beautiful cars ever designed. *Fortune* called it one of the ten most innovative products of the year. And the car-buff magazines featured it on their covers months before it went on sale.

Not since we unveiled the Mustang in 1964 have I been this excited about a new product—and this confident of success. I still remember the first time I drove the minivan at our proving grounds. They couldn't get me off the track. I just kept going around and around. I loved what the engineers had done to the handling and the ride. This car was really fun to drive.

Record profits, paying back the loan, the minivan—these were all part of our triumph.

But our success had a dark side as well. When we finally held the victory parade, a lot of our soldiers were missing. We won the war, but not without a great many casualties. A lot of people—blue-collar, white-collar, and dealers—who had been with us in 1979 were no longer around to enjoy the fruits of victory.

There was also the matter of the 14.4 million warrants we had issued to the Loan Board in June 1980, just before we received our first $500 million in guaranteed loans.

These warrants entitled the bearer to purchase 14.4 million shares of Chrysler stock at $13. When we issued them as a "sweetener," our stock was in the neighborhood of $5.00. At the time, $13 a share seemed a long way off.

But now, with our stock price hovering around $30, the government was sitting on a windfall. Moreover, they could exercise the warrants any time until 1990, when the loans were officially due.

These warrants were a sword hanging over our head. At any point over the next seven years, the government—or anyone else who owned the warrants—could demand that we issue an extra 14.4 million shares of Chrysler stock at bargain-basement prices.

As we saw it, we were already paying far too much for our government-guaranteed loans. We had borrowed $1.2 billion for ten years, but we were paying it back in three. During those three years, we had shelled out $404 million in interest, $33 million in administrative fees to the federal government, and another $67 million to the lawyers and investment bankers.

Depending on the price of the stock, the warrants could be worth as much as $300 million. Combined with the interest and the fees, this would give the government and the lenders the equivalent of 24 percent a year. When you consider that the government's money was never at risk in the first place—they had a lien on everything we owned, which was worth far more than $1.2 billion—that kind of profit was almost indecent.

But more important, of all the constituencies that had helped us in our recovery, not one was in a position to reap a windfall from our success. We had sacrificed equally when we were in trouble—so we should share equally in the rewards. If the government made a killing on the Chrysler warrants, what kind of example would that set for the workers and suppliers—and the dealers who had worked so hard?

So we quietly asked the government to surrender the warrants to us at little or no cost.

What a mistake! There was a huge uproar over our request. "Chutzpah," said *The Wall Street Journal* with a snort. "There's just no other word for Chrysler's request." This time, however, the *Journal* wasn't alone. Everybody thought we were being greedy. From a public-relations viewpoint, it was a disaster. One minute we were heroes for paying back our loan seven years early. The next thing we knew, we were bums. It was a painful experience.

We quickly retreated from our position. As a compromise, we offered the loan board $120 million for the warrants. No way. Then we raised the offer to $187 million. Nothing.

Finally, on July 13, the very same day we were paying off the loans, we offered $250 million for the warrants.

"No dice," said the Loan Board. "We're selling them to the highest bidder."

And that they did. Don Regan, a former stockbroker, reverted to type. He insisted on an auction—and, of course, lots of fees for the Wall Street crowd. But it was to be expected. From the beginning he was against the loan guarantees for ideological reasons. In three full years he never once convened a meeting of the Loan Board and never made a single move to help us.

The Reagan people, led by Don Regan, were always saying: "Whatever the Carter administration promised you is what you're going to get. We won't lift a finger to change it one way or the other. Whether it hurts you or helps you, we don't care."

As we started to recover, I said: "Embrace me, embrace me. Take some credit for our success. If nothing else, it's good politics." But Donald Regan and most of the administration said: "Ideologically we were opposed to the bailout and we still are. We don't believe in results." To the bitter end, they maintained that the government loans for Chrysler had set a bad precedent.

The issue got so hot that I went to see President Reagan twice. He said that as a matter of equity I had a strong case. On a trip I made with him on Air Force One to St. Louis he told Jim Baker to look into it.

He looked into it, all right. All he did was buck it back to Don Regan, who kept me twisting slowly in the wind. I don't know what happened in the White House, but in the end Regan prevailed.

Even now, I can't believe it. Where I come from, if I as a CEO tell someone to do something and I never get an answer back, I fire him. It's incredible that this guy Regan could sit out this guy Reagan.

In the end we were forced into bidding against our own $250 million offer and ended up buying back the warrants for over $311 million. At the time, I was furious. In fact, I still am. Why should the government be playing the stock market with our warrants? I had offered $250 million, which was a generous payment. But that wasn't enough. Their attitude was, "Screw Chrysler. Let's get every cent we can."

One congressman said: "What an opportunity! Let's take that $311 million and use it to retrain unemployed auto workers. The money came from Chrysler, so let's put it back in the auto business. Let's help the guys who lost their jobs when Chrysler had to cut back." But the government wasn't interested.

I proposed another plan. "Since you didn't expect this windfall," I said to the government, "why don't you take the money, leverage it ten to one, and use that $3 billion to help our industry become competitive with Japan?"

But the government decided to put the money back into the general fund. I'm afraid that our $311 million didn't make much of a dent in the federal deficit. But every little bit helps!

The entire episode with the warrants left a bad taste in my mouth. But what really made the Chrysler victory a mixed blessing for me is that it coincided with the greatest personal sadness of my life.

All through my career at Ford and later at Chrysler, my wife, Mary, was my greatest fan and cheerleader. We were very close, and she was always by my side.

But Mary had diabetes, a condition that led to many other complications. Both of our daughters, for example, had to be born by Caesarean section. Mary also suffered through three miscarriages.

Above all, a person with diabetes has to avoid stress. Unfortunately, with the path I had chosen to follow, this was virtually impossible.

Mary had her first heart attack in 1978, just after I was fired from Ford. She had been ailing for some time, but the trauma of that event made her condition even worse.

She had a second coronary in January of 1980. She was in Florida at the time, while I was in a Washington restaurant with all of our lobbyists. President Carter had just signed the Loan Guarantee Act, and we were celebrating our victory. In the middle of our dinner, I got a call from Florida saying that Mary had suffered another heart attack.

Two years later, in the spring of 1982, she had a stroke. On each of these occasions when her health failed her, it was following a period of great stress at Ford or at Chrysler.

Anyone who suffers from diabetes or who lives with a diabetic will recognize the symptoms. Mary was a very brittle diabetic. Her pancreas worked only part of the time. She controlled her diet very well, but her insulin injections, which she gave herself twice a day, were another story. Insulin shock, usually in the middle of the night, was very common. There would be orange juice with sugar, the stiffening of the body, the ice-cold sweats, and sometimes the paramedics struggling in the bedroom and the sudden trip to the hospital.

When I had to travel, which was often, I would call Mary two or three times a day. It got so that I was able to tell her insulin level just by the sound of her voice. On nights when I wasn't home, we would always have someone at the house with her. There was always the ever-lurking danger of shock or coma.

To the everlasting credit of my daughters, they not only accepted their mother's illness but ministered to her needs like a couple of little saints.

In the spring of 1983, Mary got very sick. Her tired heart just gave out. On May 15, she died. She was only fifty-seven and still very beautiful.

I'll always regret that she didn't live to see the loan payback only two months later, which would have made her so happy. Still, she knew we were going to make it. "The cars are really getting better," she told me before she died. "Not like the junk you were bringing home a couple of years ago."

Her last few years were not easy. Mary never understood how I could put up with Henry Ford. After the 1975 investigation, she wanted me to go public—sue him, if necessary. But even though she disagreed with my decision to stay on, she respected it and continued to support me.

During my final two years at Ford, I protected Mary and the girls from most of what was happening at the office. When I was fired, I felt worse for them than I did for myself. After all, they didn't really know how bad things had become.

After the firing, Mary was really a tower of strength. She knew I wanted to stay in the auto business, and she encouraged me to go to Chrysler—if that was what I wanted. "The Lord makes everything turn out for the best," she said. "Maybe being fired from Ford is the best thing that ever happened to you."

But after the first few months at Chrysler, our world started to fall apart again. Gasoline is the blood of the car industry, and interest rates are the oxygen. In 1979, we had both the Iran crisis and rising interest rates. If those two events had happened a year earlier, I would never have gone to Chrysler.

I didn't want to give up, but maybe events had outrun our ability to cope with them. At one point, Mary urged me to leave. "I love you and know you can do anything you set your mind to," she said. "But this mountain is straight up. There's no disgrace in walking away from an impossible task."

"I know that," I said, "but it's gonna get better." Little did I know that things would get much worse before they would finally begin to improve.

Like me, Mary was crushed by the way old friends deserted us after I was fired at Ford. But she didn't let it break her. She had always been a straightforward, gutsy person—and she stayed that way.

One day, shortly after I had joined Chrysler, she read in the paper that the daughter of some former close friends of ours was getting married. We were both very fond of the girl.

"I'm going to her wedding," Mary told me.

"You can't," I replied. "You're *persona non grata* and you haven't been invited."

"That's what you think!" said Mary. "I can certainly go to the ceremony. I like this kid and I want to see her get married. If her parents don't want anything to do with us because you've been fired, that's their problem."

She also went to the Ford annual meeting after I was canned. "I've been going for years," she said. "Why shouldn't I go now? Remember, after the Ford family, we're the biggest stockholders."

Mary was at her best when things got rough. In adversity she took charge. Once when we were visiting our good friend Bill Winn, he had a heart attack. While I panicked, she had the firemen there with a Pulmotor and a heart surgeon standing by with a heart catheter— all within twenty minutes.

Another time a close friend, Anne Klotz, called her to complain of severe head pains. Mary drove to her house, found her unconscious on the floor, called for the ambulance, got to the hospital, and stayed with her right through emergency brain surgery.

Nothing fazed her. She could be at the scene of an accident with somebody's head cut off, and her reaction would be: "What do I do next?" She just moved with dispatch, and as a result, two people owe their lives to her. When our daughter Kathi was ten years old, the brakes on her bicycle locked. She flew over the handlebars and landed on her head. Years before, my doctor had told me that the sure way of knowing if someone had suffered a concussion was that the pupils of the eyes dilated and filled the whole eye, one black mass. I took one look at Kathi's pupils—they were huge and black. I promptly proceeded to faint. Mary, meanwhile, picked her up, sped to emergency, had her in a hospital bed in half an hour, came home, made my favorite soup, had *me* in bed in half an hour, and never said a word. She was the essence of grace under pressure.

If you talked to friends about Mary today, they'd say: "Oh, God, that's what I remember about her—her strength under tough conditions. Her feistiness."

Mary cared deeply about diabetes research, and she herself was a volunteer for other diabetics. She accepted her condition with great courage and accepted death with equanimity. "You think I have it bad?" she used to say. "You should have seen the people who were with me in the hospital."

She believed in educating people about diabetes, and together we set up the Mary Iacocca fellowship at the Joslin Diabetes Center in Boston. Mary would explain that diabetes was the nation's third leading cause of death, behind heart disease and cancer. But because the word "diabetes" rarely appears on the death certificate, the public underestimates the severity of the problem. When she died, I made sure that her death certificate told the truth: complications from diabetes.

We had a lot of good times together, but Mary never got wrapped up in the corporate life. She didn't try to keep up with the Joneses. For both of us, the family was supreme. As for the responsibilities of the corporate wife, she did what was necessary and she did it with a smile. But her values—and mine—were home and hearth.

We took a lot of trips together, especially to Hawaii, which was her favorite place. But when we were in town, we spent our evenings and weekends at home, together with the kids.

Playing golf with the guys from the office has never been my idea of fun. Besides, I think that whole aspect of corporate life has been overrated. I'm not saying that you have to be a recluse. But in the end, what counts is performance. Your job takes up enough time without having to shortchange your family.

The four of us used to take a lot of motor trips, especially when the kids were young. That's when we really got close as a family. No matter what else I did in those years, I know that two sevenths of my whole life—weekends, and a lot of evenings—was devoted to Mary and the kids.

Some people think that the higher up you are in the corporation, the more you have to neglect your family. Not at all! Actually, it's the guys at the top who have the freedom and the flexibility to spend enough time with their wives and kids.

Still, I've seen a lot of executives who neglect their families, and it always makes me sad. After a young guy dropped dead at his desk, McNamara, then president of Ford, sent out a memo that said: "I want everybody to be out of the office by 9:00 P.M." The mere fact that he had to issue such an order tells you that something was screwed up.

You can't let a corporation turn into a labor camp. Hard work is essential. But there's also a time for rest and relaxation, for going to see your kid in the school play or at a swim meet. And if you don't do those things while the kids are young, there's no way to make it up later on.

One evening two weeks before her death, Mary called me in Toronto to tell me how proud she was of me. We had just announced our first-quarter earnings. Yet during those last few difficult years, I never once told her how proud I was of *her*.

Mary sustained me, and she gave everything she had to Kathi and Lia. Yes, I've had a wonderful and successful career. But next to my family, it really hasn't mattered at all.

STRAIGHT TALK

XXV

HOW TO SAVE LIVES ON THE ROAD

On the whole, we Americans are good drivers. And compared to drivers in other countries, we're terrific. Although far too many people are killed each year on roads and highways, our traffic-death rate of 3.15 per 100 million vehicle miles is the lowest in the world.

I don't pretend to be an expert on driving. But I do know a few things about cars. And I want to explain why seat belts—and not air bags—are the key to reducing traffic fatalities in the United States.

For years I've been promoting a very unpopular cause: mandatory seat-belt use. In 1972, as president of Ford, I took it upon myself to write to each of the fifty governors, letting them know that our company endorsed mandatory seat-belt use and urging them to support this life-saving cause.

Twelve years later, as I'm writing these words, not one state in our entire country has yet passed such a law. Eventually we'll come to our senses. But it's taking us far too long.

The opposition to mandatory seat-belt use comes from several directions. But here, as with so many issues, the chief argument is ideological. The idea of mandating safety just goes against the grain of some people. There are many who feel it is just another example of government intervention in their civil rights.

This is especially true in the Reagan administration. Unfortunately, their old-fashioned, laissez-faire view of economics extends to safety as well.

293

It's hard to believe, but even in this day and age there are still a lot of people who believe that telling a guy he's got to keep from killing himself (or his neighbor) just isn't the American way. In the name of ideology, they're willing to let thousands of people die and tens of thousands more be injured. As far as I'm concerned, those people are living in the nineteenth century.

But every time I come out with a statement in favor of mandatory seat-belt use, I can count on getting a big pile of negative mail from people complaining that I'm interfering with their right to go out and kill themselves if they choose.

But am I really? You have to have a license to drive, don't you? You have to stop at a red light, don't you? You have to wear a helmet in some states if you're on a motorcycle, don't you?

Are these laws examples of undue government interference? Or are they necessary rules in a civilized society? We'd have carnage at every corner if we didn't have some running rules.

And what about some state laws that say certain people can't drive unless they're wearing their glasses? I'm one of those people. If a cop pulls me over in Pennsylvania and I'm not wearing my glasses, I get a ticket. I think it's time we added another line to the driver's license, which reads: "Not valid without a seat belt."

I'm sorry, but I can't find anything in the Constitution that tells me driving is an inherent right. That's because it's not. Driving a car is a *privilege*. And like all privileges, it comes with certain responsibilities.

Would a law mandating seat-belt use constitute undue government intervention? Of course not. When it comes to government intervention, some people think you have to be either fish or fowl— completely for it or completely against.

But as with anything else, you have to look at the circumstances. There are areas of life where the government has to act to protect society. Only in America do we allow the ideologues to prevail over the demands of safety.

What these purists seem to forget is that the damage done by not using seat belts raises our taxes, increases our insurance rates, and harms us and our loved ones. And if that's not an intrusion on my freedom, I don't know what is.

But I don't want to get into a philosophical argument about seat belts, because that's the ideologue's game. We have to consider what's practical, what works in the real world.

The plain truth is that if you're wearing a combined shoulder- and lap-belt system, it's almost impossible to be killed under thirty miles per hour. Among other reasons, seat belts can prevent you from being knocked unconscious in a crash, which can happen even at relatively slow speeds.

What really gets me is that even the opponents of seat belts concede that they save lives. In case anybody still needs proof of that, a famous study by the University of North Carolina surveyed traffic accidents and determined that seat belts reduced serious injuries by up to 50 percent and fatal injuries by as much as 75 percent. And in the late 1960s, a study in Sweden examined almost twenty-nine *thousand* accidents among seat-belt users and found that not a single one had resulted in death.

The National Highway Traffic Safety Administration (NHTSA) estimates that fatalities would drop *by at least 50 percent overnight* if everybody used seat belts. But at the present time, only about one person in eight buckles up.

People are always telling me that mandatory seat-belt use is an impossible dream. But I don't think most people actively oppose seat belts. They just don't bother to wear them. Surveys have shown that consumers aren't against the *idea* of seat belts. It's just that most people find them inconvenient, intrusive, and a nuisance. Which they are.

These complaints aren't new, either. In 1956, when Ford offered seat belts as an option for the first time, about 2 percent of our customers ordered them. The indifference shown by the other 98 percent cost us a lot of money.

And you should have heard the reasons people gave for not wanting them. Some people complained that the belts clashed with the color of the interior. And I'll never forget one letter that said: "They're very bulky and uncomfortable to sit on!"

Let's deal with the other arguments, too, although they're no more compelling. I've heard people say that they don't want to be belted in case their car catches fire in an accident and they can't escape. Now, it's true that something like that *could* happen. But in actual fact, fires are the cause of only one tenth of one percent of traffic fatalities.

Besides, even if you *are* caught in a fire, it's just as easy to release your seat belt as it is to open your door. And nobody has yet suggested that we drive around with our doors open.

Another argument against mandatory seat-belt use is that you might be "thrown clear" in a crash rather than trapped inside the car.

Here, too, there's a grain of truth. After all, occasionally a passenger really *is* thrown clear in an accident.

But it doesn't happen very often. Actually, your chances of being killed are *twenty-five times higher* if you're thrown out of the vehicle than if you remain inside and let the car protect you.

Yet another argument is that seat belts are really necessary only for highway driving. But what many people don't realize is that 80 percent of all accidents and serious injuries occur in urban areas, at speeds of less than forty miles per hour.

We've come a long way since the days when seat belts were used only in airplanes. They were developed during the early days of aviation, when one of the biggest challenges of flying was simply to remain safely in the cockpit. By around 1930, federal regulations required seat belts to be worn on all passenger planes.

Today, while commercial aircraft are far more advanced and safer than they used to be, the law still mandates that you can't fly on a plane without buckling up for takeoff and landing. That's because seat belts are even more effective on the ground than in the air. If you violate that law, the airline has the right to throw you off the flight.

Originally, seat belts in cars were used only for racing. When both Ford and Chrysler offered seat belts in their 1956 models, there were few takers. A mere eight years later, in 1964, seat belts became standard equipment on all passenger cars.

I've been on a seat-belt campaign for almost thirty years. It began back in 1955, when I was part of the marketing group at Ford that decided to offer safety devices on our 1956 models. The safety package we put together seems very primitive by today's standards, but at the time it was revolutionary. In addition to seat belts, it included safety door latches, sun visors, a deep-dish steering wheel, and crash padding on the dashboard. In our ad campaign for the 1956 models, we stressed that Ford cars were safe cars.

At the time, promoting safety in cars was a revolutionary act in Detroit—so much so that some of the top guys at GM apparently called Henry Ford and told him to stop it. In their view, our safety campaign was bad for the industry, because it conjured up images of vulnerability and even death—hardly the stuff of successful marketing. Robert McNamara, whose values were markedly different from those of his fellow auto executives at Ford and elsewhere, had decided on the safety campaign. He almost lost his job because of it.

While we were selling safety, Chevrolet, our chief competitor, was promoting jazzy wheels and high-powered V-8 engines. Chevrolet clobbered us that year. By the next year, we had switched our strategy to "hot" cars with fast acceleration. Instead of safety, we marketed performance and racing, with far greater success.

Ever since the 1956 campaign, I've been quoted as having said that "safety doesn't sell," as though I were offering an excuse for not making safer cars. But that's a severe distortion of what I said and certainly of what I believe. After the failure of our campaign to promote safety features, I said something like: "Look, fellas, I guess safety didn't sell, even though we did our damndest to sell it!"

And we did. We spent millions of dollars and gave it everything we had, but the public didn't even stir. We developed the hardware, we advertised, promoted, and demonstrated it, and we couldn't give the stuff away. We had customers saying things like: "Sure, I'll take the car, but you'll have to take out those seat belts or I'm not interested."

When I first came to Detroit in 1956, I was a safety nut. I still am. But I learned the hard way that safety is a pretty poor marketing device, which is why the government has to get involved.

In this respect, at least, the cynics were right: if you stress safety, the customer starts to think about having an accident, which is the last thing in the world he wants to consider. He instinctively says: "Forget it. I'll never be in an accident. My neighbor might, but not me."

Although that particular campaign did not work out, I'm still proud that I was involved in the pioneering of safety devices back in 1956, when, for all I know, Ralph Nader was scooting around on a bicycle.

Despite the failure of our safety campaign in 1956, Ford continued to offer seat belts as an option each year, even when our competitors took them out because the public wasn't responding. I remember that a lot of people thought we were crazy: "Seat belts, like an airplane? But we're driving, not flying!"

But I also remember sitting in breakfast meetings where safety researchers would show us color slides of car accidents, so that we could understand exactly what happened in a crash. It was pretty horrible stuff, and I had to leave the room once with nausea. But it was also a good education. It made me realize that by far the most effective safety factor is the seat belt—provided you wear it.

Sometimes you have to scare people into getting the point. In 1982, I had lunch with the editors of *The New York Times*. I talked a lot about seat belts, and I gave some graphic illustrations as to how important they were in preventing serious injuries and deaths.

A few days later I got a letter from Seymour Topping, the managing editor. Until our lunch together, he had been a dedicated ignorer of seat belts. But after hearing my frightening stories, he decided to buckle up.

Later that week, as he was driving home in a storm, the car in front of him skidded and blocked his lane. He braked sharply to avoid an accident, but because of the rain, his car swerved and smashed into a containment wall. Thanks to his seat belt, he walked away unharmed. Today he's a believer.

You can be a great driver, but you still should be wearing a seat belt. Nobody thinks they'll be in an accident. But 50 percent of all accidents are caused by drunk drivers. And when *they* hit *you*, you're in big trouble if you're not protected.

About ten years ago, I realized that we weren't going to have laws mandating seat-belt use in the near future. So I came up with a plan that would force drivers and passengers to buckle up. With the help of the engineers at Ford, I developed a device called Interlock, whereby the car's ignition would not operate until the driver and front seat passenger had fastened their belts. American Motors joined us in supporting Interlock, but GM and Chrysler opposed it.

After some heated controversy, the National Highway Traffic Safety Administration mandated in 1973 that all new cars had to be equipped with Interlock. But the law was a failure. The public hated Interlock and soon found ways to get around it. Many people kept their seat belts buckled—but without wearing them. And since almost any weight in the front passenger's seat could cut off the ignition, even a heavy bag of groceries could cause problems if it weren't belted up.

The popular uprising against Interlock was so great that the House of Representatives, led by Congressman Louis Wyman, a Republican from New Hampshire, soon dismantled it. In response to public pressure, Congress took about twenty minutes to outlaw Interlock. They replaced it with an eight-second buzzer that would remind passengers to buckle up.

Interlock had its problems. But I still think that it could have been perfected and that it would have saved lives. When it was thrown out by Congress, I came up with another plan: a special light on your car that would show green when you're wearing your seat belt and red when you're not. Whenever your light showed red, you would be fined. I had in mind something similar to a radar gun, where the police don't even have to stop the offending car: they just send the driver a ticket in the mail. But in the wake of Interlock, nobody was interested.

When it comes to safety, people don't always look out for their own interests. Because so many lives are at stake here, the only solution is to have seat-belt-use legislation.

Evidently I'm not the only guy in the world who thinks this way. More than thirty countries, and five of Canada's ten provinces, already have laws on the books. In Ontario, just a few minutes from where I work, auto fatalities have dropped by 17 percent since their seat-belt-use law was passed. In France, after they enacted a similar law, the death rate in traffic accidents dropped by 25 percent.

In some places, the penalty for noncompliance is a fine. In others, you lose your insurance, and in a few cases—both. But the United States has yet to put through such legislation. The federal government generally maintains that it's up to the states, but the states have not acted. How many more people will have to die before we get smart about seat belts?

Some states now have a mandatory seat-belt-use law for children. It's time that we protected their parents as well. Nothing would be more tragic than to do only half the job—and to create a bunch of orphans in the process.

Now, I've always thought that as the home of the automobile, Michigan ought to take the lead on this issue. Whenever the question of mandatory seat-belt-use comes up before the legislature in Lansing, I either testify or publicly support it.

There are those who believe that air bags are the answer. I disagree. I've been speaking out against them since they were first developed almost twenty years ago. I sometimes have the feeling that when I die—and assuming that I go to heaven—St. Peter is going to meet me at the gate to talk to me about air bags.

Air bags were developed in the 1960s by a group of engineers at Eaton Corporation, an automotive supply company in Cleveland. In 1969, the National Highway Traffic Safety Administration decided that air bags were the best way to increase highway safety, and NHTSA began a campaign of promoting their mandatory installation in all American cars.

That same year, Congress passed a law authorizing the secretary of transportation to mandate auto safety devices. Air bags were finally mandated in 1972, but the ruling was soon reversed by a federal court. The Ford administration dropped air bags, but the Carter people revived them. In 1977, NHTSA ordered the automakers to install "passive restraint devices"—which is generally taken to mean air bags—by 1982. The question of air bags has been tied up in the courts and in Congress ever since.

The air bag itself is made of nylon coated with neoprene, which is folded inside the hub of the steering wheel and under the glove compartment—along with about a hundred grams of sodium azide. In case of an accident, special sensors are activated that cause the sodium azide to ignite immediately and to release enough nitrogen to fill the bag. When the system works, the air bag acts as a gigantic balloon, which cushions the impact of the blow.

Air bags sound like the ideal solution, but there are problems— big problems—that their proponents usually don't discuss. For one thing, although air bags are supposed to be a form of "passive restraint" —which means the consumer doesn't have to take any action at all to activate them—they are effective *only if they're used together with seat belts*. Without seat belts, the air bag works only in head-on collisions. By themselves, air bags are of no help at all in over 50 percent of accidents or on "second" hits.

Most people are still under the mistaken impression that air bags will eliminate the need to wear seat belts. I'm afraid that we in Detroit have not been very successful in explaining this point.

Air bags can also be dangerous. There's always the possibility that the bag will not inflate when it should, or that it *will* inflate when it shouldn't. Bags *can* go off inadvertently, and when this happens, they can lead to injury and even death. A bag blowing up at the wrong time can throw back the driver and lead to an accident. Even in relatively innocuous cases, an air bag blowing up prematurely can be very expensive to fix. Besides, sodium azide isn't the kind of chemical I want to be riding around with.

Whether an air bag fails to work at the proper time or whether it works prematurely, the whole business is a paradise for product liability lawyers. Because many people see air bags as a panacea, they won't hesitate to sue the manufacturers when—as would undoubtedly happen— people get killed and maimed even in cars equipped with air bags.

To be fair, the technology is now at the point where air bags are highly reliable. Let's say they'll work in 99.99 percent of cases. If all cars were equipped with air bags, and if, as now, there were 150 million cars on the road, that means that .01 percent of the air bags would not be reliable. And *that* means that about fifteen thousand times a year—which comes to about forty times a day—somebody's air bag would malfunction. If only 1 percent of those people sued, that would still be a pretty expensive proposition.

Air bags are one of those areas where the solution may actually be worse than the problem. After all, they're a pretty powerful piece of technology. Once when I was in Europe I picked up an English newspaper and was amazed to see a headline that read: "Yank Suggests Air Bags for Capital Punishment." I figured this was a gag, but apparently the proposal was made seriously. The guy who thought it up was a retired safety engineer in Michigan, and he was proposing that air bags would offer a humane alternative to the electric chair and to other forms of capital punishment.

In his application to the U.S. Patent Office, the inventor stated that by inflating an air bag directly under a condemned person's head, the force of twelve thousand pounds can instantly snap the guy's neck far more effectively than the hangman's noose, and so quickly as to preclude any pain whatsoever. I'm not sure I'd want one of those gizmos in *my* car.

Air bags are not the answer. And in fact, since the proposed legislation never actually specifies "air bags" but only "passive restraints," the legislation could be satisfied by passive belts—a kind of lap-and-shoulder belt that fastens automatically when the car doors are closed. These were developed by Volkswagen: you climb in underneath the shoulder harness, and the belt is fastened automatically. Belts that grab you whether you like it or not now come as optional equipment in the Rabbit.

Air bags have been offered only once by an American car manufacturer. In 1974, GM invested $80 million in an air-bag program and tooled up to produce three hundred thousand units. They were offered as options on certain Cadillacs, Buicks, and Oldsmobiles from 1974 through 1976. But only ten thousand customers ordered them, which means that each air bag ended up costing the company $8,000. As one GM official said at the time, "We would have been better off selling the bags and giving away the cars."

I suspect that ten years after this book is published, the government will still be debating air bags. When the crusaders get on their high horses, it's impossible to stop them. Air bags have been a red herring from the start. Barring unforeseen developments, the argument will probably continue for a long time.

But it's not air bags that we need. What we need are laws mandating seat-belt-use. The sooner we get them, the more lives we'll save.

Until we have those laws, please do yourself and your loved ones a favor. Buckle up!

XXVI

THE HIGH COST
OF LABOR

As someone who comes from a family of hardworking immigrants, I'm a strong believer in the dignity of labor. As far as I'm concerned, working people should be well paid for their time and effort. I'm certainly not a socialist, but I am in favor of sharing the wealth—so long as the company is making money.

Back in 1914, the first Henry Ford decided to pay his workers $5.00 a day and created a middle class in the process. He had the right idea, for unless the working people of this country are making a good living, we'll be wishing away our middle class. The cement in our whole democracy today is the worker who makes $15 an hour. He's the guy who will buy a house and a car and a refrigerator. He's the oil in the engine.

The mass media tend to focus on the very rich and the very poor, but it's the middle class that gives us stability and keeps the economy rolling. As long as a guy is making enough money to meet his mortgage payments, eat fairly well, drive a car, send his kid to college, and go out with his wife once a week for dinner and a show, he's satisfied. And if the middle class is content, we'll never have a civil war or a revolution.

America is different from Europe. Here auto workers are as capitalistic as management. And no wonder. When it comes to hourly workers, the UAW members are the elite of the world. And when money talks, ideology walks.

But high wages are not the real problem between management and the UAW. The real problem lies in all the fringe benefits.

As long as Detroit was making money, it was always easy for us to accept union demands and recoup them later in the form of price increases. The alternative was to take a strike and risk ruining the company.

The executives at GM, Ford, and Chrysler have never been overly interested in long-range planning. They've been too concerned about expediency, improving the profits for the next quarter—and earning a good bonus.

They? I should be saying "we." After all, I was one of the boys. I was part of that system. Gradually, little by little, we gave in to virtually every union demand. We were making so much money that we didn't think twice. We were rarely willing to take a strike, and so we never stood on principle.

I sat there in the midst of it all and I said: "Discretion is the better part of valor. Give them what they want. Because if they strike, we'll lose hundreds of millions of dollars, we'll lose our bonuses, and I'll personally lose half a million dollars in cash."

Our motivation was greed. The instinct was always to settle quickly, to go for the bottom line. In this regard, our critics were right—we were always thinking of the next quarter.

"What's another dollar an hour?" we reasoned. "Let future generations worry about it. We won't be around then."

But the future has arrived, and some of us are still around. Today we're all paying the price for our complacency.

Looking back, I see three key areas where management gave in and now we're getting killed: unlimited cost-of-living allowance; "thirty-and-out"; and cradle-to-grave medical benefits.

The first of these is the cost-of-living allowance. COLA is the engine that fuels runaway inflation. The two million workers who got it originally were in the auto industry. Today millions of American workers in industry and government are protected by COLA.

As much as I'd like to blame the unions for COLA, it really wasn't their idea. COLA was actually the invention of management, not labor. In 1946, Charlie Wilson, president of General Motors, proposed a cost-of-living allowance to deal with the temporary inflation that occurred when the government lifted price controls.

Inflation soon came down, but the unions got scared. In the 1948 settlement, GM came up with COLA, an escalator clause that provided for wage allowances based on changes in the cost of living as measured by the Consumer Price Index.

As with all new contract settlements, Ford and Chrysler soon followed with similar plans. For a few years, we managed to have a ceiling on COLA. But before too long, the auto workers struck and the ceiling came off. That's when COLA became insidious. Under the guise of fighting inflation, COLA actually *creates* it.

COLA feeds on itself: the more you try to keep up with rising prices, the more inflation you create. But like every other benefit, once COLA was introduced, it was impossible to eradicate or even to modify it. It's a rolling snowball.

During the 1950s and 1960s, it was never much of a problem. These were boom years. American industry enjoyed huge markets. Western Europe and Japan were ravaged by the war and took years to recover. All through the 1950s and 1960s, our inflation rate was low—around 2 percent a year. Meanwhile, our national productivity was high—rising by an annual rate of around 3 percent. That meant COLA was not really inflationary, because raises could always be paid out of the growth in productivity.

But in recent years, it's been the opposite: inflation has soared while productivity has dwindled. Unless we can reverse both these trends, COLA will become an even bigger problem than it already is.

When COLA was first introduced, it was a major contract gain. But over the years it's gradually turned into a ritual. By contrast, increases in productivity used to be a ritual. Now they're history. Is it any wonder, then, that labor costs are getting out of hand?

Today COLA has found its way into Social Security, Medicare, the armed forces, and plans for government workers. We taught them all dirty habits. The problems these groups suffer from today emanate from the uncapped cost of COLA.

In contrast to COLA, "thirty and out" was the union's idea—and a bad one, too. Walter Reuther, the founder of the UAW, made it the lead negotiating item with GM just before he died in 1970. Together with the demand for unlimited COLA, it was the basis for the big strike against GM that fall.

"Thirty and out" stipulates that after a guy has worked for thirty years, he has the right to retire early, whatever his age, and leave with a full pension—60 percent of his salary—just as if he were already sixty-five.

"Thirty and out" *sounds* good, and it was conceived for the purpose of creating jobs for the younger group coming into the work force, but it's the kind of program that makes America less and less competitive. Why? We get a good, hardworking guy at eighteen, train him for years, and at forty-eight he goes home for good. Not only do we lose a skilled worker, but we also have to pay his pension for the rest of his life—which on average will be for another thirty years!

According to the rules, this "retired" guy is not allowed to work. If he does work, he loses his pension. But if he's forty-eight, he's not going to stay home for long. Typically, he becomes a cabdriver or picks up odd jobs and works for cash. As a high union official once admitted to me: "They don't stop working. They just change jobs. The rules say the guy can't work, but who's going to check up on him?"

As a result, some of the best electricians who once worked for me at Ford and Chrysler are now driving cabs. And the irony of it all is that if I want to hire new guys to be electricians, I have to train a bunch of cabdrivers who don't know the first thing about the auto business. It's crazy! The country has been stood on its head in a headlong rush into mediocrity.

"Thirty and out" makes me furious. It's a crime to retire a guy just because he's worked thirty years. At fifty he's just hitting his stride. By then he has a wealth of experience and a variety of skills. Instead of using those skills, he's out driving a cab or sitting home twiddling his thumbs.

I'm not arguing with the idea of a good pension. But we can no longer afford to give pensions to guys who are fifty or fifty-five. I'd like to modify the "thirty and out" rule to one where the guy could still take early retirement with a full pension if he's worked for thirty years—as long as he's reached the age of sixty or higher.

Otherwise, we're paying the guys who should be helping us take on the Japanese $800 a month *not* to come to work. Does that really make any sense?

The third major abuse in the system has been the medical benefits. When I came to Chrysler, I saw that Blue Cross/Blue Shield had already become our largest supplier. They were actually billing us more than our suppliers of steel and rubber! Chrysler, Ford, and GM are now paying $3 billion a year just for hospital, surgical, medical, and dental insurance (H-S-M-D), plus all pharmaceutical bills. At Chrysler, that comes to $600 million or about $600 per car. All told, that adds up to over $1 million a day!

Like every other benefit that management provides to labor, the medical plans began modestly. But over the years, we've gone from paying no medical bills to the point where the company now pays for everything you can think of: dermatology, psychiatry, orthodontics—even eyeglasses.

To make matters worse, there's no deductible for doctor's fees or hospital costs. There is a small one for prescription medicines: the guy has to pay the first $3.00 himself. That's my great claim to fame. The deductible used to be $2.00, and I got it up to $3.00. Twenty-five years of negotiating and that was my only clear-cut victory.

The real nut of the problem is there's no buyer/seller relationship left in the delivery of medical goods and services. The attitude is always to let Uncle Sam or Uncle Lee pick up the tab. "So what if you're charging me too much for the tests or the surgery—*I'm not paying for it.*"

Like Medicaid, this system leads to incredible abuse. I recently found four podiatrists who were each making $400,000 a year just from the families of Chrysler workers. How the hell can a podiatrist see that many patients? They must be treating these people one toe at a time! I also found that in a single year we paid for two hundred forty thousand blood tests. That's a lot of blood to check at a time when we had only sixty thousand employees.

Health care costs us $600 for every car and truck we manufacture. For some of our smaller cars, that comes out to as much as 7 percent of the sticker price. In 1982, for example, we paid $373 million in health insurance premiums for employees, retirees, and their dependents. In addition, we also paid $20 million in Medicare taxes. And finally, we estimate that about $200 million of our payments to suppliers went to cover *their* employees' health insurance premiums.

Every time we strike a deal with the union, we have to give similar benefits to our white-collar people, from the chairman on down.

A couple of years ago Mary was in the hospital for two weeks. The total bill came to around $20,000. Guess how much they asked me to pay? A grand total of $12! (And that was for the TV set.) Chrysler got a bill for $19,988. The fact that I wasn't even asked to pay the first $1,000 is a scandal. But that's the way the system works.

We've worked hard to get some of these abuses out of the system, but we still have a long way to go. One reasonable solution to the problem might be for the government to tax employees on the contributions we make for their health insurance premiums. That way, people would think twice before going for extra tests. As the system works now, the doctors and the hospitals are killing us.

Those are the three big areas where we gave in too quickly to union demands. But there was almost a fourth—the four-day week. This is something the union has been talking about for years, although they never call it by its right name, which is five days of pay for four days of work.

Whenever this one comes up, I always think back to World War II: France was on a four-day week, and Germany was on a six-day week. Remember who got creamed?

The union is much too smart to talk openly about a four-day week. They know full well that the public would never accept it. Leonard Woodcock, then-president of the UAW, once said to me: "Lee, I'll have a four-day week and you won't even know it's happening." His roundabout plan was to petition for so many days off that the union would soon have the equivalent of a four-day week.

That's the origin of that brilliant invention called paid personal holidays, where each worker gets a certain number of days off a year just for the hell of it. In 1976 the union won twelve paid personal holidays—five in the second year of their contract, and seven in the third. For a while, even a guy's *birthday* was a paid holiday. But that one was a big headache, so the union agreed to change it. These days, we celebrate everybody's birthday at the same time—usually by counting the last Sunday before Christmas as a workday.

All of these plans—unlimited COLA; "thirty and out"; unlimited medical benefits; and paid personal holidays—violate common sense. No matter how sophisticated something like paid personal holidays sounds, there's no logical way you can pay a guy just to stay home.

If we're going to survive, it's absolutely essential that labor and management figure out a new and more practical method of working together. The kind of joint effort that saved Chrysler will have to become standard operating procedure.

I know it won't be easy. For one thing, workers have long memories. Some of the violent confrontations with the auto companies earlier in this century are still not forgotten. It hasn't been *that* long since the National Guard was called to Flint in 1937 to quell the rebellious GM workers and their union organizers.

In addition, workers and management represent different social classes, which is always a source of tension. The worker on the assembly line is resentful of the managers who, he imagines, drink coffee all day and don't really work very hard.

The seniority system is another factor that leads to union militancy. The younger guys are always the first to be laid off in hard times. In the UAW, unemployed workers have the right to vote on contracts for six months after their unemployment benefits expire. After that, they have to fill out forms every month if they want to keep their voting rights. Most workers just don't bother.

So whenever there's a referendum on a new contract or a proposed concession, the workers who vote are the guys with the most seniority. Older workers can afford to be militant, because they're protected from losing their jobs unless the whole place shuts down. But what about the younger worker who's temporarily out of a job? He's willing to make concessions in order to get his job back, but usually he has no say in the matter.

The union was established to protect the rights of the workers, who were mistreated and underpaid. And it's been more than successful. But today it represents an elite group that is well paid and highly protected. In a way, the UAW has made it harder for a young, unskilled worker to get himself a job in the auto industry. In many cases the union has priced him right out of the market.

How did this sad state of affairs come to pass? It began when the auto industry was golden.

Even when I left Ford in 1978, we had just finished our three most profitable years *ever*. Until then, with a few exceptions, the history of the Big Three was a series of variations on a single theme: success.

This was especially true in the aftermath of World War II. Back then, cars were almost as important as food, and the ability to produce them was like a license to print money. GM was—and still is, for that matter—more like a country than a corporation. Ford was the third largest industrial corporation in America. Even Chrysler, the smallest of the Big Three, was until recently the tenth largest manufacturing corporation in the world.

It took two very different groups to produce this great success. On one side was management, led by a group of highly paid executives. Today management is dominated by M.B.A.'s. But it wasn't always that way. For most of its history, the car industry was led by a group of rugged individualists—arrogant, high-powered, and rich.

On the other side were the unions. The United Auto Workers, which really came into its own after World War II, was in its own way as powerful as management. The UAW has always been a monopoly—it alone has supplied the labor force that has kept the entire industry going.

The United Auto Workers began in the 1930s as part of the Congress of Industrial Organizations (the CIO), which broke away from the American Federation of Labor in 1935. Before that, the AFL had tried repeatedly to unionize the auto industry, but to no avail. Finally, after major and often violent battles with each of the major automakers, the UAW established itself as a force to be reckoned with.

I was too young to have known Walter Reuther, the union's founder and its president from 1946 to 1970. He died in a plane crash around the time I got to be president of Ford. But I do know that he was pretty enlightened. His attitude could be summed up very simply: labor's task is to carve up the pie as advantageously as possible. And the bigger the pie, the more money in it for the workers.

According to the old-timers in Detroit, Reuther would actually sit down at the negotiating sessions and draw a picture of a pie. "It's the job of management to bake this pie," he'd announce. Then he'd point to the various segments of the pie and explain—as if he were talking to schoolchildren: "This much goes for raw materials, this much for overhead and rent, this much for executive salaries, and this much for labor. We're here today, gentlemen, because we're not entirely satisfied with the way this pie has been divided. We want to cut it up just a little bit differently."

Walter Reuther's speeches became something of a joke around town because he'd say exactly the same thing at every session. It was like a record. Some of the reporters used to write up their stories in advance and they never guessed wrong.

Because Reuther cared about profits and productivity and because he understood that the fate of labor was inherently linked to the fate of the company, he gained the respect of management as well as workers. In fact, I sometimes like to remind the present union leadership of his attitude. Although Reuther founded the UAW, they don't invoke his name very much these days. And for good reason. The union is still clamoring for a bigger serving, but the pie is getting smaller.

Reuther never fought automation. He never opposed industrial progress, even when the short-term interests of labor seemed to be threatened. From the very start, he supported the installation of robots. "Never fight the new machinery," he would tell his people, "because it's the way to get more productive. And if the companies get more productive and earn bigger profits, we'll be in a better position to negotiate."

With this attitude, management and labor prospered together. And both groups have made more money in Detroit than their counterparts anywhere else in the world.

For all my complaints about the UAW, I have to admit that Reuther's enlightened outlook put his union far ahead of other unions, such as the railroad workers or the printers, with all their featherbedding and make-work. When the diesel locomotive was developed, for example, the railroads no longer needed a fireman to shovel coal into the engine. But the union insisted that the fireman had to stay on, even though his job was now obsolete.

Walter Reuther could be tough and even unreasonable. Still, he was a real visionary. Journalist Murray Kempton once said that Reuther was the only man he ever met who could reminisce about the future.

In 1948, under Reuther's leadership, management and the union developed a pattern of multiyear contract negotiations. Before that there had been annual bargaining sessions, a situation that was bound to create an unstable working environment. The 1948 labor agreement ran for two years instead of one. It was followed in 1950 by a five-year contract. Eventually the union settled into a series of three-year contracts with each of the Big Three.

In some industries, such as rubber or steel, companies have banded together at times and done industrywide collective bargaining. But the auto workers have always negotiated separately with General Motors, Ford, and Chrysler. Every three years, the union would choose a pattern company, and—often after a strike or at least the *threat* of a strike—they'd work out an agreement with that company that became the model for the others.

Pattern bargaining made life easier for everybody. One advantage was that no company could undercut the competition on wages. On the other hand, pattern bargaining helped make management complacent when it came to dealing with the unions. After all, if the same labor agreement was in force for all four auto companies (American Motors was part of this arrangement), there was less incentive for management to cut a better deal during the negotiations.

I was involved in a number of labor talks during the 1970s when I was president of Ford. Throughout those years, I always felt that the companies were at a real disadvantage in dealing with the union. It had us over a barrel, because included in the union's arsenal was the ultimate weapon: the right to strike. And the mere threat of a work stoppage was the most frightening thing we could imagine.

Everybody in Detroit has a clear memory of the 1970 strike against General Motors, which lasted sixty-seven days in the United States and ninety-five days in Canada. It was a disaster for labor and management alike. The four hundred thousand workers who were idled lost $760 million in wages. The union's strike fund was quickly depleted, and the workers had to live off their savings.

GM had an equally rough time of it. Their income in 1970 fell by 64 percent from the previous year. As a result of the strike, GM failed to produce at least 1.5 million cars and trucks that were scheduled for production, which would have resulted in more than $5 billion in sales. I remember thinking that any union with the power to bring GM to its knees must be pretty strong.

Back in 1950, Chrysler had sustained a 104-day strike. It was then that Ford overtook Chrysler, so in a way the effects of that strike are still being felt today. We at Ford had our share of strikes, too, during which time our losses ran to around $100 million a week. At that rate, pretty soon you're talking about real money.

Because the strikes were so devastating, the leaders of the industry would do almost anything to avoid one. In those days, we could afford to be generous. Because we had a lock on the market, we could continually spend more money on labor and simply pass the additional costs along to the customer in the form of price increases.

A lockout would have been the answer, a kind of strike in reverse, where management closes down the plants. It would have been expensive, of course, but we might have had a final bloodletting. It's just possible that we could have changed the pattern between union and management before it was too late.

But there's never been a lockout in the auto industry. When I was at Ford, I urged that solution. But GM was always in favor of acquiescing to union demands, because for them money wasn't a problem. Chrysler wanted to give in, too, for the opposite reason—as the marginal player, they would be the first to go broke in the event of a prolonged strike.

Before each negotiating session, when the heads of the Big Three used to meet to plan our strategy, the possibility of a lockout would always come up. We used to go through the motions, but we were always too divided among ourselves to take any joint action. Ford, GM, and Chrysler could not agree on anything all year long—there was no reason to think they'd make an exception for something as important as this. The union had absolutely nothing to fear.

XXVII

THE JAPANESE
CHALLENGE

Shortly after I joined Chrysler, I flew over to Japan for a series of meetings with the top people at Mitsubishi Motors. Back in 1971, Chrysler had purchased 15 percent of Mitsubishi and arranged to import some of their excellent small cars under the Dodge and Chrysler names. We've been partners ever since.

The talks were held in the shrine city of Kyoto. During one of the breaks, I went out for a walk with Dr. Tomio Kubo, the dynamic chairman of Mitsubishi. As we strolled through the private shrines and temple gardens of the city, I asked my new friend why his company had built its giant engine plant in this peaceful and rural environment.

Kubo laughed and replied: "Actually, our Kyoto factory started out as Japan's major aircraft plant. This is where we built our bombers during the war."

"But why here," I asked, "in the middle of all this beauty?"

"That's why," he replied. "You see, before the war, your President and Mrs. Roosevelt came here on a vacation. They fell in love with this city. And when the war began, Mr. Roosevelt gave orders that Kyoto was not to be bombed. As soon as our military intelligence learned of this order, we decided to build our aircraft plant in a place whose safety was already guaranteed."

When I heard this story, I just shook my head. "I guess all's fair in love and war," I said.

Kubo nodded in agreement. "What would you have done?" he said. "We in Japan look out for our self-interest. What I don't understand is why your country doesn't always do the same."

I don't understand it either. Right now, we're in the midst of another major war with Japan. This time it's not a shooting war, and I guess we should be thankful for that. The current conflict is a trade war. But because our government refuses to see this war for what it really is, we're well on the road to defeat.

Make no mistake: our economic struggle with the Japanese is critical to our future. We're up against a formidable competitor, and all things being equal, we'd be lucky to stay even with them.

But all things are not equal. The field where this game is being played is not level. Instead, it's strongly tilted in favor of Japan. As a result, we're playing with one hand tied behind our back. No wonder we're losing the war!

To begin with, Japanese industry is not playing by itself. It's backed to the hilt in its close relationship to the Japanese government in the form of MITI, the Ministry of International Trade and Industry. MITI's job is to determine the industries that are critical to Japan's future and to help out in their research and development.

To the American observer, MITI might sound like a meddlesome collection of low-level bureaucrats. It's not. In Japan, government service attracts many of the best and the brightest young people. When you also consider that the ministries of trade, economics, and finance are the most prestigious areas within government, you get some idea of the kind of talent that MITI draws. MITI has made some classic mistakes, but its overall impact on Japanese industry has been incredible.

When Japan started to rebuild after the war, its government targeted autos, steel, chemicals, shipbuilding, and machinery manufacturing as critical industries. In other words, Japan's economic destiny was not left up to the free play of laissez-faire economics. Now, Japan is not Russia, which has a totally planned economy. Far from it. But Japan does have a system of goals and priorities that allows government and industry to work together to achieve their national objectives.

As a result, Japan's auto industry has been wrapped in a cocoon of protection: government loans, accelerated depreciation, R&D assistance, protection from imports, and a prohibition against foreign investment. Because of this concerted effort, Japan's auto production has gone from a hundred thousand vehicles back in the mid-1950s to eleven million today.

But regardless of how the Japanese manufacturers were helped, they also deserve our respect and admiration. They've shown themselves to be prudent planners and engineers. They didn't sit back behind the barriers and grow fat.

Instead, management, shareholders, the government, bankers, suppliers, and workers all pulled together. They designed products that were world class, using state-of-the-art technology. They built fuel-efficient cars, motivated by a national energy policy of high gasoline taxes for a scarce resource. No wonder the Japanese were prepared for the Arab-Israeli war of 1973 and the Shah's hasty departure in 1980.

Another Japanese advantage is that their taxes are the lowest of any industrial country in the world. And one reason they can afford such low taxes is that they don't spend very much on defense. Ever since the end of World War II, we've taken care of that burden for them. After they surrendered, we said to them, "Listen, you guys, stop making arms. You can see where that got you. Don't worry, we'll defend your country for you. We want you to start making some nice, peaceful things for a change—like cars. We'll even show you how. The people in Detroit will give you a hand!"

And we did. In the process, we gave birth to a monster. Today he's about thirty-five years old, fully grown, with big muscles. He's running amok through the American car market, and he's going to continue doing so unless we put a stop to it.

But how do you compete with a country that is spending only $80 annually per citizen on defense when we're spending more than ten times as much? While we're busy protecting *both* countries, the Japanese are free to spend *their* money on research and development.

Still another major advantage for the Japanese is the artificial weakness of the yen. Their currency manipulation is enough to bring you to your knees. Their banks and their industry have conspired to keep the yen weak so that the price of their exported goods can remain attractive to Western markets.

Unfortunately, the manipulation of the yen is very difficult to prove. Whenever I complain about it in Washington, the government asks me for evidence. Everybody wants to know exactly how Japan is going about it.

I haven't the slightest idea. And I don't have an embassy in

Tokyo or London or Zurich to help me with the answers. The U.S. Treasury has 126,000 employees. Let *them* figure it out!

All I know is that if it walks like a duck and quacks like a duck, the chances are pretty good that it *is* a duck. And when our prime rate goes from 10 percent up to 22 percent and back down to 10 percent—and during all those fluctuations the yen stays locked in at 240 to the dollar—you know that something is rotten in Tokyo.

At a minimum, the yen is undervalued by 15 percent. That may not sound like much, but it works out to a cost advantage of over $1,000 on a new Toyota. How the hell are we in Detroit supposed to compete with something like that?

Whenever this subject comes up, the Japanese always say it's not the yen that's too weak but the dollar that's too strong. There's certainly some truth to that charge, and our recent fiscal policies haven't helped. The Reagan administration has to accept some of the blame, because its policy of tight money and high interest rates has made our dollar too attractive to foreign capital.

One of my biggest fears is that in ten years we'll have an incredibly efficient operation at Chrysler, with an increased profit margin of $1,000 per car. And then suddenly the yen will take a big swing and wipe out that advantage we worked so hard to create.

We can't go on like this. It's time for our government to call the kid in after class and ask him to explain his behavior. His excuses aren't convincing any longer, and his actions are disrupting our economy. We should give the Japanese ninety days to tell us why the yen is undervalued—and what they intend to do about it.

Finally, there's the problem of free trade. Or perhaps I should say the *myth* of free trade. As far as I can tell, free trade has been practiced only four times in all of history. One is in textbooks. The three real-world practitioners were the Dutch, briefly; the English at the beginning of the Industrial Revolution; and the United States after World War II.

The English could do it two hundred years ago because they had no real competition. As soon as other industrial economies developed, England abandoned free trade.

Similarly, the United States once had the world to itself. Over the years our dominance has eroded, but in our heads, we're still trapped in 1947.

Free trade is fine—as long as everyone is playing by the

same rules. But Japan has its own rules, so we're constantly at a disadvantage.

Here's how it works. When a Japanese car is put on a boat for the United States, the Japanese government rebates about $800 to the manufacturer. That's a commodity tax rebate, and it's perfectly legal under the General Agreement on Tariffs and Trade (GATT). In other words, a housewife in Tokyo pays more for a Toyota than she would in San Francisco.

How should we respond? Well, in Europe they routinely slap on a border tax to offset the rebate that the Japanese provide for their exports.

Is that free trade? Of course not. Is it sensible? You bet!

Take a Toyota that sells for $8,000 in Japan. As soon as it arrives in San Francisco, the price drops to $7,200. But if that same Toyota goes to Frankfurt, its price goes up to $9,000. If it goes to Paris, it sells for $10,500. Because we see ourselves as the last bastion of free enterprise, we're being played for suckers.

Now, how can we give the imports 25 percent of a twelve-million-car market and then plead with them not to take 35 percent. It's unheard-of in the annals of history that we would offer up our labor-producing goods and then tell the Japanese: "Take anything you want. Let us worry about the social consequences."

Until some equilibrium is reached in our national trade deficit, we should limit the Japanese share of our domestic auto market by saying: "You guys can have 15 percent—and that's it."

Europe is a lot older than we are and a lot more experienced. If free trade is so important, then why are they setting limits on their imports?

Italy says two thousand Japanese cars a year is the most they'll tolerate. France says the limit is 3 percent. And what about Germany, that great free-trader? They don't like such strict limits. But when the Japanese share reached 11 percent in Germany, what did they do over there? They said: "Ten percent and no more." England did the same.

Unfortunately, our government finds this course of action difficult to imagine. Many of our leaders seem to think that we're still the only producers around and we have to be magnanimous. But forty years have passed since World War II, and it's time to acknowledge that the situation has changed.

Meanwhile, do the Japanese play fair with imported goods from America? Not on your life! Recently, some of our trade representatives met with the Japanese to discuss these inequities. Our people wanted to talk about beef and citrus products, which are protected in Japan, and about opening up new markets for our exports there.

But the Japanese said none of this was negotiable. Without cracking a smile, they said they'd be willing to take the tariff off tomato puree. Mind you, not tomatos—just tomato puree. Terrific! That should cut our $30 billion trade deficit with Japan by over a thousand bucks.

Meanwhile, Japan restricts the sale of American pharmaceuticals. They bar our telecommunications equipment and our fiber optics. They've created a web of almost five hundred government-protected cartels that practice two-tiered pricing and closed bidding on contracts. The Japanese marketplace is protected by a festival of crazy performance requirements and bureaucratic red tape that make it all but impossible to sell many kinds of American goods there.

For example, their system of product reclassification is an absolute sham. Take potato chips, which the Japanese really like. Potato chips were initially classified as a processed food, carrying a 16 percent tariff. But when an American manufacturer threatened to make significant inroads into the Japanese market, guess what happened? Potato chips were suddenly redesignated as "confectionery," and a 35 percent duty was slapped on.

My favorite example is cigarettes. They allow our cigarettes to be sold in Japan—but in only 8 percent of the tobacco shops. Moreover, there's a duty of fifty cents a pack. Does that sound like free trade?

Until 1981, American cigarette manufacturers were not allowed to advertise in Japan—except in English. Maybe, to even the score, we ought to force Datsun and Toyota to advertise here only in Japanese. Can you imagine the screams of anguish if we did that? I wonder how you say "Oh, what a feeling" in Japanese?

When people ask me whether I'm in favor of free trade or protectionism, my response is: None of the above. I'm opposed to protectionism. I'm also opposed to local content legislation. But the United States is just about the only industrial country left in the world that doesn't have an enlightened, modern-day trade policy. We're the only country in the world that comes close to practicing free trade—and we're getting clobbered.

That's why I take a middle road that I call *fair* trade. Fair trade involves some selective—and temporary—restraints against the one country in the world that is running such a lopsided negative trade balance with us.

Let's look at what is really going on here. We ship them wheat, corn, soybeans, coal, and timber. And what do they ship us? Cars, trucks, motorcycles, oil well equipment, and electronics.

Question: What do you call a country that exports raw materials and imports finished goods?

Answer: A colony.

Now, is *that* the kind of relationship we want to have with Japan? We were in a similar situation once before, and we ended up throwing a lot of tea into Boston Harbor!

But this time we're just sitting by and watching the Japanese take aim at one industry after another.

They've already taken electronics. They've taken sporting goods. They've taken copiers. They've taken cameras. They've taken a quarter of the automobile industry.

Along the way, they've taken a quarter of the steel industry, too. The Japanese have a clever way of smuggling their steel into the United States. They paint it, put it on four wheels, and call it a car.

While the Japanese are shipping us Toyotas, they're really exporting something more important than cars. They're sending us unemployment. Their subsidies are aimed at maintaining full employment in Japan, and the policy is working. Their unemployment is 2.7 percent. Ours is three to four times as high.

What's next? It's no secret, because they've been kind enough to tell us: airplanes and computers.

Now, I don't want to give anyone the wrong impression about my attitude toward the Japanese. Yes, I'm angry about the tilted playing field. And I'm angry that we're sitting passively while all this is going on. But Japan is really doing nothing wrong. As Kubo said, they're simply dealing in their own self-interest. It's up to us to start dealing in *ours*.

Because I speak out on these inequities while many of my colleagues in the auto industry are silent, people get the impression that I'm anti-Japanese. There's even a story going around the country these days about a third-grade history class where the teacher is giving a little quiz:

"Now, class," says the teacher, "who said, 'I only regret that I have but one life to give for my country'?"

A little Japanese girl in the first row stands up and replies: "Nathan Hale, 1776."

"Excellent," says the teacher. "Now, who said, 'Give me liberty or give me death'?"

The little Japanese girl stands up again. "Patrick Henry, 1775."

"Good work!" says the teacher. "Boys and girls, I think it's wonderful that Kiko over here knows the answers. But the rest of you should be ashamed of yourselves. Remember, you're American and she's Japanese."

Just then, a boy at the back of the room mutters, "Ah, screw the Japanese."

"All right," snaps the teacher, "who said that?"

Whereupon a voice calls out: "Lee Iacocca, 1982!"

It's a cute story, but in reality I'm a great admirer of the Japanese. Why? Because they know where they've come from, they know where they're at, and they know where they're going. And most important, they have a national strategy to get them there.

They also know how to make good cars. During the 1970s, their cars were actually better than ours. That's not true any longer, but many Americans still believe it.

How did Japan's cars get so good? It starts with the workers. To begin with, labor costs over there are much lower than ours. Japanese workers earn about 60 percent of what their American counterparts take home. They don't have automatic cost-of-living increases tied to the Consumer Price Index, as American workers do. And they don't have the same array of company-paid medical benefits that cost the consumer several hundred dollars a car.

Japan's workers are also more productive than ours. I don't mean that they're *better*, merely that they operate by a different set of rules.

There are really only two job classifications in Japan: skilled and unskilled. Depending on what needs to be done on a given day, a worker may perform a variety of jobs. If the floor is dirty, he'll pick up a broom and sweep it without worrying about whether that's part of his job definition. Naturally, this sense of responsibility leads to much greater efficiency.

Such a system would be unthinkable in Detroit, where every worker has a specific set of duties. Next to the simplicity and common sense of the Japanese factory, our own system of union rules and regulations looks pretty ridiculous. The UAW now has about 150 job classifications. Whereas the attitude of the Japanese worker is, "How can I help?," the attitude of his American counterpart is, all too often, "That's not my job."

Japanese labor unions work very closely with management. Each side understands that its fate is bound up in the other guy's success. The relationship between labor and management is one of cooperation and mutual respect. That's a far cry from the antagonism and mutual suspicion that has long been the tradition in our country.

The Japanese worker is highly disciplined. If something's crooked, he'll straighten it. If there's a problem on the assembly line, he'll stop the line until it's fixed.

These guys have a lot of pride. They see their work as a mission. You don't hear stories in Japan about workers showing up with a hangover. There's no industrial sabotage and no visible worker alienation.

In fact, I once read that some Japanese companies had to fine their supervisors because so many of them insisted on working on holidays as well as on their days off. Could you imagine that happening in Michigan or Ohio?

Japanese management, too, operates by a set of assumptions that might seem strange to us but that contribute to their overall success. The typical Japanese auto executive doesn't earn anything close to what his counterparts are making in Detroit. Nor does he receive any stock options or deferred compensation.

At some point in his career, he may have worked on a production line. American managers would probably be shocked to learn that the chief executive officer of Mitsui was once the head of his company's labor union. Unlike his counterparts in Detroit, the Japanese executive lives in the same world as the workers rather than in a completely rarefied environment.

What it all boils down to is that in Japan, government, labor, and industry are all working on the same side. In our country, industry and labor are traditional adversaries. And despite what the public may believe, private industry and government don't work together, either.

Here, again, I blame the ideologues who seem to think that *any* government involvement in the national economy somehow undermines our free-market system. Certainly there can be such a thing as too much intervention. But as we continue to fall behind Japan, it's become increasingly clear that there's also such a thing as too little.

We have to take action. We must replace free trade with fair trade. If Japan—or any other nation—protects its markets, we should be doing the same. If they encourage local industry, we should respond in kind. And if they play tricky games with their currency, we should take steps to equalize the exchange rate.

I don't know when we're going to wake up, but I hope it's soon. Otherwise, within a few years our economic arsenal is going to consist of little more than drive-in banks, hamburger joints, and videogame arcades.

Is that really where we want America to be by the end of the twentieth century?

XXVIII

MAKING AMERICA
GREAT AGAIN

T hese days, *everybody's* talking about the national deficit. But because we almost lost Chrysler a few years ago, I had the dubious honor of starting to worry about this problem a little earlier than most people. We were being killed by high interest rates, and it was clear that as long as the government was using up more than 50 percent of the nation's credit, interest rates could never come down very much.

So back in the summer of 1982, I wrote a piece for *Newsweek* where I proposed a simple way of cutting the national deficit in half. At the time, the deficit was only—*only!*—$120 billion. My plan involved cutting $30 billion from government spending while raising another $30 billion in revenues.

I had already learned firsthand that Chrysler was alive only because of the combined efforts of management, labor, the banks, the suppliers, and the government. And so I wondered: Why couldn't the principle of "equality of sacrifice" be applied to the federal deficit as well?

My plan was simple. First I would cut 5 percent a year out of the defense budget. That would come to $15 billion, and it could be done without affecting a single hardware program.

Then we'd call in the Democrats and say to them: "Okay, boys, I want you to match this $15 billion cut with an equal cut in the social programs you've put in over the past forty years."

Then comes the hard part. Once we've cut $30 billion in spending, we match it dollar for dollar on the revenue side. First, we raise $15 billion with a surtax on imported oil, designed to help OPEC keep their oil prices at $34 a barrel. Then we add a fifteen-cent tax to gas at the pump, which raises another $15 billion.

Even with these new taxes, American gas and oil would still be cheaper than anywhere else outside the Arab world. And in addition to all that revenue, we'd finally be creating an energy policy. The next time OPEC struck, we'd be ready for them.

Taken together, these "four 15s" would cut the deficit by $60 billion a year. The beauty of this program is that it spreads the sacrifice equally among all our people—Republicans and Democrats, business as well as labor.

When I came up with this plan, I went to every CEO I knew on Wall Street and asked them: "What would happen if the President went on TV and announced that he was cutting the federal deficit in half?" They all agreed that this announcement would trigger the biggest investment binge in our history. It would restore our credibility as a country. It would prove that we knew what we were doing.

Needless to say, we didn't do it. But it's not as if nobody was listening. Thousands of *Newsweek* readers wrote to tell me they liked my plan. I even got a call from the White House asking me to come and see the President.

When I walked into the Oval Office, President Reagan greeted me with the *Newsweek* article in his hand. "Lee," he said, "I like what you've written here. And I'm worried about the size of the deficit, too. But Richard Wirthlin, my pollster, tells me that a gas tax is the most unpopular thing I could do."

"Wait a minute," I thought. "Are we running this country by the polls? Is that what leadership is all about?"

The President wanted to talk about the defense budget. "We spent too little under Carter," he told me. "We've got to spend a lot more for our national security. You don't understand the whole picture."

"That's true," I replied. "I don't understand it all. And I don't want to be presumptuous. But the defense budget is now more than $300 billion. I'm a businessman. Believe me, I can cut 5 percent out of *anything* and you'll never know I did it. In fact, I've been doing that all my life."

Well, we didn't cut the deficit in August 1982. And now it's grown to over $200 billion. As I write these words in the spring of 1984, we're still wringing our hands about what to do.

*   *   *

Unfortunately, the budget deficit is only the tip of the iceberg. If anyone doubts that we've lost some of our economic greatness, let's consider the following questions:

Why does the country that produced Walter Chrysler, Alfred Sloan, and the original Henry Ford have so much trouble making and selling cars competitively?

Why does the country of Andrew Carnegie have so much trouble competing in steel?

Why does the country of Thomas Edison have to import most of its phonographs, radios, television sets, videorecorders, and other forms of consumer electronics?

Why does the country of John D. Rockefeller have oil problems?

Why does the country of Eli Whitney have to import so many of its machine tools?

Why does the country of Robert Fulton and the Wright brothers face such heavy competition in transportation equipment?

What became of the industrial machine that was once the envy and the hope of the rest of the world?

How, in less than forty years, did we manage to dismantle the "arsenal of democracy" and wind up with an economy that is flabby in so many critical areas?

Our loss of leadership did not come about overnight. The gradual erosion of our strength and power began in those halcyon years following World War II. But in no period of our history has America showed more vulnerability than in this past decade.

First, we woke up one morning and discovered that something called OPEC had the power to bring America to its knees. Like Pavlov, who rang a bell to achieve his desired results, OPEC rang its bell and we responded. And now, more than ten years later, we still have no real program to respond to this monumental economic danger.

Second, in the name of free trade, we're sitting by and watching Japan systematically capture our industrial and technological base. By combining the skills and efficiencies of their culture with a whole host of unfair economic advantages, Japan appears capable of looting our markets with impunity.

In Washington this is known as laissez-faire economics, and they love it. In Tokyo they call it *Veni, Vidi, Vici* economics, and believe me, they love it even more. The Japanese have come, they've seen, and they are conquering. And our dependence on Japan will continue to grow until we establish some practical limits to their enjoyment of our markets.

Third, the Soviet Union has caught us in overall nuclear capability. America no longer has a decisive military edge. We've now defined a program to regain that edge, but its dominance of the national agenda has been so total that I'm beginning to wonder what all these new weapons are going to *protect*. Without a strong, vital industrial infrastructure, we're a nation bristling with missiles that surround a land of empty factories, unemployed workers, and decaying cities. Where is the wisdom in this policy?

Finally, at some point in our recent past America lost sight of its true source of power and greatness. From a nation whose strength has always flowed from investments in the production and consumption of goods, we have somehow turned into a nation enamored with investing in paper.

And so our biggest companies are pouring huge sums of money into buying up the stock of other companies. Where is all this capital ending up? In new factories? In new production equipment? In product innovation?

Some of it is, but not very much. Most of that money is ending up in banks and other financial institutions who are turning around and lending it out to countries such as Poland, Mexico, and Argentina. That doesn't help America much. But at least when these countries went broke and the banks cried wolf, they accomplished what Chrysler, International Harvester, and the housing industry could never have done: they persuaded the Federal Reserve to back off of tight money.

Each month, some new type of financial instrument is created for the express purpose of absorbing consumer purchasing power and enriching the brokerage houses. Looking back on this period of deep-discount this and zero-coupon that, I can't help but think that never before in history has so much capital produced so little of lasting value.

Right now, our biggest industrial employers are in autos, steel, electronics, aircraft, and textiles. If we want to save millions of jobs, we've got to preserve these industries. They're the ones that create markets for the service sector as well as for high technology. They're also critical to our national interest. Can we really maintain the backbone of our defense system without strong steel, machine tool, and auto industries?

Without a strong industrial base, we can kiss our national security good-bye. We can also bid farewell to the majority of our high value-added jobs. Take away America's $10 to $15-an-hour industrial jobs and you undercut our whole economy. Oops—there goes the middle class!

So we've got to make some basic decisions. Unless we act soon, we're going to lose both steel and autos to Japan by the year 2000. And worst of all, we will have given them up without a fight.

Some people seem to think that this defeat is inevitable. They believe we should even hasten along the process by abandoning our industrial base and concentrating instead on high technology.

Now, I don't for a moment dispute the importance of high technology in America's industrial future. But high tech alone won't save us. It's important to our economy precisely because so many other segments of American industry are its customers.

Especially the auto industry. We're the ones who use all the robots. We've got more computer-aided design and manufacturing facilities than anyone. We're using computers to get better fuel economy, to clean up emissions, and to get precision and quality in the way we build our cars.

Not many people know that the computer industry's three biggest customers (excluding defense) are GM, Ford, and Chrysler. There can't be a Silicon Valley without a Detroit. If somebody is producing silicon chips, somebody else has to *use* them. And we do. There's now at least one computer on board every car we build. Some of our more exotic models have as many as eight!

You can't sell your silicon chips in a brown paper bag down at the hardware store. They've got to have a use. And America's basic industries are the users. Close us down and you close down your market. Close down autos and you close down steel and rubber—and then you've lost about one of every seven jobs in this country.

Where would that leave us? We'd have a country of people who serve hamburgers to each other and silicon chips to the rest of the world.

Don't get me wrong: high technology is critical to our economic future. But as important as it is, high tech will never employ the number of people that our basic industries do today. That's a lesson we should have learned from the demise of the textile industry. Between 1957 and 1975, 674,000 textile workers were laid off in New England. But despite that region's booming high-tech industries, only 18,000 of those workers—about 3 percent—found work in the computer industry.

Nearly five times as many ended up in lower-wage retail trade and service jobs. In other words, if you lost your job in a textile mill in Massachusetts, you were five times as likely to end up working at K-Mart or McDonald's than at Digital Equipment or Wang. You just can't take a forty-year-old pipefitter from Detroit or Pittsburgh or Newark, put a white coat on him, and expect him to program computers in Silicon Valley.

So the answer isn't to promote high technology at the expense of our basic industries. The answer is to promote *both* of them together. There's room for all of us in the cornucopia, but we need a concerted national effort to make it happen.

In other words, our country needs a rational industrial policy.

These days, "industrial policy" is a loaded term. It's like yelling "fire!" in a crowded theater. A lot of people panic whenever they hear the phrase.

Don't they want America to be strong and healthy? Sure they do. But they want it to happen without any planning. They want America to be great *by accident.*

The ideologues argue that industrial policy would mark the end of the free-enterprise system as we know it. Well, our wonderful free-enterprise system now includes a $200 billion deficit, a spending program that's out of control, and a trade deficit of $100 billion. The plain truth is that the marketplace isn't always efficient. We live in a complex world. Every now and then the pump has to be primed.

Unlike some people who talk about industrial policy, I don't mean that the government should be picking winners and losers. The government has proved again and again that it's not smart enough to do that.

And I don't want the government interfering in the operations of my company—or any other company, for that matter. Believe me, the existing regulations are bad enough.

As I see it, industrial policy means restructuring and revitalizing our so-called sunset industries—the older industries that are in trouble. Government must become more active in helping American industry meet the challenge of foreign competition and a changing world.

Almost everyone admires the Japanese, with their clear vision of the future; the cooperation among their government, banks, and labor; and the way they lead from their strengths. But whenever somebody suggests that *we* ought to follow their lead, the image suddenly shifts to the Soviets and their five-year plans.

But government planning doesn't have to mean socialism. All it means is having a game plan, an objective. It means coordinating all the pieces of economic policy instead of setting it piecemeal, in dark rooms, by people who have only their own vested interests at heart.

Is planning un-American? We do a great deal of planning at Chrysler. So does every other successful corporation. Football teams plan. Universities plan. Unions plan. Banks plan. Governments all over the world plan—except for ours.

We're not going to make progress until we give up the ridiculous idea that any planning on a national level represents an attack on the capitalist system. Because of this fear, we're the only advanced country in the world without an industrial policy.

Actually, that's not entirely true. America already *has* an industrial policy, and it's a bad one. Nobody who's familiar with Washington can claim that the government would somehow violate free enterprise if it helped American industry. Washington is Subsidy City! And each subsidy adds up to an industrial policy.

Let's start with federal loan guarantees. (I'm an expert in this area.) Chrysler wasn't the first. Before we came along, there were $409 billion in guaranteed loans. Now the figure is up to $500 billion and still climbing. That's industrial policy.

Then there's defense. Eisenhower warned us about this one when he talked about the military-industrial complex. That complex has us spending over $300 billion a year. It's the only protected industry we have left in this country. It's the only industry where, by law, the Japanese are not allowed to compete.

That's why when we at Chrysler sold our tank division to General Dynamics, a lot of people asked: "Why don't you sell the car business and keep the tanks? The tanks are making you $60 million a year guaranteed and protected!"

Then there's NASA and the space program. That's industrial policy, too. The moon shot is what sent our computer industry into high gear.

There's the Export-Import Bank. Eighty percent of everything it does supports four aircraft companies. I can understand that, but what bothers me is their lending $95 million in taxpayers' money to Freddie Laker. To do what? To buy $95 million worth of DC-10s so he could undercut Pan Am and TWA, two American companies, on the transatlantic runs. But Freddie Laker went broke, and that $95 million is gone. What kind of industrial policy was that?

Or what about the International Monetary Fund? It bails out foreign countries that have borrowed beyond their means and can't keep up the payments. Not long ago Paul Volcker gave Mexico another $1 billion to keep its credit intact and to relieve some big U.S. banks that lent them the money in the first place. Volcker made his loan overnight, without a hearing. But in order to get $1.2 billion to save Chrysler—an American company—we had to tie up Congress for weeks. What kind of industrial policy is that?

In the past, the U.S. government has made loans to Poland at 8 percent while we ask Polish Americans to buy houses at 14 percent. If the Democrats can't make hay out of that, they *deserve* to lose.

And what about tax policy? The auto industry in the aggregate pays 50 percent of its income in taxes. The banking industry pays only 2 percent. That's another form of industrial policy.

So we *do* have an industrial policy—or more accurately, *hundreds* of industrial policies. The only problem is that they're all over the lot and do little if anything for our basic industries.

Is industrial policy some kind of radical new idea? Not at all. We had an industrial policy in America even before we had a nation. Back in 1643, Massachusetts granted a new smelting company exclusive iron-producing privileges for twenty-one years to encourage this developing industry.

More recently, in the nineteenth century, our industrial policy included extensive government support for our railroads, the Erie Canal, and even our universities.

In the twentieth century, we've seen government support for our highways, for synthetic rubber, modern jet travel, the moon shot, integrated-circuit industries, high technology, and much more.

Over the past few decades we've had a phenomenally successful industrial policy—in agriculture. Three percent of our population not only feeds the rest of us—they feed much of the rest of the world to boot. Now, *that's* productivity!

How did that happen? Well, there's more going on here than good climate, rich soil, and hardworking farmers. We had all those things fifty years ago, and all we got were dust bowls and disasters.

The difference lies in a wide range of government-sponsored projects. There are federal research grants; county agents to educate people; state experimental farms; rural electrification and irrigation projects such as the TVA; crop insurance; export credits; price supports; acreage controls; and now Payment in Kind—which pays farmers *not* to grow certain crops. That program alone now comes to over $20 billion a year.

With all of that government help (or, some would say, interference) we've created a miracle. Our agricultural industrial policy has made us the envy of the world.

Now, if we've got an agricultural-industrial policy and a military-industrial policy, why the hell can't we have an *industrial*-industrial policy?

I guess my attitude toward an industrial policy is the same as Abraham Lincoln's when somebody told him that Ulysses S. Grant got drunk a lot. Lincoln said: "Find out what kind of whiskey he drinks and send it to my other generals."

Here's my six-point program that could form the basis for a new industrial policy.

First, we should provide for energy independence by 1990 by taxing foreign energy, both at the port and at the pump, in order to restore the conservation ethic and rekindle investments in alternate sources of energy. We must not be lulled by the current depressed demand. OPEC will always act in its own interest, and that interest will always be served best by high prices and tight supplies. The American people are willing to pay a price for energy independence. They know it can't be achieved without a sacrifice.

Second, we should provide for specific limits to Japan's market share for certain critical industries. We should declare a state of economic emergency for those industries and unilaterally set aside the restrictive GATT provisions during this period. We don't have to apologize for taking this commonsense approach to trade with Japan. At this point in our history, we can't afford a trading partner who insists on the right to sell but who refuses to buy.

Third, as a nation, we've got to face reality on the costs and funding mechanisms for federal entitlement programs. They're studying this to death in Washington because it's a political hot potato. But the answer has always been right in front of our noses: we can't continue to pay out more than we take in, and that will mean some very painful adjustments.

Fourth, America needs more engineers, scientists, and technicians. On a per-capita basis, Japan graduates about four times as many engineers as we do. (But we graduate fifteen times as many lawyers!) Special education grants and loans should be provided for high-technology fields of study. The Soviets and the Japanese are both dedicated to building up their technological competence—and we are not keeping up.

Fifth, we need new incentives to increase research and development efforts in the private sector and to accelerate factory modernization and productivity in critical industries. One approach is to offer investment tax credits for R&D and twelve-month depreciation write-offs for productivity-related investments.

Finally, we need to establish a long-term program for rebuilding America's arteries of commerce—our roadways, bridges, railroads, and water systems. Our infrastructure, which is vital to any strengthening and expansion of our industrial power, is deteriorating at an alarming rate. Something must be done. Such a program could be partially funded by the OPEC energy tax. It would also provide a major buffer from the future employment dislocation that will inevitably result from productivity gains and industrial automation.

To put all these programs into practice, we should set up a Critical Industries Commission—a forum where government, labor, and management could get together to find a way out of the mess we're in. We have to learn how to talk to each other before we can take joint action.

This tripartite coalition would recommend specific measures to strengthen our vital industries and to restore and enhance their competitiveness in international markets.

Let me make clear that I am *not* proposing a welfare system for every company that gets into trouble. *We need a program that kicks in only when troubled American companies have agreed to equality of sacrifice among management, labor, suppliers, and financial backers.* It worked for Chrysler, and it can work for the rest of America.

When an industry or a company comes looking for help, as I did five years ago in Washington, the commission should ask on behalf of the taxpayers, who are going to take the risk: "What's in it for us?" What's in it for the people? In other words, "What are management and labor bringing to the party?"

I've lived through this, and it's simple. It's management agreeing to do something *before* the government does *anything*—such as loan guarantees, or import restraints, or investment tax credits, or R&D help. Management might have to agree to plow back its earnings into job-creating investments—in *this* country. It might have to agree to profit sharing with its employees. It might even have to agree to keeping a lid on prices.

As for the unions, they would have to come out of the dark ages.

They'd have to agree to changes in the many work rules that hamper productivity—such as having 114 job classifications in assembly plants where about 6 would do fine. They might even have to agree to restraints on the runaway medical costs that are now built into our system.

If neither management nor labor is going to make sacrifices, then the meeting's over. You can't expect to get government help if you're not willing to get your own house in order. In other words, there's no free lunch. Whoever applies for assistance will have to understand that there are strings attached.

If all of this sounds a little like a Marshall Plan for America, that's exactly what it is. If America could rebuild Western Europe after World War II, if we could create the International Monetary Fund and a dozen international development banks to help rebuild the world, we ought to be able to rebuild our own country today. If the World Bank—which is a profit-making institution—can successfully help out underdeveloped countries, why couldn't a new national development bank do as well in helping out troubled American industries?

Maybe what we need is an *American* Monetary Fund. What's so terrible about a $5 billion national development bank to get our basic industries competitive again?

Early in 1984, the Kissinger Commission requested $8 billion for the economic development of Central America. Now, I always thought that Central America meant places like Michigan, Ohio, and Indiana. (Shows you how simpleminded I am!) What about *our* Central America? How can we spend $8 billion to strengthen the economies of other countries while neglecting ailing industries in our own backyard?

Some people say that an industrial policy is nothing more than lemon socialism. If it is, I'll take a crateful—because unless we act fast, our industrial heartland is going to turn into an industrial wasteland.

Any realistic industrial policy for America will have to include a monetary and fiscal policy.

We can't have a stable, healthy economy with high interest rates— or with interest rates that fluctuate every ten minutes. High interest rates are man-made disasters. And what man makes, man can unmake.

I look back on October 6, 1979, as a day of infamy in this country. That's when Paul Volcker and the Federal Reserve Board let the prime rate float. That's when the monetarists said: "The only way to break inflation is by controlling the supply of money—and to hell with interest rates."

As we all learned the hard way, that decision unleashed a tidal wave of economic destruction. There's got to be a better way to control inflation than to break it on the backs of the workers in the auto and housing industries. When future historians look back on our way of curing inflation and all the pain the cure caused, they'll probably compare it to bloodletting in the Middle Ages!

Detroit got hit first. We suffered the longest car-sales depression in fifty years. The housing industry came next. After that, almost everybody else in the country got hit.

Before the prime rate came unglued, interest rates had gone as high as 12 percent only once in our entire history, and that was during the Civil War. But now, once they hit 12 percent, they kept on going. At one point they reached as high as 22 percent. That's legalized usury. Some states have laws that kick in at 25 percent, suggesting criminal intent. The Mafia calls it vigorish.

But as tough as 20 percent interest rates are, what's even worse is the yo-yo effect. From October 6, 1979, to October 1982, rates went up (or down) eighty-six times, which comes out to once every 13.8 days. How can you plan anything on that?

When interest rates are high, consumers divert a lot of money into short-term securities. But making money on money isn't productive. It doesn't create any jobs. And those of us who *do* create jobs, who invest in productivity and want to expand and are willing to pay our fair share of taxes, end up downstream waiting for a few measly drops of credit to get through so we can put a few more people back to work.

High interest rates encourage the big boys to play their new game of making money on money. When money is expensive, investment in research and development is risky. When rates are high, it's cheaper to buy a company than to build one.

Of the ten largest corporate mergers in U.S. history, nine have taken place during the Reagan administration. One of the biggest involved U.S. Steel. While protected by trigger prices (which cost us $100 more per car to buy American steel), U.S. Steel paid $4.3 billion to buy Marathon Oil. Most of that money was borrowed. It should have been used to buy modern basic oxygen furnaces and continuous casters to compete with the Japanese.

When the steel workers saw what was going on, they were so mad they demanded that any wage concessions they made be plowed back into the steel business. It's almost unbelievable that American management should have to be lectured to by the workers on just how our system works.

Or what about DuPont buying Conoco for $7.5 billion, and in the process tripling its debt to $4 billion? It costs DuPont $600 million a year in interest just to service that debt. Wouldn't we all be better off if DuPont used that money to develop the kind of new and inventive products that made them world-famous?

And what about Bendix, United Technologies, and Martin Marietta borrowing $5.6 billion to fund their corporate cannibalism—without creating a single new job in the process? That three-ring circus ended only when Allied threw a tent over it all and put a stop to the whole thing.

Think of this: in the decade between 1972 and 1982, the total number of employees in America's five hundred largest industrial companies actually declined. All the new jobs—well over ten million—came from two other sources. One was small business. The other, I'm sorry to say, was government—which may be the only real growth industry left.

Why don't we pass a law that says when you borrow money to buy somebody else and cannibalize him, the interest payments on those loans are not deductible? That would get the excesses out of the system pretty fast.

Right now, if you want to buy up a competitor, generally you can't. That would violate the antitrust laws. But if you want to buy a company that does something else entirely, that's okay.

Where's the sense in that? Why should a guy who's been in the steel business suddenly become an oil man? It's a completely different world. It will take him years to learn about it. And most important, it's not productive.

If we lowered interest rates and ended this merger madness, we could get the money changers out of the temple of the national economy. We could get back to doing business the American way, by reinvesting and competing instead of buying each other up. And by creating more jobs so more people could participate in our economic growth. Welfare costs for local, state, and federal governments would come down. Capital would begin to accumulate. Plants would expand again.

As everyone knows, the way to lower interest rates is to make big cuts in the federal deficit. It's time somebody took away the government's charge card. Today Washington uses more than half of all the available credit (54 percent to be exact) to finance the national debt.

Despite all of President Reagan's campaign promises, the national debt is out of control. Back in 1835, the federal deficit was a mere $38,000. In 1981, the annual deficit broke $100 billion for the first time in history. Today it's about $200 billion. And, over the next five years it's expected to total over $1 *trillion!*

We picked up a deficit that big once before—during the period from 1776 through 1981. Think of it. It took us 206 years, with eight wars, two major depressions, a dozen recessions, two space programs, the opening of the West, and the terms of thirty-nine presidents to do that. Now we're going to duplicate that record in just five years while we're at peace—and during a so-called economic recovery.

To put it another way, there are sixty-one million families in this country and we're going to put all of them in hock for $3,000 a year *without their permission.* It's like Uncle Sam is using your credit card without asking. As a result, we're mortgaging the futures of our kids and our grandchildren. Since most of them can't vote yet, they've given us their proxy. And we're not using it very well. In my book, the boys in Washington—all of them—get an F on the budget.

We have to attack the budget deficit and our other economic problems before they completely overwhelm us. Of course, to solve big problems you have to be willing to do unpopular things. As a child of the Great Depression, I've always been a great fan of F.D.R. He did a lot for this country, even though the ideologues were fighting him every step of the way. He melted the pot. He included the excluded. He had the audacity to take people off the street corners where they were selling apples and put them to work.

Above all, he was pragmatic. When he was confronted by big problems, he *did* something—and that always takes more courage than doing nothing. Roosevelt did not attack the problems of the Depression with charts and graphs, with Laffer curves, or with Harvard Business School theories. He took concrete action. He was always willing to try something new. And if that didn't work, he was willing to try something else.

We need a little more of that spirit in Washington today. Our problems are huge and they're complicated. But there *are* solutions. They aren't always easy, and they aren't always comfortable. But they do exist.

The great issues facing us today are not Republican issues or

Democratic issues. The political parties can debate the means, but both parties must embrace the end objective, which is to make America great again.

Can we succeed in this undertaking? Someone once said that in great undertakings there is glory even in failure. So we must try, and if we do, I believe that we'll make it.

We are, after all, a resourceful people in a nation that has been blessed with abundance. With direction, leadership, and the support of the American people, we can't miss. I'm convinced that this country can once again be that bright and shining symbol of power and freedom—challenged by none and envied by all.

THE GREAT LADY

W hen President Reagan asked me to serve as chairman of the Statue of Liberty–Ellis Island Centennial Commission, I was up to my ears at Chrysler. But I accepted anyway. People asked me: "Why did you take this on? Don't you have enough to do?"

But this was a labor of love for my mother and father, who used to tell me about Ellis Island. My parents were greenhorns. They didn't know the language. They didn't know what to do when they came here. They were poor, and they had nothing. The island was part of my being—not the place itself, but what it stood for and how tough an experience it was.

But my getting involved in the restoration of these two great symbols is more than just a memorial to my parents. I, too, can identify with their experience. And now that I'm involved, I've found that almost every other American I meet feels the same way.

Those seventeen million people who passed through the gates of Ellis Island had a lot of babies. They gave America a hundred million descendants, which means that close to half of our country has its roots there.

And roots are what this country is yearning for. People are aching to return to basic values. Hard work, the dignity of labor, the fight for what's right—these are the things the Statue of Liberty and Ellis Island stand for.

Except for the American Indians, we're all immigrants or the children of immigrants. So it's important that we go beyond the stereotypes we've lived with. The Italians brought more to this country than pizza and spaghetti. The Jews brought more than bagels. The Germans brought more than knockwurst and beer. All the ethnic groups brought their culture, their music, their literature. They melted into the American pot—but somehow they also managed to keep their cultures intact as each rubbed off on the other.

Our parents came here and were part of the industrial revolution that changed the face of the world. Now there's a new high-tech revolution and everyone's scared out of their wits. When you're in a mode of change, as we're in right now, the great fear is that a lot of people are going to get hurt—and that one of those people might just turn out to be you. That's why so many people are worried. They're asking themselves: "Will we be as good as our parents in coping with these new changes, or will we be left out in the cold?" And our kids are beginning to ask: "Do we have to lower our expectations and our standard of living?"

Well, I want to say to them: It doesn't have to be that way. If our grandparents could overcome, maybe you can, too. You may never have thought about it, but they went through hell. They gave up a lot. They wanted your life to be better than theirs.

When the chips were down, my mother found nothing wrong with working in the silk mills so I could have lunch money for school. She did what she had to do. When I got to Chrysler I found a royal mess, but I did what I had to do.

Think about it. The last fifty years can give you a vision for the next fifty. What the last fifty taught us was the difference between right and wrong, that only hard work succeeds, that there are no free lunches, that you've got to be productive. Those are the values that made this country great.

And those are the values that the Statue of Liberty represents. The Statue of Liberty is just that—a beautiful symbol of what it means to be free. The reality is Ellis Island. Freedom is just the ticket of admission, but if you want to survive and prosper, there's a price to pay.

I've had a terrific career, and this is the country that gave me the chance to do it. I seized the opportunity, but I was no ninety-day wonder. It took me almost forty years of hard work.

People say to me: "You're a roaring success. How did you do it?" I go back to what my parents taught me. Apply yourself. Get all the education you can, but then, by God, *do* something! Don't just stand there, make something happen. It isn't easy, but if you keep your nose to the grindstone and work at it, it's amazing how in a free society you can become as great as you want to be. And, of course, also be grateful for whatever blessings God bestows on you.

Since most of my life has been selling—selling products, or ideas, or values—I guess it would be out of character to close this book without asking for the order. So here goes:

Please help me in the restoration of Ellis Island and the Statue of Liberty. Send your tax-deductible contribution to: Statue of Liberty–Ellis Island Foundation, Box 1986, New York, NY 10018. Don't let the flame in the Statue go out!

Remember, if nothing else, Christopher Columbus, my father, and I will be forever grateful.

INDEX